Other books by the author

British Cultural Identities (with Mike Storry)
An Encyclopedia of Contemporary British Culture (with Mike Storry)
An Introduction to Post-colonial Theory (with Patrick Williams)
Paul Scott's Raj Quartet: *History and Division*
The Twentieth Century in Poetry
Modernism
Post-colonial Theory and English Literature
Reading Fiction: Opening the Text
A Source Book on A Passage to India

Contemporary Novelists

British Fiction since 1970

Peter Childs

First published 2005 by
PALGRAVE MACMILLAN
Houndmills, Basingstoke, Hampshire RG21 6XS and
175 Fifth Avenue, New York, N.Y. 10010
Companies and representatives throughout the world

PALGRAVE MACMILLAN is the global academic imprint of the Palgrave Macmillan division of St. Martin's Press, LLC and of Palgrave Macmillan Ltd. Macmillan® is a registered trademark in the United States, United Kingdom and other countries. Palgrave is a registered trademark in the European Union and other countries.

ISBN 1–4039–1119–3 hardback
ISBN 1–4039–1120–7 paperback

This book is printed on paper suitable for recycling and made from fully managed and sustained forest sources.

A catalogue record for this book is available from the British Library.

Library of Congress Cataloging-in-Publication Data
Childs, Peter, 1962–
        Contemporary novelists : British fiction since 1970 / Peter Childs.
          p. cm.
        Includes bibliographical references and index.
        Contents: Martin Amis – Pat Barker – Julian Barnes – Angela Carter – Kazuo Ishiguro – Hanif Kureishi – Ian McEwan – Salman Rushdie – Zadie Smith – Graham Swift – Irvine Welsh – Jeanette Winterson.
            ISBN 1–4039–1119–3 (cloth) — ISBN 1–4039–1120–7 (pbk.)
            1. English fiction – 20th century – History and criticism. I. Title.
    PR881.C53 2004
    823'.91409—dc22   2004052828

10 9 8 7 6 5 4 3 2 1
14 13 12 11 10 09 08 07 06 05

Printed and bound in China

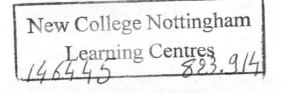

Contents

Introduction: The Novel Today and Yesterday

An article in *The Observer* newspaper by the BBC's political editor Andrew Marr on 27 May 2001 claimed that the novel no longer provided a way of understanding the world freshly. In the article, Marr wonders if the novel has a life cycle of invention, full expression, and formal decay. His conclusion is that the 'truths' the novel is best equipped to convey have already been accepted.

The occasion of this doom-mongering, harping on the death of the novel, helps to place it in context. Chair of a panel of judges awarding a prize for the best non-fiction book of the year, Marr was so impressed by what he read that he thought it must be better than contemporary fiction. Such a belief reinforces a distinction between fiction and non-fiction that some novelists themselves now question, but it is worth recalling that the novel's obituaries had already been written on several occasions before 2001 – most prominently over 30 years earlier in the 1960s – only for them to be found premature when fiction showed itself to be full of life in the 1980s.

Pronouncements on the death of the novel in the 1960s and 1970s were followed by a wave of new writers in the ensuing decade. These were largely the figures identified in 1983 by the Book Marketing Council's list of the 'Best Twenty Young British Novelists', which included Pat Barker, Salman Rushdie, Graham Swift, Ian McEwan, Martin Amis, Julian Barnes, and Kazuo Ishiguro. Sample work by the writers on this '20 Under 40' list, which was unashamedly a promotional exercise for contemporary literature, was showcased in an issue of the literary periodical *Granta*, whose editor Bill Buford took it upon himself to produce a new list in 1993, with the help of A. S. Byatt, Salman Rushdie, and John Mitchinson of Waterstone's booksellers.

The 1983 list has since served to mark a watershed in the postwar British novel, flagging up the time at which an old guard gave way to a new generation, a large number of who have since become the celebrated stalwarts of contemporary fiction. Compared to the first, the second list in 1993 contained only a handful of figures who have gone on to become major figures, but it still featured many impressive novelists, including Jeanette Winterson, Will Self, Ben Okri, and Hanif Kureishi. These writers, along with others such as Iain Banks, Louis de Bernières, A. L. Kennedy, and Caryl Phillips, have become established and celebrated authors if less well known internationally than the likes of Rushdie and Amis.

Written in 2001, 18 years after the turning-point signalled by the first *Granta* list, Andrew Marr's polemic capitalized on the fact that it came at a time which can be described as both the beginning of a new century (implicitly provoking comparisons with the upheaval of fiction wrought, at least in retrospect, by Conrad, James, and others around the beginning of the twentieth century) and a moment in literary history when few young, new voices had recently broken through into the public consciousness. Instead, from Marr's perspective, it might be said that the complexion of literature from 1993 to 2001 had been marked by three things: the emergence of post-Amis 'lad lit.', from Irvine Welsh and John King to Nick Hornby and Tony Parsons; the appearance of even more media-friendly writers of 'chick lit.', including Helen Fielding and Allison Pearson; and the remarkable success in children's literature of J. K. Rowling. In other words, the 'literary' novel (which can only be loosely recognized in its broad distinction from 'genre fiction') appeared overshadowed by emerging competition from more 'popular' fiction, and Marr took the opportunity to declare the novel also eclipsed by publications in history, science, and autobiography.

The latest discussion of fiction's decline certainly coincided with a promotion of the past, especially via the television programmes of 'media dons' such as Simon Schama, David Starkie, and Niall Ferguson, as though literature and history were not only disconnected but also opposed: a curious impression after the call 'to historicise' became the rallying-cry of University literature departments in the 1990s. Yet, for many critics, science, and to lesser extent history, has appropriated a significant proportion of the narrative power traditionally associated with fiction; and not even Shakespeare, let alone any novelist, could be considered a serious rival for the title of the 'Greatest Briton' in the BBC's 2002-poll, when in competition with Brunel and Churchill.

Since which time, a new *Granta* selection has appeared. The 20 'best young novelists' list of 2003 prominently featured a handful of authors who have appeared on shortlists for prizes, such as Zadie Smith, David Mitchell, and Sarah Waters, but, with a certain degree of inevitability, has generally been considered inferior to the two previous ones. It remains to be seen how the list will appear with hindsight, but it takes a place alongside the numerous other 'best ofs' that are perhaps now the primary means of marketing literary fiction, with 2003 also seeing the BBC's compilation of Britain's 100 best loved novels, accompanied by similar rival lists from literary pundits such as Robert McCrum (see Further Reading below; see also Table 0.1 below).

Certainly the novel is not in decline in publishing terms; indeed it is in a boom period. The number of works of fiction published each year doubled between 1950 and 1990; currently, about 100 new British novels are released each week. Approximately 130 works of fiction are submitted for the Booker Prize, while around 7000 novels eligible for the prize are published in Britain and the Commonwealth annually. While quantity is not the same

Table 0.1. Young British novelists

1983	1993	2003
Martin Amis	Iain Banks	Monica Ali
Pat Barker	Louis de Bernières	Nicola Barker
Julian Barnes	Anne Billson	Rachel Cusk
Ursula Bentley	Tibor Fischer	Susan Elderkin
William Boyd	Esther Freud	Peter Ho Davies
Buchi Emecheta	Alan Hollinghurst	Philip Hensher
Maggie Gee	Kazuo Ishiguro	A. L. Kennedy
Kazuo Ishiguro	A. L. Kennedy	Hari Kunzru
Alan Judd	Philip Kerr	Toby Litt
Adam Mars-Jones	Hanif Kureishi	David Mitchell
Ian McEwan	Adam Lively	Andrew O'Hagan
Shiva Naipaul	Adam Mars-Jones	David Peace
Philip Norman	Candia McWilliam	Dan Rhodes
Christopher Priest	Lawrence Norfolk	Ben Rice
Salman Rushdie	Ben Okri	Rachel Seiffert
Lisa de Terán	Caryl Phillips	Zadie Smith
Clive Sinclair	Will Self	Adam Thirlwell
Graham Swift	Nicholas Shakespeare	Alan Warner
Rose Tremain	Helen Simpson	Sarah Waters
A. N. Wilson	Jeanette Winterson	Robert McLiam Wilson

as quality, there is evidence here of a healthy literary scene, albeit one that is changing.

To open wider the critical discussion of the health of the novel, it is necessary to begin to historicize it, and so I'd like shortly to turn to concerns over the novel's mortality in the 1960s and 1970s; but first I want to sketch the decades since 1970 from two different perspectives: trends in politics and in fiction.

0.1. Politics

From the early 1950s, the Conservative Party broadly accepted policies, such as nationalization and the development of the Welfare State, more readily associated with the Labour Party. This led many commentators to speak of post-war Britain up to the mid-1970s as having a 'consensus politics' in which there was not a great difference between the programmes of the governments formed by the two major parties. However, after the repeated clashes between government and unions in the early 1970s, the Tory party under Margaret Thatcher moved away from 'One Nation' Conservatism towards a set of policies aimed at promoting business, consumerism, and the interests of those who aspired to be 'upwardly mobile'. Thus, the values of the Conservatives, once the party of the Establishment (the civil service, the armed forces, and the Church), shifted from general agreement with those of the upper middle classes and the professions to align with those of the new entrepreneurs and self-employed traders. In simplest terms, the Party was seen as becoming associated with the commercial sections of society under the leadership of a greengrocer's daughter. The different world this ushered in can be sensed at the end of Hanif Kureishi's first novel *The Buddha of Suburbia* (1990), which registers the mood of the country on election night in 1979, at the moment of the rise of the 'new right' after two decades of the so-called 'permissive society'. Early life under Thatcherism is more fully explored in texts such as Pat Barker's novel *Union Street* (1982) and Ian McEwan's filmscript *The Ploughman's Lunch* (1983).

Thatcher was the longest serving Prime Minister of the twentieth century, from 1979 to 1990. Her years in power saw radical reforms that sought forcefully to express Britain's transition from a prevailing atmosphere of consensus to the radically new mood in which there was a clear division between political left and right. After the economic and social crises of previous Labour and Conservative governments, Thatcherism aimed towards objectives that centred on a drive to change working practices: privatization of nationalized industries, regulation of professions such as medicine and teaching, an end to strike-bargaining, and a curtailment of union power. Accordingly, many political commentators have suggested that the 'Thatcher Revolution' shifted power through government reforms away from bureaucrats, the trade unions, and the Establishment to individual consumers and the free market. This could be seen in almost every economic and social sphere: parents were encouraged to take control of their schools by becoming governors; the Community Charge, or Poll Tax, was designed to recoup money more evenly for local amenities; privatization initiatives were concentrated on key public utilities like gas, electricity, telecommunications, and water, turning many of them into private monopolies. Amongst this, the influence of class supposedly diminished as the marketplace took over and the power of collective action was replaced with that of consumerism – the target of much of Irvine Welsh's fiction from *Trainspotting* (1993) to *Porno* (2002).

Many of Thatcher's reforms in the 1980s, including sharp reductions in the highest rates of personal and company tax, the removal of exchange controls, City de-regulation, the expansion of the private sector, and the weakening of trade unions, clearly benefited business, but the financial bedrock of British society arguably changed little. The modern socio-economic elite was still based on individuals with a common class background and close social contacts. This fact is bitingly satirized in Jonathan Coe's novel *What a Carve Up!* (1994), just as the preceding state of the pre-Thatcher nation is comically presented in his later book *The Rotters' Club* (2001), which opens with two teenagers trying to imagine 'a country that neither of us would recognize, probably Britain, 1973'.

The privileged sections of 1980s society in economic and cultural terms were the self-employed, who had long been the staunchest supporters of the Conservative Party. During the decade, advertising focussed a great deal of its energies on popularizing the self-made businessperson. This climate in which 'greed was good', in the words of Michael Douglas's character Gordon Gekko in the Hollywood film *Wall Street* (1987), made the entrepreneur the individual most valorized by government and the media, such that in Britain the Department of Trade and Industry actively promoted an 'enterprise culture' as a method of social engineering (the spirit of the times is most scathingly presented in fiction by Martin Amis in *Money* (1984)). However, the financial crash of 1987 ended most dreams of making a quick fortune; especially as the housing market temporarily collapsed.

After its 1987 election defeat, the Labour Party's powerbrokers realized that Thatcherism had changed the agenda of British politics once and for all. By the early 1990s, the party was retreating from such policies as unilateral nuclear disarmament and the re-nationalization of core industries. The political ascendancy of the modernizing tendency was confirmed in 1994 when, following the death of John Smith, Tony Blair assumed leadership. Under Blair, Labour sought to provide greater powers to individual members, curtailing the former dominance of the trade unions over the party. In 1995, the party revised Clause Four of its constitution and thus ended Labour's historic commitment to state ownership. Blair promoted a centrist social democratic programme under the slogan 'New Labour' and led the Party to its largest-ever parliamentary majority at the General Election in May 1997, while the Conservative Party was foundering on a reputation for scandals and sleaze (cf. Ian McEwan's novel *Amsterdam* (1998)). The most significant achievements of the early New Labour government, which consciously set out to rebrand Britain, were in constitutional reform. Referendums in September 1997 established the Scottish Parliament and Welsh Assembly, and significant progress was made in Northern Ireland with the signing of the multiparty peace declaration in April 1998.

But the changes enacted at a macro-political level can best be seen in the ways that they affected people's lives at work and in the home. So, while in 1979 white male manual workers formed an overwhelming majority of the workforce and most of these men belonged to trade unions, by 2000, nearly 50% of the workforce was female or a member of an ethnic minority while the membership of trade unions had fallen from 13 million to below 7 million. Also, while unemployment never rose above 1.5 million from 1951 to 1979, since 1979, as governments focussed on keeping inflation at a minimum, it has been as high as 3.5 million and rarely below 2 million. In the 1980s and 1990s these changes led to talk of the development of an 'underclass' in Britain: individuals cut off from the consumer society, poor and sceptical of the authorities. This was the most striking feature of a new 'two nations' society under the Conservatives, such that the percentage of the population living at the lowest rate of social security benefit rose from 6% in 1979 to 19% by the mid-1990s. Alongside the growth of poverty and homelessness in the 1980s came riots in poor urban areas such as Toxteth (Liverpool), Moss Side (Manchester), Handsworth (Birmingham), and Brixton (London). This picture of a divided Britain was reflected across literature: in Tony Harrison's poem *V* (1985), in David Hare and Howard Brenton's play *Pravda* (1985), and in Pat Barker's early novels, such as *Blow Your House Down* (1984).

As a response to perceptions of Britain as a country of 'haves' and 'have nots' under the Conservatives, Tony Blair promoted the notion of a 'classless society' through his rhetoric of a meritocracy of 'stakeholders'. Yet many people perceived Labour to have done little to help the less well-off and to be chiefly characterized by 'spin'. So, after coming to power on an agenda of 'education, education, education', New Labour proceeded to set its targets high (e.g. 50% participation in Higher Education) while simultaneously offering little new state funding and maintaining that individuals should pay for their own education.

Again, with regard to the effects on people's lives, the difference between pre- and post-Thatcher Britain can be seen in terms of legislation relating to women's rights, childbirth, marriage, and sexuality. In the dozen years before the Thatcher government came to power, there were key reforms, such as: the Abortion Act of 1967, legalizing termination of pregnancy; the Sexual Offences Act in the same year, decriminalizing homosexuality; the Divorce Reform Act in 1969, making divorce available through mutual consent; and the Sex Discrimination Act in 1975, banning employment and education discrimination against women. However, with campaigns centred on 'family values', the Conservative rule from 1979 to 1997 saw several comparatively regressive steps, such as Clause 28 in 1987, outlawing positive gay and lesbian images in schools, and the Child Support Agency in 1993, a Government authorized body pursuing child maintenance. When Thatcher took office, she promised to end the enlarged role of the state. But, as suggested by bodies such as the Child Support Agency, this did not in fact happen – there had merely been a change in emphasis. In 1979 the state was responsible for 43% of the economy and in 1990 the state was still responsible for 43%. Indeed, Britain remains the most centralized state among all the major western industrial democracies. Power has increasingly been concentrated in the hands of the Prime Minister and the Cabinet: in the 1994 Police Act, the police, previously organized on a local basis were brought under the control of the Home Secretary; while schools now operate a National Curriculum, in 1988 British universities came under central research and teaching regulation for the first time; regional health authorities have been abolished and the National Health Service is now under the control of the Health Secretary; the power of local government has been dramatically weakened from 1979 to the present and local authorities no longer have the right to build homes.

Lastly, one of the most significant changes in the years since 1970 has been the apparent alteration in people's attitudes to national politics. In the General Elections since 1970 the share of the votes of the two major parties has fallen from 92% to below 75%, while the number of floating voters who switch their votes to different parties at each election has grown. People are now less attached to a specific political party than ever before. In 1964, 48% of voters said they identified strongly with one party, but in 1992 this figure had fallen to 21%, while the number of non-voters has steadily increased up to the 2001 election. This is especially true of the 18–24 age group (less than half of whom vote) and indicates a shift from the widespread belief in party politics in the 1970s to the greater concern with consumer power since the 1980s.

0.2. Fiction

Since the early 1970s, both literature and popular culture have witnessed a number of trends in response to changes in perceptions of identity in relation to sexuality, ethnicity, and gender. Against these currents has been a counterforce led by the Conservative government and dubbed 'Victorian values' in the 1980s, 'family values' in the early 1990s. In the 1980s, the backlash was confidently spearheaded by Thatcher, who once said, 'We are reaping what was sown in the 1960s ... The fashionable theories and permissive claptrap set the scene for a society in which the old virtues of discipline and self-restraint were denigrated.'

It is a striking phenomenon that the most politically repressive decade in post-war British history should also be one in which fiction was believed to have undergone a renaissance. The 1980s saw the best early work of a new group of novelists that had begun to emerge in the previous decade – many of whom are discussed in this book and now constitute the established names of British fiction. These were novelists who had known little at first-hand of the Second World War or the British Empire, but had grown up instead with a decreasing division between 'high' and popular culture, with an awareness of the literary tradition alongside the new experiences that ranged from television and rock music to the Welfare State and the Cold War. Martin Amis's early novels, such as *Dead Babies* (1974), expressed a new ethos for a younger generation, centred on drugs, sex, money, hedonism, consumer culture, and a sometimes-morbid treatment of sexuality which was also apparent in the first short fictions of Ian McEwan. No less a product of the times, an alternative fantastic, ornate, and erotic prose style became recognizable in the works of Angela Carter, such as *The Passion of New Eve* (1977), an allegory of the rebirth and self-fashioning of the women's movement in the 1970s, and *The Bloody Chamber and Other Stories* (1979), a series of macabre, lush, sexualized versions of traditional fairy tales.

Carter combined writing fiction with university teaching and critical writing. This is also the case with David Lodge and Malcolm Bradbury, who produced different strains of the 'campus novel' in the 1970s. Bradbury's *The History Man* (1975) satirized the sexual politics of redbrick universities, while Lodge's *Changing Places* (1975) and *Small World* (1984) poked fun at literary theory, the international conference scene, and transatlantic differences between the glamorous academic world of Euphoria State, California, and the low-budget drabness of Rummidge, England (modelled on Birmingham University).

Politically, these novels sprang out of the growing failure of the liberal consensus in the 1970s. Also from this perspective, Doris Lessing's *The Golden Notebook* (1962) and *Children of Violence* (1952–69) quintet combined an intense interest in socialist politics with an unprecedented investigation into the forces that shaped women's emotional and social lives since the war, while others of her novels appraised her own and southern Africa's post-colonial predicament. Also trying to assess the failure of liberalism, Paul Scott dissected the end of Empire in *The Raj Quartet* (*The Jewel in the Crown* (1966) to *A Division of the Spoils* (1974)), a sustained attempt to deal with the imperial legacy that most writers, with the exception of Lessing, J. G. Farrell, and Anthony Burgess seemed to want to ignore, despite the growing stature of 'Commonwealth novelists' like V. S. Naipaul and Sam Selvon. Lessing also published allegorical fantasy and science fiction in the 1970s, from *Briefing on a Descent into Hell* (1971) to her *Canopus in Argus: Archives* series. Since then, other more popular science fiction novelists (such as Brian Aldiss, Michael Moorcock, and J. G. Ballard) and fantasy writers (such as Iain Banks, Douglas Adams, Clive Barker, and Terry Pratchett) have pushed their genres into different realms of philosophical and psychological extremity, while retaining undercurrents of social comment, and gained cult status alongside horror movies and SF television series – products of the mainstream mass-consumer culture which was widely and wrongly anticipated to bring about the commercial failure of the novel.

The dominant themes of 1970s writing reflected in myriad ways the maturation of the post-war shift in social attitudes, sexual mores, religious consciousness, and youth movements, underpinned by a growing Americanization of British culture. By contrast in some respects, the 1980s showed novelists returning to the postmodernist styles of the 1960s. In the decade running up to 1970 there had been many self-conscious fictions which experimented with previous genres, toyed with literary theory, questioned traditional character-representations of a stable personal identity, and complicated familiar narrative organizations of space and time, expressing the liberationist impulse of the decade in prose techniques: John Fowles's *The French Lieutenant's Woman* (1969), Christine Brooke-Rose's *Such* (1966), B. S. Johnson's *Alberto Angelo* (1964), Eva Figes's *Winter Journey* (1967), Andrew Sinclair's *Gog* (1967), and Muriel Spark's *The Driver's Seat* (1970). Developing from this, fiction in the 1980s, including Graham Swift's *Waterland* (1983), Alasdair Gray's *Lanark* (1981), and Julian Barnes's *A History of the World in* $10\frac{1}{2}$ *Chapters* (1989), showed a fresh postmodernist concern with history and its narrative construction (discussed by Linda Hutcheon as historiographic metafiction), which suggested that, while novelists sought to historicize their stories, analysts of historiography needed to pay attention to the same prose effects as literary critics: discourse, metaphor, fantasy, narration (different but related explorations in chronology, history, and loss came in Martin Amis's *Time's Arrow* (1991), Marina Warner's *The Lost Father* (1988), and Ian McEwan's *The Child in Time* (1987)). Julian Barnes's earlier novel, *Flaubert's Parrot* (1984), played similar tricks with biography, as did D. M. Thomas's *The White Hotel* (1981) and Peter Ackroyd's *The Last Will and Testament of Oscar Wilde* (1983). Ackroyd went on in the 1990s, with his studies of Charles Dickens and William Blake, to contest the boundary between biography and fiction from the other side, introducing overt rhetorical or literary techniques into his life-stories. The comic social novel, along the lines of Evelyn Waugh and Kingsley Amis, continued in the work of writers as varied as William Boyd, Beryl Bainbridge, and Tom Sharpe, while A. S. Byatt, in her tour de force *Possession* (1990), brought together satirical slants on post-structuralist theory, the academic novel, detective fiction, the late Victorian Romance, and literary biography. Most significantly, Byatt succeeded in blending the social perspective of the liberal realist novel with a dissection of history, identity, and language more typical of postmodernist writing.

Byatt has never explicitly presented herself as a feminist novelist, but Emma Tennant, Fay Weldon, and Pat Barker produced assertive yet questioning novels that confronted chauvinism, patriarchy, and male violence. More recent feminist novelists like Zoë Fairbairns and Sarah Dunant have remodelled masculinist genres such as the sci-fi novel, detective fiction, and crime thrillers. Fairbairns also founded the very productive Feminist Writers group with Sara Maitland, Michelene Wandor, and Michèle Roberts, while a number of new women's presses were founded in the 1970s and 1980s after the success of Virago. From the momentum gained by an increasingly militant movement in the 1970s, gay writing broke into the mainstream in the 1980s with Jeanette Winterson and Alan Hollinghurst, followed by such writers as Maureen Duffy and Jackie Kay. Gender criticism, body politics, queer theory, and media interest in (usually food-related) 'hysterical illnesses' all led to increased emphasis on sexuality and identity politics.

As implied at the start of this section, inasmuch as it is useful to talk of literary decades, the 1980s has generally been seen as the foremost period for British fiction since the war. There are many reasons for this but the beginning of the decade might be considered in terms of a signal transition. In 1980 the Booker Prize was won by William Golding's *Rites of Passage* (1980), the first volume in his *To the Ends of the Earth* trilogy: a sequence of sea novels which demonstrated his continuing concern with the interlocking of the material and spiritual planes. Golding's vision of the metaphysical complexity of human existence led him in 1983 to become, until V. S. Naipaul's award in 2001, Britain's only Nobel prize-winning novelist since the war. Golding was perhaps considered Britain's most important novelist at the end of the 1970s, but the year after Golding's Booker success, the prize was won by Salman Rushdie's second novel, *Midnight's Children* (1981) – which was also named the 'Booker of Bookers' in 1993: the outstanding winner of the first 25 years. Rushdie has since become, for literary and non-literary reasons, Britain's best-known novelist; yet his preoccupations, with politics, ethnicity, and national identity, are hugely different from Golding's spiritual concerns. More generally, as can be seen from prize lists in the 1980s, many other new names started to gain prominence: an older school of writers from Golding and Angus Wilson to Iris Murdoch and Doris Lessing were gradually being eclipsed by a new generation, from Amis and McEwan to Timothy Mo, A. S. Byatt, D. M. Thomas, and William Boyd. The most controversial work of fiction in the 1980s was Rushdie's fourth novel, which brought book-burning to Britain's streets and the *fatwa* from Iran. Rushdie's earlier excoriation of Pakistan's history since independence, *Shame* (1983), had been banned in several countries and brought him many political enemies, but *The Satanic Verses* (1988), a novel of migrants and post-colonial reinscriptions, mainly set in Ellowen Deeowen (London), provoked greater controversy on religious grounds. A defining moment in itself, the Rushdie Affair became the backdrop to Hanif Kureishi's 1995-novel of racial tension and multicultural failure, *The Black Album* (1995). Kureishi also considered the meeting of East and West in *The Buddha of Suburbia* (1990), a critique of 1970s trends that exposed England's partial appropriation of India's 'spirituality' alongside its wider rejection of the transnationals that Britain had actively recruited from the Commonwealth since the 1950s. Kazuo Ishiguro also provided an understated but probing examination of English values in *The Remains of the Day* (1989), a novel which took the formality and the adherence to traditional hierarchies partly explored in his earlier Japanese stories and transferred them to an analysis of English class and nostalgia, where emotional repression and the restraints imposed by master–slave relationships were shown to have infected and stultified both personal feelings and political action.

The Scottish novel has undergone a transformation since the early 1980s every bit as great as that in English fiction. Alasdair Gray, Scotland's most experimental contemporary novelist, at the very least in terms of typography and the marriage of text and image, has been followed by such writers as James Kelman, Janice Galloway, Andrew Grieg, A. L. Kennedy, and Alan Warner. The most well known recent Anglo-Welsh novelists are Alice Thomas Ellis and Bernice Rubens, though there are new writers starting to emerge, such as Russell Celyn Jones (*The Eros Hunter*, 1998), Niall Griffiths (*Sheepshagger*, 2001), and Stephen Knight (*Mr Schnitzel*, 2001). Overall, the 1990s might be most readily drawn in terms of post-colonial themes such as decolonization and diaspora. For example, Indian fiction in English, concerned with migrant identity and colonial relationships, has revealed some of the most exciting writers of the last 30 years: Vikram Seth, Ruth Prawer Jhabvala, Kamala Markandaya, Amit Chaudhuri, Shashi Tharoor, and Sunetra Gupta. Alongside these has developed a plethora of highly respected award-winning British writers with Caribbean or African roots, such as Caryl Phillips and Ben Okri.

Steven Connor has argued that amid these cultural cross-currents, transnational tensions, and international writings 'it is now hard to be sure of what "the British novel" may be said to consist' (Connor 1996: 27). Yet, the place at which the modern British novel has arrived might be described in terms of a number of tendencies or cultural dominants. For example, the majority of novels published in the early twenty-first century are likely to be written in the first person. Belief in the appropriateness of the narratorial hierarchy of discourse declined over the last century and many novelists now seem to prefer to render one consciousness or narrator in the first person, rather than write in the omniscient third person, which is a way of rendering the world that they might see as antithetical to everyday experience. Alongside this trend has been an increase in 'life-writing'. The first person narrator has very commonly been an individual in many ways similar to the author. Such books use the autobiographical mode and are written in a meditative, confessional style, while their authors often seek neither to equate the narrator with themselves nor to pretend that the narrator is simply a fictional character. Books in this mode range from Naipaul's 1987 *The Enigma of*

Arrival ('fiction') and Amis's 2000 *Experience* ('autobiography') to Winterson's 1992 *Written on the Body* and Kureishi's 1998 *Intimacy* ('autobiographical fiction' or 'fictional autobiography'). In many cases, fiction over the last 35 years has also eschewed the novel's traditional attempt to render depth, preferring to tell a story, which, instead of seeking to offer truth, deep meaning, or philosophical belief, depicts particular aspects of the modern world refracted through the life experience of individuals. It is also fair to say that the most striking characteristic of the contemporary novel is variety, epitomized by the wide range of authors whose reputations are perhaps still in the ascendant, such as Iain Sinclair, Adam Thorpe, Sarah Waters, Jim Crace, Monica Ali, Hari Kunzru, Lawrence Norfolk, Rachel Cusk, David Mitchell, Andrew Miller, and Diran Adebayo. As we will see, this emphasis on plurality has been dominant for at least the last 15 years, as the novels and novelists themselves become increasingly diverse.

0.3. Criticism

In 1977, Malcolm Bradbury edited a collection entitled *The Novel Today*. The book was subtitled 'Contemporary Writers on Modern Fiction' and included a range of essays from Iris Murdoch's 'Against Dryness', first published in 1961, to Gerald Graff's 'The Myth of the Postmodernist Breakthrough' from 1973. Most of the contributing writers were British, a few American, and one European: Michel Butor. The book was reissued in a new edition in 1990, presumably because either the publishers or Malcolm Bradbury felt that the first edition had been in some sense eclipsed or superseded. Yet, the essays chosen for inclusion were the same as in the first edition with two exceptions. The two new selections were not directly concerned with British, or even American writers, but reserved for the Europeans Milan Kundera and Italo Calvino. Graff's 'The Myth of the Postmodernist Breakthrough' was omitted, presumably because in the intervening years it was realized that it wasn't a 'myth', confirmed by the introduction of two heavyweight postmodernists in Calvino and Kundera. From the evidence of the negligible changes to the list of 12 essays, it seems that Bradbury in fact wanted, or at least felt able, to convey the idea that the novel 'Today' in 1990 could be represented by the novel 'Today' in 1977, or rather from 1961 to

1973. Yet, the world into which this reissue masquerading as a new edition emerged, had changed dramatically. Looking inside the pages of the two editions of *The Novel Today* provokes some noteworthy comparisons between Bradbury's two Introductions.

In the first Introduction, Bradbury is much exercised by the concerns of the 1960s: 'the Death of the novel', 'the literature of exhaustion', 'the nouveau roman', the 'anti-novel', 'metafiction', and so forth. Yet, this debate leads him to conclude that 'the novel does indeed seem to have become, in criticism, the exemplary literary object, displacing the poem, and, to a lesser extent, the play, as *the* type of literary experience, an ultimate example of what we do when we tell a story, report a fact, devise an order for events' (NT, 10). In this Introduction of 1977, the importance of the novel is not in question for Bradbury, and arguably its importance was signalled precisely by fiction being in some sense 'in crisis': fiction was important enough to have a crisis. The excitement surrounding the novel has often come precisely from this concern over its form and function. Bradbury says that there is an international debate in which the business of the novel is put under question, and in which certain preoccupations are evident: the fictiveness of fictions, the role of narrative, and the relationship between fictional structures and other types of prose-writing.

With respect to the British novel, while declining to cite Lessing and Golding, Bradbury considers the interrogation of realism in Angus Wilson, Iris Murdoch, Muriel Spark, David Storey, John Fowles, and B. S. Johnson, novelists who questioned the associations of British fiction with sociological writing, with a persistent liberalism, and with what the critic Bernard Bergonzi labelled 'predictable pleasures'. Overall, in its interest in the future of the novel, Bradbury's 1977 Introduction is concerned with form and experiment, with the ways in which the modern novel has refracted as well as constructed contemporary reality.

After this, it perhaps comes as a surprise to read the Introduction to the 1990 edition, published subsequent to fiction's prominent resurgence in the 1980s. It is, first of all, half the length of the earlier prefatory chapter, as though there were only half as much to say. The novel, Bradbury argues, now has a 'clear character' having 'regained much of its stature and its artistic and intellectual interest' (NT2, 2). In other words, after the 1980s, the novel is no longer 'in crisis'. The reasons for this that Bradbury instances are largely extraneous to the novel: 'There has been an increase in public discussion, major publishers have concentrated on [the novel], and even the proliferation of literary prizes for fiction has done much to draw attention to contemporary talents.' Next, this new Introduction again reviews the development of the novel in the twentieth century from Henry James to the 1960s, from modernism to postmodernism, but has little to say about 'the Novel Today'. Only on the closing page does a sense of the change emerge:

> In the previous edition of this book, I made much of the emphasis on 'fictionality'. The argument seemed particularly necessary then because, in Britain at least, there did seem to be a tradition of obstinate and often provincialized realism which limited the invention of the novel [although] by that time we were already seeing the emergence of a striking new generation of writers in Britain – as various as Angela Carter, Ian McEwan, Martin Amis, Julian Barnes, Bruce Chatwin, Graham Swift and Salman Rushdie – who had broken away from the provincializing spirit of much post-war British fiction. That general widening of horizons has led to a much more expansive and interesting discussion of the novel ...   (NT2, 11)

The reader expecting this discussion to then follow is disappointed because in one more paragraph Bradbury has finished the essay. He adds some remarks on Milan Kundera and concludes that there is no 'distinctive contemporary movement' in fiction so 'it is better not to seek a critical finality'. The essay finishes, forestalling discussion and signalling not the death of the novel but an end to the critic's attempt to describe it. The baton is then handed to the novelists themselves to discuss their work and its position in contemporary fiction, or rather, with the two exceptions of Kundera and Calvino, in the fiction of the 1960s and the early 1970s.

To find the discussion that Bradbury sets up but elects not to have, we might turn to an essay first given as a talk at the same time. Also speaking in 1990, one of the contributors to Bradbury's collection, David Lodge, takes up the same 'state of the novel' debate in what was later to become the preface to his own essay collection entitled *The Practice of Writing* – a title that again exhibits a concern to move away from criticism to performance. Lodge's talk also considers pluralism to be the foremost characteristic of

contemporary fiction at the end of the 1980s. He says: 'The astonishing variety of styles on offer today, as if in an aesthetic supermarket, includes traditional as well as innovative styles,
minimalism as well as excess, nostalgia as well as prophecy.'
(PW, 11) Without a dominant literary mode or any consensus
about aesthetic value, as Lodge believes there was in the 1930s or
1950s, some other value system may take over. He argues therefore that: 'given the nature of our society it is not surprising that
a somewhat materialistic notion of success, as measured by sales,
advances, prizes, media celebrity etc., has filled the vacuum'.
Lodge thinks that 'success' has supplanted the fashions of literary
judgement.

Here then, we seem to enter the 'aesthetic supermarket', the
meeting point of two ways of considering the novel, the aesthetic
and the commercial. Lodge is thus viewing the novel through the
political and social reformation of the Thatcher years:

> It is a commonplace that the literary novel acquired a new
> commercial significance in the 1980s, and it is no coincidence
> that it was a decade dedicated to Enterprise culture and the
> deregulation and internationalisation of high finance. ...
> Prestigious literary writers became valuable assets, like brand
> names in the commodity market, worth far more than the
> income they actually generated. ... The literary bestseller was
> born, a concept that would have seemed a contradiction in
> terms to F. R. and Q. D. Leavis.   (PW, 12)

In revising this talk into an essay for publication in 1996, Lodge
considers the economic recession earlier in the decade. He sees
publishing houses streamlining their lists as well as their staff,
reviews dedicated to hyped rather than innovative fiction, and
the mass marketing of competent writers alongside the down
ward spiral of sales of less accessible novels.

> Today, novelists with a reputation do not send off a manuscript
> for publication but enter into negotiations between agent and
> publisher, with the prestigious novel itself possibly even going
> up for auction. Acceptance for publication is only the beginning
> of a campaign involving sales and marketing departments,
> designs teams, bookshop tours, interviews, production sched-
> ules, and an eye on the movie rights as much as the calendar of

book prizes. The Death of the author in the academy coincided with the birth of the modern literary celebrity in the media. While some writers recoil from this whole process, few manage to avoid it entirely, and the creative writer, a term which itself now smacks of institutionalisation, creative writing commonly being a course rather than a solitary activity, is encouraged to consider themselves as 'professionals in a business partnership with their publishers'.   (PW, 14)

Lodge descries and decries the 'contamination of literary values by considerations of fame and money', as though literary values might exist separately from society, but his point remains that the majority of novelists today are embarking on a career as much as if not more than a vocation (while it is mooted that novels in 2004 can receive commercial payments for product placements, Fay Weldon's 2001 novel *The Bulgari Connection* was the first to be sponsored: Weldon was committed to a dozen product placements but the decision to put 'Bulgari' in the book's title was her own). In an expression which itself fixes Lodge's essay in our time, he remarks that a major repercussion of this situation is that the modern novel, even an experimental one, will be 'reader-friendly'.

Lodge hints at publishing changes in the 1990s that have had an impact on literary fiction. The first of these embraces various takeovers and mergers among publishing houses and their parent organizations that have increasingly resulted in conglomerates who perceive literature as they might any other part of their business: as a source of profit and prestige, generating cultural if not always financial capital. The other major, but now familiar, factor is the collapse of the net book agreement, which means that consumers need only pay the full price for a popular novel if they choose to – and may benefit by a 50% discount from a promotional offer, even on much literary fiction such as those works on the Booker Prize short list. This will potentially be compounded by the proposed move to remove prices from book covers altogether.

Alongside this shift, Lodge draws attention to the digital revolution in print and communications technology which has led to a proliferation of media outlets: newspapers, magazines, supplements, TV channels, and radio stations not only have an appetite for fiction but for the gossip that now surrounds it. All of which suggests that fiction at the start of the twenty-first century is very different from how it was at the beginning or even the middle of the twentieth.

0.4. Twelve Novelists

Any selection of contemporary novelists is likely to be partial and in some ways arbitrary, but this book concentrates solely on British authors born since 1940. Indeed, with the significant exception of Zadie Smith, who alone represents authors from the 2003 *Granta* list, all the novelists considered here were born in the 40s and 50s. They have all produced their best work since 1970. Others I have not included, such as Doris Lessing, V. S. Naipaul, Alasdair Gray, and A. S. Byatt are studied alongside writers like Ishiguro and Carter on contemporary fiction courses but were born in the interwar years – and in the case of Lessing and Naipaul they produced a good proportion of their significant work before 1970. Some other important writers producing key works after 1970, such as Anthony Burgess, Iris Murdoch and William Golding, are clearly of an earlier generation: each of them published a first novel in the mid-50s, alongside *Lucky Jim*, the first novel by Kingsley Amis, Martin's father. It is perhaps a sign of this shift in culture and in reputations that Kingsley is now more often likely to be referenced this way than Martin Amis is likely to be introduced as his son.

The dozen novelists discussed here represent a cross-section of the most prominent writers born since the beginning of the Second World War. They are in a sense, for the most part, from the *Granta*-list generation, though Angela Carter was too old and Zadie Smith far too young to be included in the first list of 1983. Though others born in the period could have been chosen, from Iain Sinclair, Timothy Mo, Peter Ackroyd, Nick Hornby, and Ben Okri to Iain Banks, James Kelman, Janice Galloway, and Bruce Chatwin, the novelists I have selected for inclusion are among those most often encountered on contemporary fiction courses. Also, while Zadie Smith is included because *White Teeth* has become the most likely British novel of the new millennium to be studied at University, the writers born in the 60s and 70s have generally not yet had the same impact, as a group, or appeared to critics as a generation, though certain writers have gained some prominence on syllabi: for example, John Lanchester, Will Self,

Jonathan Coe, and A. L. Kennedy. Others, such as David Mitchell and Sarah Waters, are increasingly likely to appear on courses over the next ten years. A further group appear more regularly on post-colonial literature courses for reasons that may increasingly seem anachronistic: Caryl Phillips, Joan Riley, Buchi Emecheta, and David Dabydeen.

If a question mark is more and more likely to be placed over the usefulness of the first adjective in 'black British fiction', one can also be placed over the second. On one level 'British' fiction is simply a matter of passports and residency, just as it is one of language. For example, an author such as W. G. Sebald did not write in English, was not born in Britain, but, as a long-term resident, could be claimed to be a British writer as much as Joan Brady, who was born and raised in the USA, but, now living in Devon, won the Whitbread novel award, which is open only to British writers, with a book about the USA. Another salutary example could be David Mitchell, who has to date lived most of his adult life in Japan, and has primarily written about other countries, such that he is in a sense not a British writer because he has not made his career in Britain (which was the criteria for inclusion in Merritt Moseley's book on *British Novelists Since 1960*). Irish writers, such as Brian Moore, Roddy Doyle, Patrick McCabe, John Banville, and William Trevor, have not been included as they are more than worth a separate book and the resurgence of Irish literature in recent decades has made for a distinctive literary scene with, in many cases, different if parallel concerns.

Just as Irish writing (and increasingly Scottish writing) is likely to be taught as a distinct element on courses across the British Isles, the 12 chapters here concentrate on a selection of the writers that are most often studied at University under the umbrella term 'contemporary British fiction'. There is clearly a sense therefore that they are considered to shed light on British society, culture, or literature since the 1970s. Alongside the perennial trinity of sex, love, and death, some themes recur across their work: war, apocalyptic cities, queer and gender identities, the family in crisis, serial killers, childhood, new ethnicities, and American influences. Youth subculture in its broadest sense has been a constant subject, as has the individual's relation to history and heritage. Fabulation and dirty realism have existed side-by-side, and the dominant mode has accentuated irony and first-person narrative.

The authors under consideration here are concerned with a range of subjects and they can be grouped in varying and surprising ways on topics such as national identity and post-imperial Britain (Kureishi and Smith), science (McEwan and Winterson), art and love (Barnes and Winterson), vernacular language and colonialism (Welsh and Rushdie), war and history (Barker and Swift), gender and mythology (Barker and Carter), detectives and unreliable narrators (Amis, Swift, and Ishiguro). However, if we consider what Graham Swift calls the 'here and now', then, with the notable exceptions of writers like Amis and Welsh, it does remain true that a remarkable amount of British fiction concerns the past, just as it is true that a great deal concerns other countries. A scan of the Booker and Whitbread prize winners listed below will reveal few novels about the present-day UK, which suggests that one unusual thing that can be said about the contemporary British novel is that comparatively little of it, outside of subgenres such as ladlit and chicklit, seems to be set in contemporary Britain. This is a major contrast, for example, with the American novel.

Critics have argued that British fiction has few writers with a claim to be considered alongside US novelists like Saul Bellow, Philip Roth, John Updike, or Don DeLillo. Some, like Amis for example, certainly take a large number of cues from such writers and attempt to transfer their style to a transatlantic if not always British scene. Alternatively, it could be argued that a more appropriate comparison is with European writers, and novelists like McEwan and Barnes look more often to Germany or France for the sense of a broader, international cultural position. This is arguably an acknowledgement, consciously or unconsciously, that European politics and culture provide a key context for British life and literature that can be obscured when the modern world most often 'dreams itself American', in Stuart Hall's phrase.

In much contemporary fiction, Britain's imperial past and post-colonial present provide a third geographical perspective alongside the US and Europe. Several of the writers covered in this study, notably Rushdie, Kureishi, and Smith, depict an 'inbetween' experience and viewpoint in their novels, aware of the changes needed to be wrought on traditional ideas of British identity in order to include the migrant's experience and also recognize the new British ethnic mix brought about by the post-war diaspora. With regard to the continued importance of imperial history, it may also be worth noting that a British novelist has not won the Booker prize in the last five years – the Commonwealth has instead provided winners from South Africa, Canada, and Australia.

Kazuo Ishiguro, who has won the Booker for what is by far his most 'English' novel, is another writer who poses a question for any easy understanding of what exactly 'British' fiction is: resident and educated in England, he was born in Japan and writes about an internal world that ranges across diverse national landscapes as well as real and imagined memories. By contrast, the works of Graham Swift and Pat Barker rarely move outside the confines of England for much of their narrative (though Greece and France, for example, do feature as locations in their novels), just as Irvine Welsh mostly depicts a localized life in and around Leith, though sometimes with a European perspective and with, for example, American or Australian scenes. Different again are Carter and Winterson, who deal with myriad imaginative worlds that are likely to transport characters across borders and continents to explore ideas and emotions that are often more central than issues of geographical place.

Any conclusions about the contemporary novel have to recognize the startling diversity of subject matter and experience that characterize British fiction. Benedict Anderson has argued that print capitalism, Protestantism, and vernacular languages allowed the 'imagining' of the modern nation, and remembering that national fiction is an imagined rather than an empirical phenomenon, reinforced by capitalism and the state infrastructure, is important in trying to describe the British novel. Nation states have become more pluralistically imagined since the eighteenth century and the same has to be true for 'British' fiction, which has a number of repeated themes and concerns, including the subject of national identities, but is less amenable to definition than it ever was. Indeed the resistance to homogenizing or defining is the most important characteristic of contemporary British writing – as opposed to a 'national literature' – which bears the hallmark of diversity alongside the qualities of energy and imagination that ensure its continued importance.

Timeline

	Events and non-fiction	Included fiction	Other fiction	*Booker winner	Whitbread best novel
1970	Labour lose general election to Edward Heath's Conservatives; Beatles split; Death of E M Forster; Thalidomide scandal; Ted Hughes' *Crow*		Muriel Spark *The Driver's Seat*	Bernice Rubens *The Elected Member*	
1971	Decimalization; Immigration Bill; Open University begins; Industrial Relations Bill to halt unofficial strikes; Greenpeace founded; Edward Bond's *Lear*	Carter *Love* (revised 1987)	Doris Lessing *Briefing for a Descent into Hell*; E. M. Forster *Maurice*; B. S. Johnson *House Mother Normal*	V. S. Naipaul *In a Free State*	Gerda Charles *The Density Waltz*
1972	Miners' Strike; 'Bloody Sunday' in Northern Ireland; John Betjeman becomes Poet Laureate; Tom Stoppard's *Jumpers*	Carter *The Infernal Desire Machines of Doctor Hoffman*	Margaret Drabble *The Needle's Eye*; Richard Adams *Watership Down*	John Berger *G.*	Susan Hill *The Bird of Night*

1973	After a referendum, Britain enters European Economic Community; oil crisis; Virago founded	Amis *The Rachel Papers*	Graham Greene *The Honorary Consul*; J. G. Ballard *Crash*	J G Farrell *The Siege of Krishnapur*	Shiva Naipaul *The Chip Chip Gatherers*
1974	Wilson Labour Government formed; Philip Larkin's *High Windows*	Amis *Dead Babies*; Carter *Fireworks: Nine Profane Pieces*	Doris Lessing *The Memoirs of a Survivor*	Nadine Gordimer *The Conservationist*; Stanley Middleton *Holiday*	Iris Murdoch *The Sacred & Profane Love Machine*
1975	Thatcher becomes Conservative Party leader; North Sea Oil; Record levels of inflation; Sex Discrimination Bill; Seamus Heaney's *North*; Harold Pinter's *No Man's Land*	McEwan *First Love, Last Rites*; Rushdie *Grimus*	Malcolm Bradbury *The History Man*; David Lodge *Changing Places*; Sam Selvon *Moses Ascending*; Paul Scott *The Raj Quartet*	Ruth Prawer Jhabvala *Heat and Dust*	William McIlvanney *Docherty*
1976	Start of Punk Rock; National Theatre opens; Race Relations Act; Notting Hill Riots; Callaghan takes over from Wilson as Labour PM;	Rosamond Lehmann *A Sea-Grape Tree*		David Storey *Saville*	William Trevor *The Children of Dynmouth*

Continued

	Events and non-fiction	Included fiction	Other fiction	*Booker winner	Whitbread best novel
1977	Concorde's maiden passenger flight; David Edgar's *Destiny*	Carter *The Passion of New Eve*	Margaret Drabble *The Ice Age*; Barbara Pym *Quartet in Autumn*	Paul Scott *Staying On*	Beryl Bainbridge *Injury Time*
1978	David Hare's *Plenty*; Craig Raine's *The Onion, Memory*	Amis *Success*; McEwan *In Between the Sheets*; McEwan *The Cement Garden*	Fay Weldon *Praxis*; Emma Tennant *The Bad Sister*	Iris Murdoch *The Sea, The Sea*	Paul Theroux *Picture Palace*
1979	Soviet Union invades Afghanistan; 'Winter of Discontent'; Thatcher wins election with Conservatives	Carter *The Bloody Chamber and Other Stories*	V. S. Naipaul *A Bend in the River*; William Golding *Darkness Visible*	Penelope Fitzgerald *Offshore*	Jennifer Johnston *The Old Jest*
1980	Ronald Regan elected President of USA; Brian Friel's *Translations*	Barnes *Metroland*; Swift *The Sweet Shop Owner*	Anthony Burgess *Earthly Powers*	William Golding *Rites of Passage*	Merritt Moseley *How Far Can You Go?*

1981	Prince Charles marries Diana Spencer; city riots; first personal computers	Amis *Other People: A Mystery Story*; McEwan *The Comfort of Strangers*; Swift *Shuttlecock*; Rushdie *Midnight's Children*	D. M. Thomas *The White Hotel*	Salman Rushdie *Midnight's Children*	Maurice Leitch *Silver's City*
1982	Falklands Conflict; Britain's first official Aids-related death; Social Democrat Party founded; Greenham Common women protestors; Launch of Channel 4; Caryl Churchill's *Top Girls*; Blake Morrison and Andrew Motion (eds) *Contemporary British Poetry*	Barker *Union Street*; Barnes *Before She Met Me*; Ishiguro *A Pale View of Hills*; Swift *Learning to Swim and Other Stories*	William Boyd *An Ice Cream-War*; Timothy Mo *Sour Sweet*; Bruce Chatwin *On the Black Hill*; Graham Greene *Monsieur Quixote*	Thomas Keneally *Schindler's Ark*	John Wain *Young Shoulders*
1983	Cruise Missiles arrive in UK; Conservatives re-elected; William Golding wins Nobel Prize	Rushdie *Shame*; Swift *Waterland* (revised 1992)	Fay Weldon *The life and Loves of a She Devil*	J. M. Coetzee *The Life and Times of Michael K*	William Trevor *Fools of Fortune*
1984	Miners' Strike; Band Aid; Ted Hughes becomes Poet Laureate; IRA bomb Tory Brighton Conference	Amis *Money: A Suicide Note*; Barker *Blow Your House Down*; Barnes *Flaubert's Parrot*; Carter *Nights at the Circus*	David Lodge *Small World*; Iain Banks *The Wasp Factory*; Alasdair Gray *Lanark*; Kingsley Amis *Stanley and the Women*	Anita Brookner *Hotel du Lac*	Christopher Hope *Kruger's Alp*

Continued

	Events and non-fiction	Included fiction	Other fiction	*Booker winner	Whitbread best novel
1985	London and Birmingham riot; Live Aid; *EastEnders* starts; Tony Harrison's *V*; Carol Ann Duffy's *Standing Female Nude*	Carter *Black Venus*; Winterson *Oranges Are Not the Only Fruit*; Winterson *Boating for Beginners*	Caryl Phillips *The Final Passage*; Peter Ackroyd *Hawksmoor*; John Fowles *A Maggot*	Keri Hulme *The Bone People*	Peter Ackroyd *Hawksmoor*
1986	Lockerbie Disaster	Barker *The Century's Daughter* (*Liza's England*); Ishiguro *An Artist of the Floating World*	Jim Crace *Continent*; Timothy Mo *An Insular Possession*	Kingsley Amis *The Old Devils*	Kazuo Ishiguro *An Artist of the Floating World*
1987	Stock Market Crash; Wind Storms; Thatcher wins third term; Churchill's *Serious Money*	Amis *Einstein's Monsters*; Barnes *Staring at the Sun*; McEwan *The Child in Time*; Winterson *The Passion*	Peter Ackroyd *Chatterton*; Margaret Drabble *The Radiant Way*; V. S. Naipaul *The Enigma of Arrival*	Penelope Lively *Moon Tiger*	Ian McEwan *The Child in Time*
1988	Stephen Hawking's *A Brief History of Time*; Education Reform Act Introduces National Curriculum	Rushdie *The Satanic Verses*; Swift *Out of this World*	Alan Hollinghurst *The Swimming Pool Library*; Bruce Chatwin *Utz*; David Lodge *Nice Work*	Peter Carey *Oscar and Lucinda*	Salman Rushdie *The Satanic Verses*

1989	Berlin Wall torn down; End of Cold War; Fatwa against Rushdie; 'poll tax' introduced in Scotland	Amis *London Fields*; Barker *The Man Who Wasn't There*; Barnes *A History of the World in 10½ Chapters*; Ishiguro *The Remains of the Day*; Winterson *Sexing the Cherry*	James Kelman *A Disaffection*; Rose Tremain *Restoration*; Janice Galloway *The Trick is to Keep Breathing*	Kazuo Ishiguro *The Remains of the Day*	Lindsay Clarke *The Chymical Wedding*
1990	East and West Germany reunified; John Major takes over as Prime Minister from Thatcher; 'poll tax' introduced in England and Wales	Kureishi *The Buddha of Suburbia*; McEwan *The Innocent*	Beryl Bainbridge *An Awfully Big Adventure*; Nicholas Shakespeare *The Vision of Elena Silves*	A. S. Byatt *Possession*	Nicholas Mosley *Hopeful Monsters*
1991	Gulf War; apartheid ends in South Africa; Francis Fukuyama's *The End of History*	Barker *Regeneration*; Amis *Time's Arrow: The Nature of the Offence*, Barnes *Talking it Over*; Carter *Wise Children*	Iain Sinclair *Downriver*; Caryl Phillips *Cambridge*; Gordon Burn *Alma Cogan*	Ben Okri *The Famished Road*	Jane Gardam *The Queen of the Tambourine*
1992	Creation of World Wide Web; Clinton elected President in US; John Major wins UK general	Barnes *The Porcupine*; McEwan *Black Dogs*; Swift *Ever After*; Winterson *Written*	Michèle Roberts *Daughters of the House*; Gilbert Adair *The Death*	Barry Unsworth *Sacred Hunger*; Michael Ondaatje *The English Patient*	Alasdair Gray *Poor Things*

Continued

	Events and non-fiction	Included fiction	Other fiction	*Booker winner	Whitbread best novel
	election; Polytechnics made into Universities; European Single Market	On the Body	of the Author; Adam Thorpe Ulverton		
1993	Jamie Bulger killing; Stephen Lawrence murder; Launch of UK satellite TV; Fred D'Aguiar's British Subjects	Barker The Eye in the Door; Carter American Ghosts and Old World Wonders; Welsh Trainspotting	Caryl Phillips Crossing the River; Vikram Seth A Suitable Boy; Sebastian Faulks Birdsong	Roddy Doyle Paddy Clarke Ha Ha Ha	Joan Brady Theory of War
1994	Opening of Channel Tunnel from Folkestone to Calais; National Lottery commences; Church of England ordains first women priests	Rushdie East, West; Welsh The Acid House; Winterson Art & Lies: A Piece for Three Voices and a Bawd	Romesh Gunesekera Reef; Jonathan Coe What a Carve Up!; Louis de Bernières Captain Corelli's Mandolin; Alan Hollinghurst The Folding Star	James Kelman How Late It Was, How Late	William Trevor Felicia's Journey
1995	Treaty halts fighting in Bosnia; O. J. Simpson trial; Oklahoma bombing	Barker The Ghost Road; Amis The Information; Ishiguro The Unconsoled; Kureishi The Black Album; Rushdie The Moor's	Kate Atkinson Behind the Scenes at the British Museum; Nick Hornby High Fidelity; Nicholas Shakespeare	Pat Barker The Ghost Road	Salman Rushdie The Moor's Last Sigh

1996	Opening of 'Shakespeare's Globe on Thames; Prince and Princess of Wales divorce; Clinton reelected	Last Sight; Welsh Marabou Stork Nightmares	Barnes Cross Channel; Swift Last Orders; Welsh Ecstasy: Three Tales of Chemical Romance	The Lancer Upstairs; Alex Garland The Beach; Lawrence Norfolk The Pope's Rhinoceros; Helen Fielding Bridget Jones's Diary	Graham Swift Last Orders	Beryl Bainbridge Every Man for Himself
1997	Death of Princess of Wales; Tony Blair forms Labour Government; Scottish and Welsh devolution referendums; Hong Kong reverts to Chinese rule; first cloned sheep, Dolly	Amis Night Train; Kureishi Love in a Blue Time; McEwan Enduring Love; Winterson Gut Symmetries	Jim Crace Quarantine; Iain Sinclair Lights Out for the Territory; J. K. Rowling Harry Potter and the Philosopher's Stone		Arundhati Roy The God of Small Things	Jim Crace Quarantine
1998	Northern Ireland Peace Agreement; Ted Hughes' Birthday Letters	Barker Another World; Barnes England, England; Kureishi Intimacy; McEwan Amsterdam; Welsh Filth; Winterson The World and Other Places	John King England Away; A. L. Kennedy Original Bliss; James Kelman The Good Times; Giles Foden The Last King of Scotland		Ian McEwan Amsterdam	Justin Cartwright Leading the Cheers
1999	Ethnic cleansing in former Yugoslavia; Andrew	Amis Heavy Water; Kureishi Midnight All Day; Rushdie The	Peter Ackroyd The Plato Papers; Jim Crace Being Dead; Meera Syal		J. M. Coetzee Disgrace	Rose Tremain Music and Silence

Continued

	Events and non-fiction	Included fiction	Other fiction	*Booker winner	Whitbread best novel
			Life Isn't All Ha Ha Hee Hee		
2000	Motion becomes Poet Laureate; Simon Armitage's *Killing Time*	*Ground Beneath Her Feet*			
	Putin becomes President of Russia; George Bush jnr becomes President of US; human genome deciphered	Barnes *Love, etc.*; Ishiguro *When We Were Orphans*; Smith *White Teeth*	Philip Pullman *The Amber Spyglass*; David Mitchell *Ghostwritten*	Margaret Atwood *The Blind Assassin*	Matthew Kneale *English Passengers*
2001	September 11 attack destroys Twin Towers in New York; Blair re-elected with Labour; V. S. Naipaul wins Nobel Prize	Barker *Border Crossing*; Kureishi *Gabriel's Gift*; McEwan *Atonement*; Rushdie *Fury*; Welsh *Glue*; Winterson *The PowerBook*	Rachel Seifert *The Dark Room*; Andrew Miller *Oxygen*	Peter Carey *The True History of the Kelly Gang*	Patrick Neate *Twelve Bar Blues*
2002	Golden Jubilee of Queen Elizabeth II; First 'cloned' baby announced in US	Kureishi *The Body*; Smith *The Autograph Man*; Welsh *Porno*	Sarah Waters *Fingersmith*; Barry Unsworth *The Song of the Kings*	Yann Martel *The Life of Pi*	Michael Frayn *Spies*
2003	Second Gulf War; 'SARS' outbreak	Swift *The Light of Day*; Amis *Yellow Dog*; Barker *Double Vision*	Fifth Harry Potter novel, *Order of the Phoenix*; Monica Ali *Brick Lane*	D. B. C. Pierre *Vernon God Little*	Mark Haddon *The Curious Incident of the Dog in the Night-Time*

* The Man Booker Prize is awarded for the best full-length novel written in English by a citizen of the Commonwealth or the Republic of Ireland. The Booker was established in 1969, when the first winner was P. H. Newby with *Something to Answer for*. It has become the best-known literary prize in Britain, is rarely without controversy and a split-jury, and is now something on which one can place a bet at Ladbrokes – some authors have been known to place bets on themselves. Literary prizes are also increasingly pluralistic: Nick Hornby was on the long list (which is pared down to a shortlist of six) of the Booker in 2001, while J. K. Rowling was widely tipped to win the Whitbread in 1999. It has been said that this has resulted in a further stapling together of the literary and the commercial, not least because the most readily quantifiable calibrations of success are book sales and media coverage. Publishers choose the novels in the running for the Booker, whose small management committee includes three publishers, an agent, a librarian, a public relations consultant, and one author (the awarding panel itself has an academic, a critic or two, a writer or two, and a 'celebrity' who, a little paradoxically, represents the 'person in the street'). The Whitbread Book Awards are open to British writers only. Awards are given in the categories of Biography, Novel, First Novel, Poetry, and Children's Novel. Set up by Whitbread plc and the Booksellers Association, it is the richest annual literary award. Angela Carter said of Kureishi's *The Buddha of Suburbia* that it may be 'the first novel ... designed *on purpose* to exclude itself from the Booker list' (one would also be surprised if a novel by Amis, Welsh, or Winterson ever won). The fact that it won the Whitbread 'best first novel' prize helps to illustrate the difference between the two prizes, with the Booker sometimes accused of being middle-brow and populist whereas the Whitbread, perhaps because it is less well-known, cast as a more worthy 'alternative' award: in music terms, the Mercury Music Awards to the Booker's Brits. The same book has never won both prizes.

References and Further Reading

Malcolm Bradbury (ed.),. *The Novel Today* (NT), London: Fontana, 1977. A collection of essays, mainly by practitioners, on fiction from the 1960s and 1970s.

—— (ed.), *The Novel Today* (NT2), Second Edition, London: Fontana, 1990. A new edition of the above.

——, *The Modern British Novel, 1878–2001*, Revised Edition, Harmondsworth: Penguin, 2001. One of the most comprehensive overviews of twentieth-century fiction.

John Brannigan, *Orwell to the Present: Literature in England 1945–2000*, London: Palgrave, 2003. Good general coverage of postwar fiction focussing on notions of 'Englishness'.

Steven Connor, *The English Novel in History 1950–95*, London: Routledge, 1996. An incisive and wide-ranging appraisal with some excellent short analyses.

Dominic Head, *The Cambridge Introduction to Modern British Fiction, 1950–2000*, Cambridge: Cambridge University Press, 2002. Wide-ranging thematic analysis of key novels in the second half of twentieth century.

Richard J. Lane, Rod Mengham, and Philip Tew (eds), *Contemporary British Fiction*, Cambridge: Polity, 2003. Valuable collection of original essays on a wide range of much-studied authors.

Zachary Leader (ed.), *On Modern British Fiction*, Oxford: Oxford University Press, 2002. Conference based essay-collection with contributions by Martin Amis and Ian McEwan. Essays cover a wide range of subjects from 'ladlit' and Scottish fiction to commissioning and reviewing novels.

David Lodge, *The Practice of Writing* (PW), Harmondsworth: Penguin, 1996. A collection of Lodge's recent essays concerned with both fiction and creative writing.

Randall Stevenson, *The British Novel Since the Thirties*, London: Batsford, 1986. An immensely readable, if a little dated, introductory survey.

D.J. Taylor, *After the War: The Novel and England Since 1945*, London: Chatto & Windus, 1993. A highly selective account, from an author with an axe to grind about the state of the novel, in the tradition of liberal criticism.

Richard Todd, *Consuming Fiction: The Booker Prize and Fiction in Britain Today*, London: Bloomsbury, 1996. Wide-ranging analysis of the contemporary novel in relation to competition-culture and consumerism.

Patricia Waugh, *Harvest of the Sixties*, Oxford: Opus, 1995. A comprehensive and authoritative review of literature since the sixties.

Richard Weight, *Patriot: National Identity in Britain 1940–2000*, London: Macmillan, 2002. One of the best single volumes for understanding the social, political, and cultural changes of the second half of the twentieth century in Britain.

Lists Online

http://books.guardian.co.uk/news/page/0,8097,869641,00.html

Guardian newspaper site covering the *Granta's* Best Young British Novelists, 2003

http://www.bbc.co.uk/arts/bigread/index.shtml

The BBC's 2003 'Big Read' page containing its poll of voters' 'top 100 books.'

http://observer.guardian.co.uk/print/0,3858,4772541-102280,00.html

Robert McCrum's 100 greatest novels of all time, for *The Observer*, Sunday 12 October 2003. A list that sets out to counter that of the 'Big Read'.

1
Martin Amis: Lucre, Love, and Literature

1.1. Literary History

In one of Martin Amis's novels, a character complains: 'That's not realism That's – it's vandalism' (M, 226). The accusation has also been levelled at the novel's author more than once. Amis (b.1949) is principally seen as a stylist and a satirist; his books are often more praised for their use of language than for their subject matter, which has been criticized for its WASP insularity. The emphasis on style is in accord with Amis's own views on what is important in fiction. His major collection of essays and reviews was published in 2001 under the title of an article he wrote about James Joyce's *Ulysses*: *The War Against Cliché*. The book's title expresses a stance Amis has inherited from one of his chief literary influences, Vladimir Nabokov, who 'regarded cliché as the key to bad art' (WAC, 245).

A comment that Nabokov once made about Gustave Flaubert, the progenitor of the view that style is of supreme importance in fiction, best summarizes the approach Amis adopts in his work: 'The subject may be crude and repulsive. Its expression is artistically modulated and balanced. This is style. This is art This is the only thing that really matters in books' (WAC, 251). Again, in his autobiography *Experience* (2000), Amis writes: 'style *is* morality: morality detailed, configured, intensified. It's not in the mere narrative arrangement of good and bad that morality makes itself felt. It can be there in every sentence' (E, 121).

Amis is thus more interested in good and bad writing than in literature that attempts to delineate the good and the bad. In another essay from *The War Against Cliché*, Amis picks up on a

35

strand running through V. S. Pritchett's criticism which distin-
guishes between two kinds of writer: the masochist and the
imposer (WAC, 66–7). Pritchett appears to align himself with the
first kind of writer, as one who lets 'their characters speak
through them', but Amis remarks that generally 'Male writers
tend to be imposers, female writers masochists'. Even without
this last comment one would still place Amis as an 'imposer': a
writer who contrives a plot in which the reader is expected not to
sympathize with the characters but to appreciate the aims of the
author. Indeed he has quoted Nabokov as saying that art tries to
make the reader 'share not the emotions of the people in the book
but the emotions of its author' (WAC, 251). Elsewhere he writes:

> The contexts, the great forms of the eighteenth- and nineteenth-
> century sagas, have been exhausted; realism and experimenta-
> tion have come and gone without seeming to point a way
> ahead. The contemporary writer, therefore, must combine these
> veins, calling on the strengths of the Victorian novel together
> with the alienations of post-modernism.   (WAC, 78–9)

The characters of Amis's postmodernist novels are thus alienated
and usually socially marginalized; his plots, like those of his men-
tor Nabokov, are self-consciously analogous to games of chess:
driven by defensive moves and offensive strategies, by the protagonists' manoeuvrings and manipulations. The metafictional
aspect of Amis's work can be seen in his characters' relationship
with their author. John Self meets 'Martin Amis' as a character in
Money, while the narrator of *London Fields* thinks he exists 'in a
book written by somebody else' (LF, 409), and the narrator of *The
Information* turns out to be 'Mart' himself (I, 281).

To date Amis has published nine novels, two collections of
short stories, and six works of non-fiction, including his copiously annotated autobiography *Experience* and the book that is in
part its sequel as well as being a study of Stalin's reception in the
West: *Koba the Dread: Laughter and the Twenty Million* (2002). In the
light of his later fiction, Amis's early novels, *The Rachel Papers*
(1973), *Dead Babies* (1974), *Success* (1978), and to a lesser extent
Other People: A Mystery Story (1981), appear as apprentice work.
Though not derivative, they are clearly written under the influence of other writers: Angus Wilson and Pritchett, Borges and
Nabokov. It is only with *Money: A Suicide Note* (1984) that Amis

moves away from a tight control on form and gives free rein to his linguistic exuberance. With its author appearing as a character, its original narrative voice, and its anatomy of an entire transatlantic culture on-the-make in the 1980s, *Money* has been critically positioned as a key British novel of and about the decade.

Amis's next work of fiction was *Einstein's Monsters* (1987): a collection of five stories set in the shadow or the aftermath of nuclear destruction and preceded by a polemical anti-nuclear essay entitled 'Unthinkability'. This was followed by his most controversial novel, *London Fields* (1989), which takes the style of *Money* and applies it to the pre-millennial apocalyptic concerns of *Einstein's Monsters*. It describes a rain-soaked London under threat of a global disaster that never actually occurs, though the murder that metonymically stands in for it arrives with a pronounced degree of inevitability. *Time's Arrow; Or, The Nature of the Offence* (1991) unfolds in reverse chronology, beginning with the end of a man's life and tracing it sequentially backwards to his involvement with running the Nazi gas chambers. Amis explains that the novel is 'narrated by the soul of one of Mengele's lesser assistants at Auschwitz-Birkenau' (E, 289). An important departure from the three long novels that surround it in his oeuvre, *Time's Arrow* is Amis's most serious fiction, exploring the holocaust in terms of a literal separation of action from conscience, of mind and body from soul or spirit: 'Something isn't quite working: this body I'm in won't take orders from this will of mine' (TA, 13). The story appears to have been meticulously researched and the narration eschews the verbal inventiveness of his other mature novels. Amis once wrote that 'Nearing the Holocaust, a trespasser finds that his imagination is decently absenting itself, and reaches for documentation and technique. The last thing he wants to do, once there, is make anything up' (WAC, 13).

The publication of 1995's novel of literary envy, *The Information*, was surrounded by controversy as Amis's personal life, his financial situation, and even his dental bills were discussed in the press. Not as much as, but in a similar way to *The Satanic Verses*, *The Information* appeared to be overshadowed by the reactions of individuals who were less concerned with the merits of the fiction than with the perceived failings of its author. Amis's next book was *Night Train* (1997), a hardboiled crime thriller that gradually shifts its concerns from that of a whodunit to that of an existentialist 'whydunit'.

Yellow Dog was released in 2003 and billed as a post-9/11 comedy. It received poor reviews, largely because the novel struck critics as, in comparison with his best work, diluted and self-derivative. For many critics, Amis appeared to have little new to say despite the usual, if occasional, bursts of linguistic invention. The narrative itself implies that Amis thinks religious fundamentalism and postmodern relativism are the twin evils faced by a humanity which can only break the circle of violence by an overhaul of secular human consciousness, largely through self-reinvention: an awareness, on the part of those with the power to do so, of the need and the ability to re-imagine humanity. *Yellow Dog's* characters range from a good husband turned 'bad', an exploitative 'yellow' journalist called Clint Smoker (an attenuated version of Amis's earlier loutish protagonists), a porno magnate named after a novel by Henry Fielding, and a faithless king Henry IX.

One of the chief subjects of the novel is masculinity, but here it is allied to a wider sense of the relationship between patriarchy and violence, within which pornography figures as the pervasive symbol and characteristic industry of a fallen world. Amis has said that he sees little but futility in writers attempting to respond to 11 September directly in fiction, but *Yellow Dog* has been written in the belief that radical Islamicism and American foreign policy are fuelled by a male insecurity that has returned the world to pre-1989 fears: 'We had a period when we were congratulating ourselves on having survived nuclear destruction. 11 September plunged us back into the omnipresence of violence' (*Times* 21 October 2002). However, despite the grand themes – *Yellow Dog* climaxes on Valentine's Day with gang violence and a royal abdication as well as a comet narrowly missing the earth and a plane disaster – the novel lacks coherence and direction, its multiple strands underdeveloped and insufficiently intertwined.

Heavy Water and Other Stories, published in 1999, seemed to confirm that Amis, unlike Angela Carter, or Ian McEwan, has a style that is not well suited to the short story, and it is his long novels that have remained his key works. Amis's non-fiction, in *Invasion of the Space Invaders* (1982), *The Moronic Inferno: And Other Visits to America* (1986), *Visiting Mrs. Nabokov and Other Excursions* (1993), and *The War Against Cliché*, is idiosyncratic in the sense that it provides a unique and valuable guide to Amis's psychological and literary make-up. Amis has also written a movie screenplay, for *Saturn 3* (1980), and his experience of this informed the writing of *Money*, in which Lorne Guyland, for example, has been said to resemble *Saturn 3*'s star, Charlton Heston.

What remains constant in most of Amis's fiction is an attempt to reflect, and reflect upon, his own preoccupations at each stage of his life. His first novel, published when he was 24, is structured around the countdown to its protagonist's twentieth birthday; *Money*, published when Amis was approaching forty, details the addictions of a 35-year-old; *The Information*, published when Amis was 46, begins with the crisis-point of the central character's fortieth birthday. The introspection of Amis's narrative concerns has produced three important novels, considered in section three below, but in his mature work he has shown a consistent interest in the relationship the individual bears both to contemporary society and to the long nightmare of twentieth-century history. For many critics, Amis is the key English social novelist of the 1980s, but his work over the last ten years has raised a question as to whether he can continue accurately to dissect the times into the twenty-first century.

1.2. Themes: The Aesthetics of (Self-) Abuse and Apocalypse

Amis's principal male characters are addicted to excess, particularly with regard to drinking and smoking: Richard Tull, in *The Information*, is 'approaching the point where smoking and drinking were *all* he liked to do' (I, 335). The world these characters inhabit is surrounded by TV, pornography, threats of child abuse, and nuclear threat, each of which can be considered in turn.

Long before the advent of 'Reality TV', in Martin Amis's novels TV is reality. John Self, for whom 'Watching television is one of my main interests, one of my chief skills' (M, 67), notes its appropriation of his mind in *Money*: 'Television is cretinizing me – I can feel it. Soon I'll be like the TV artists. You know the people I mean. Girls who subliminally model themselves on kid-show presenters, full of faulty melody and joy, Melody and Joy. Men whose manners show newscaster interference, soap stains, film smears. Or the cretinized, those who talk on buses and streets as if TV were real' (M, 27). Seemingly falling into this last category,

Keith Talent in *London Fields* struggles with describing his hobbies
on a form and 'in the end ... put TV':

> It was no less than the truth. He watched a very great deal of
> TV, always had done, years and years of it, aeons of TV. ... It
> was the world of TV that told him what the world was ... TV
> came at Keith like it came at everybody else; and he had noth-
> ing whatever to keep it out. He couldn't grade or filter it. So he
> thought TV was real ... an exemplary reality, all beautifully
> and gracefully interconnected, where nothing hurt much and
> nobody got old.   (LF, 55)

Amis writes in one of his essays that 'we inhabit the postmodern
age, an age of mass suggestibility, in which image and reality
strangely interact' (WAC, 16). He suggests that modern culture
consists for some people in *striving* to watch television. He notes
for example that Andy Warhol writes in his diaries that 'I tried to
watch TV but nothing good was on' (WAC, 41). Even Keith Talent
needs his television programmes videotaped so they can be either
stepped through (for 'sex, violence, and sometimes money') or
accelerated (everything else): 'he could no longer bear to watch
TV at the normal speed, unmediated by the remote and by the
tyranny of his own fag-browned thumb. Pause. SloMo. Picture
Search' (LF, 165). It is not just the pleasurable aspects of control
and consumption that attract Amis's lowlifes to TV, it is also the
promise of what's on the other side of the camera: 'I see you,
Keith, as a young boy in the street with your nose crushed up
against the glass. But it's not a shop window. It's a TV screen.
We're talking TV stardom here, Keith. Behind the screen is where
you've got to get to. That's where all the other stuff is – all the
stuff you want' (LF, 288). TV in fact becomes all but synonymous
with culture in *London Fields*, just as darts, the ultimate televisual
wallpaper sport, stands for heritage: the pilgrims are thought to
have played the game on the *Mayflower* and King Arthur is 'said
to have played a form of darts' (LF, 313), while Stonehenge is considered to be designed like a dartboard (LF, 396).

For Keith Talent, addicted to simulation, pornography is similarly modern art: 'Pornography awakened all his finer responses.
It wasn't just the sex. He really did think it was beautiful' (LF,
332). Similarly, in *Yellow Dog* Amis consciously and repeatedly
describes a 'Porno' world, while in *Money* pornography is the

highest form of art, its actors self-admiring sack-artists. At one point, John Self is shown by Vron, who they both think is going to become his stepmother, a copy of her porn-mag debut to appreciate. She scans the pages with him, saying 'I'm so proud' (M, 149) and 'I've *always* been creative' (M, 177). In *The Information*, Gwyn Barry typically argues that he doesn't watch pornography because it objectifies women, while, just as typically, Richard Tull argues that he should watch it because it will keep him up-to-date with sexual styles (I, 362). We are told that Nicola Six in *London Fields* 'disliked pornography, or she disliked its incursion into her own lovelife. Because it was so limited, because there was no emotion in it (it spoke straight to the mental quirk), and because it stank of money. But she could do pornography. It was easy' (LF, 191). And it is precisely pornography that Nicola makes for Keith, who watches it in her bedroom while Nicola tells Guy that she is a virgin, pandering to his alternative stereotype (Nicola declares herself explicitly as 'a male fantasy figure', LF, 260). Like TV becomes reality in Amis's fiction, pornography becomes the sexual norm: 'Keith knew that he had no resistance to pornography. He had it on all the time, and even that wasn't enough for him. He wanted it on *when he was asleep*. He wanted it on *when he wasn't there*' (LF, 295). However, it is Steve Cousins in *The Information* for whom pornography has the greatest interest: 'Here's what struck Steve Cousins about pornography: at last he had found something that was as interested in sex as he was. ... Steve Cousins didn't *read* pornography (words were no use here), but he read everything he could find that was about pornography – that was all about the thing that was all about sex' (I, 410).

In one essay, Amis writes that pornography's 'industrial dimensions are an inescapable modern theme' (WAC, 161), and this stretches even to children. Marmaduke, Guy Clinch's unruly son in *London Fields*, 'looks as though he is already contemplating a career in child pornography' (LF, 158). Child abuse features periodically throughout *Yellow Dog*; it is a staple of *London Fields*, where it is applied in a mild form to Guy's child Marmaduke, who is finally if sadistically taught to behave by Nicola's violent nannying, and in more persistent parental ways to Keith and Kath's child Kim. The abuse of the defenceless innocent appears to become the last recourse for put-upon adults who, through the torturing of others, seem also to attempt to punish something in themselves. In *The Information* it is a constant subject, in the press

('every other day on the cover of my newspaper there is a photograph of a murdered child', I, 124) and in the story's chilling end
when Richard's child Marco is nearly brutally attacked by Steve
Cousins (I, 478, 492–3), whose interest in pornography has its
roots here: 'Many times he had read that many of the actors and
almost all of the actresses on the pornographic screen had been
abused as children. That meant that he and they formed ... not a
happy family. But a big one. [...] They were all children together
in this – this big family. All children, until they weren't.
Pornography was the story of his life' (I, 410–11).

   Nuclear disaster is discussed at great length in the essay and
stories of *Einstein's Monsters*. It is here that Amis explains why
nuclear threat infects his novels: 'the modern situation is one of
suspense: no one, no one at all, has any idea how things will turn
out. What we are experiencing inasmuch as it can be experienced
is the experience of nuclear war. Because the anticipation ... the
anxiety, the suspense, is the only experience of nuclear war that
anyone is going to get ... So this is it, this is nuclear war – and it
is ruining everything' (EM, 17). In an essay published soon after
Einstein's Monsters, Amis explains further

> the error of SDI, or Star Wars, is ... [i]t presupposes a situation
> of unique desperation and catastrophic failure, one in which
> everyone has already 'lost'. It presupposes nuclear war. 'Well,
> things do go wrong,' the layman will say with a shrug. But this
> thing isn't like other things. For the first time in history, human
> beings have come up with something that may eliminate all
> second chances, something that therefore *must never go wrong*.
> (WAC, 51)

There is consequently a sense of apocalypse overhanging much of
Amis's work. In *London Fields* there is the prediction of a
'Horrorday': 'That at the moment of full eclipse on 5 November,
as the Chancellor made his speech in Bonn, two very big and very
dirty nuclear weapons would be detonated, one over the Palace
of Culture in Warsaw, one over Marble Arch ... That the conflu-
ence of perihelion and syzygy would levitate the oceans. That the
sky was falling –' (LF, 394).

   Amis's work might best be seen as an attempt to make sense of
a world that doesn't make any. This is clearest in *Time's Arrow*
where the narrator, who does not know that everything is working

in reverse, struggles to understand why venerated doctors inflict so much harm, why murderers are hated when they bring people back to life, why the avaricious give so much to the world. Amis uses the metaphor of time running backwards to express the apparent 'nature' of the holocaust, the inhumane but all-too-human offence of genocide or 'ethnic cleansing'. While Amis's characters are addicted to the excesses of their times, the times appear in his work to be addicted to personal and global forms of destruction, all of which will appear on TV.

1.3. Key Works: *Money, London Fields, The Information*

It has been observed that Amis's three long novels, though they do not have the continuity of characters or plot to constitute a trilogy, do form a triptych: a set of three pictures of West London and contemporary Britain with its American influences.

The first of them is set in 1981 against a backdrop of urban riots and royal weddings, British pubs and Californian saunas, Thatcherism and Reaganomics. *Money* is narrated by John Self, and Amis writes in *Experience* that it is 'the novel that John Self, the narrator, had in him but would never write'. Amis also suggests that the book is akin to 'a series of dramatic poems about the thoughts of so-called ordinary people' (E, 6). Self is a director who has previously worked on advertisements but is now moving on to his first feature film. He jets back and forth across the Atlantic talking to his producer, to actors, to cabbies and hotel clerks, to his girlfriend Selina, and his father Barry, owner of the Shakespeare pub. In Britain Self meets the writer Martin, whom he persuades to rewrite his movie script, and in the US he meets Martina, who persuades him to read a book.

The subtitle of the novel is *A Suicide Note*, and this can be taken to describe John Self's entire narrative or simply to refer to his suicide message at the close of the book; also, the 'suicide note' may be read as Amis the author's as much as Self the narrator's, and this interpretation is sharpened by the fact that Self's closing suicide note is addressed to someone of the same name as Amis's then-wife, Antonia (M, 380). However, as with everything else in this book, the first reference is to money, specifically to banknotes: 'Dollar bills, pound notes, they're suicide notes. *Money* is a suicide note' (M, 116). The suicide depicted in the book is therefore primarily that of a society engulfed by a money-culture. As the psychoanalyst and critic Adam Phillips recently observed, 'We're living in a money cult. … In the 14th century, if you'd asked people what they wanted they'd have said, "To be saved". Now they'd say, "To be rich and famous" ' ('The Pleasure Principle', *The Times Magazine*, 6 July 2002, 40).

John Self's surname conceivably suggests that the character might be in some respects a portrait of the artist (Amis has said that its concerns were also his at the time of writing) but more importantly it suggests the push towards individualism that defined the twentieth century from the ego-theory of Freud, through the increasingly intense popular cults of celebrity and fame, to the commercial greed of the 1980s. In an essay, Amis at one point refers to the 'herd opinions and social anxieties, vanities, touchinesses, and everything else that makes up a self' (WAC, xiii). This is therefore taken to be especially true of John Self, a British-American whose narration is as candid as it is unreliable: his improbable monologue apparently takes place in the present as he even manages to tell his story while having sex (M, 275). Although readers will feel that Self tells them too much, he does not tell everything, partly because of his 'blackouts', partly because there are things he doesn't like to admit to, such as crying at Charles and Diana's royal wedding (M, see 271 compared with 263).

The novel was published in 1984, and Orwell's fiction of that name is a reference point in the story, as is Bulwer Lytton's play *Money* of 1840. But the key intertext is Orwell's earlier novella, *Animal Farm*, which John Self reads unaware that it is an allegory of the Russian revolution or that its depiction of a society taken over by its porcine characters might offer an insight into his world, which is equally the reader's society – not least because the book's suicide note, according to Amis's author's 'note', is addressed to the 'you out there, the dear, the gentle'. Cementing the sense of the *hypocrite lecteur's* complicity, the reader is also addressed by the narrator, a *self*-proclaimed non-reader who would never pick up a book such as *Money* (though he does pick up the economist John Kenneth Galbraith's 1976 classic of the same name). Self professes to hating the educated sections of society and then challenges the reader directly: 'And you hate me, don't you. Yes you do. Because I'm the new kind, the kind who has money but can never use it for anything but ugliness' (M, 58).

All of Self's relationships are defined by money: he sees no point in 'friends', remunerates his girlfriend to have sex with him, and accompanies every other human interaction with a payment – a characteristic possibly inherited from his father, who invoices Self 'for all the money he had spent on my upbringing' (M, 178). As Self says, 'Money is always involved' (M, 19); but what is more, his narrative implies that 'good money' and 'bad money' are now interchangeable (M, 106). The title of Self's movie shifts between these two titles, 'good money' and 'bad money', such that the novel itself can dispense with any adjectives, because, as in economic theory, bad money drives out good. Self at one point says: 'Me, I couldn't even blame money. What is this state, seeing the difference between good and bad and choosing bad – or consenting to bad, okaying bad?' (M, 26). Self, an ultimately incompetent arriviste in the movie world, is in most respects a cipher for his times rather than a 'true' figure (hence the reader looking for character consistency will marvel at a self-confessed illiterate such as Self describing his thoughts as 'A dance of anxiety and supplication, of futile vigil' (M, 60)). Amis has eschewed realism throughout his career and Self's only consistency is to his persona as an addict of the twentieth century (M, 91). One of the significances of this addiction is that it points to Self's downfall (Amis goes to some lengths to parallel the plot of the book to that of *Othello*). His producer, and nemesis, Fielding Goodney explains this to him: 'Always endeavour, Slick, to keep an eye on the addiction industries: you can't lose. The addicts can't win. Dope, liquor, gambling, anything video – these have to be the deep money-veins' (M, 93).

Yet, for many readers, John Self does have a human side that elicits sympathy, especially as he turns out to be only a pantomime villain: the unwitting victim of others, from Goodney to 'Martin Amis'. When one of his ageing stars wants reassurance 'about the nature of his role' as well as his youthfulness, athleticism, and general popularity, Self thinks: 'Me too, pal. Lorne, I sympathize' (M, 182). A couple of pages later Self reflects pathetically on his ignorance: 'Oh Christ, the exhaustion of not knowing anything. It's so tiring and hard on the nerves. It really takes it out of you, not knowing anything. You're given comedy and miss all the jokes. Every hour, you get weaker. Sometimes as I sit alone in my flat in London and stare at the window, I think how dismal it is, how hard, how heavy, to watch the rain and not know why it falls' (M, 184). Though he fails to deflect himself from the frenetic, self-destructive lifestyle he has chosen, Self does at least imagine another possibility: 'Perhaps there are other bits of my life that would take on content, take on shadow, if only I read more and thought less about money' (M, 223). This could be said to stand as the book's advice to the reader, and to the 1980s, but its emphasis is more on eschewing money-culture than on the moral improvement that a postmodernist novel like *Money* might seek to achieve – as 'Martin Amis' himself tells Self: 'Reading's overrated' (M, 372).

* * *

Following the disquiet in Amis's breakthrough novel over living in a money-cult, his next novel shifted to a more sinister agenda:

> We used to live and die without any sense of the planet getting older, of mother earth getting older, living and dying. We used to live outside of history. But now we're all coterminous. We're inside history now all right, on its leading edge, with the wind ripping past our ears. Hard to love, when you're bracing yourself for impact. And maybe love can't bear it either, and flees all planets when they reach this condition, when they get to the end of their twentieth centuries.   (LF, 197)

After the transatlantic world he depicted in *Money*, Amis moved the narrative back to England for his next long book, though this new story is told by an American writer living in London. The animus of the novel is suggested by this passage which references another key writer for Amis: 'in *More Die of Heartbreak* Bellow says that America is the only place to be, because it contains "the real modern action". Everywhere else is "convulsed" in some earlier stage of development. That's true. But England feels like the forefront of something, the elegiac side of it, perhaps' (LF, 101). A state-of-the-nation novel, a murder mystery, an anti-love story, and a satire, *London Fields* is a postmodernist apocalyptic take on the millennium's finale. Suffused with death and war, attended by constant rain and images of ecological disaster, it is also, as the above quotation hints, an elegy: a mournful lament for the future dead it envisages and for the long-lost fields of London: 'this is London; and there are no fields. Only fields of operation and observation, only fields of electromagnetic attraction and repulsion, only fields of hatred and coercion' (LF, 134). London Fields is in fact an area of Hackney, but Amis's novel is not set in this part of the city and the book's title represents for the narrator not a place but an ahistorical, prelapsarian time of innocence when he, if not all of London, lived 'outside history':

> I must go to London Fields before it's too late.
> If I shut my eyes or even if I keep them open I can see the parkland and the sloped bank of the railway line. The foliage is tropical and innocuous, the sky is crystalline and innocuous. In fact the entire vista has a kiddie-book feel. There in his van putts Postman Pat: Postman Pat and his black-and-white cat. It is all outside history.   (LF, 323)

The novel has three principal characters, whose perspectives take it in turn to dominate the 12 chapters that make up the first half of the novel. However, all twenty-four chapters are supplemented by a coda provided by Samson Young, the British-born American novelist in London who is also the book's (dead) narrator. Together with the three protagonists, Samson is a point in the novel's 'black cross', which marks the locations of the narrative for death, disease, and possible mass destruction. The most influential of the three main characters, because she is also the source and manipulator of the plot, is Nicola Six (pronounced 'nuclear sex'), a post-Christian embodiment of quasi-satanic destruction: 'Necropolitan Nicola, in her crimson shoes' (LF, 467), a 'goodtime girl' who supposedly, if only metaphorically, goes out with the Devil 'because it was good fun and it made God mad' (LF, 122–3). Not least because Necropolis is the name Amis gives to any post-nuclear city in 'Unthinkability' (EM, 15), Nicola is a nuclear Cassandra. All importantly, her best friend as a child was 'Enola Gay': the name of the plane that dropped the 'Big Boy' A-bomb on Hiroshima in 1945. It is she who foretells London's doom: 'On television at the age of four she saw the warnings, and the circles of concentric devastation, with London like a bull's-eye in the centre of the board. She knew that would happen too. It was just a matter of time' (LF, 16). The reference to the rings of a nuclear explosion radiating from the centre of London like the bands of a dartboard reminds the reader of the book's 'bad guy' (LF, 4), the arrows-man Keith Talent: 'Keith was the key: Keith, and his pub charisma. Keith was the pub champ. The loudest, the most booming in his shouts for more drink, the most violent in his abuse of the fruit machine, the best at darts – a darts force in the Black Cross' (LF, 36; the Black Cross pub, in which the principal characters first meet, appears again in *The Information*, 486). The third protagonist is the well-off, handsome, tall, and healthy Guy, who: 'had everything. In fact he had two of everything. Two cars, two houses, two uniformed nannies, two silk-and-cashmere dinner jackets, two graphite-cooled tennis rackets, and so on and so forth' (LF, 28). It is Guy's downfall that he has idle time on his hands and so 'looked round his life for a dimension through which some new force might propagate' (LF, 35). The narrator describes him as 'lifeless' and 'wide open' (LF, 27). He is thus ripe both for Nicola's devil-work and for the 'dark force in the Black Cross' to exploit him.

The significance of each of these characters is embodied in their names. Guy's first name intimates that he is not just the story's 'good guy' (LF, 27), but the dupe of the novel's plot, while his surname, Clinch, implies the pincer movement he will be caught in by the other two main characters. 'Guy' is also a reminder of Guy Fawkes, the defeat of whose attempt to blow up Parliament is celebrated on 5 November the threatened date of destruction in the novel. Nicola Six's name has two principal layers of meaning beyond an allusion to a character at the start of Dickens's *Hard Times*. Her forename puns on 'nuclear' but is also, in its diminutive form, one of the devil's names, while her surname gestures towards his Biblical 'number of the beast', 666. Keith Talent's name is of course also significant (it echoes that of the London actor Keith Allen who has played many characters similar to Keith Talent). His first name has evidently been chosen for its image of wide-boy sensibilities. His surname has several resonances: 'talent' is slang for the opposite sex but primarily describes an innate ability to do something admirably well. Yet Keith, for all his facility to influence or coerce people and to exploit various business opportunities, is seemingly devoid of talent, a quality Amis describes in his foreword to *The War Against Cliché* as a natural barrier to the forces of democratization that in many ways Keith might be said to represent:

> Some citadels, true, have become stormable. You can become rich without having any talent (via the scratchcard and the rollover jackpot). You can become famous without having any

talent (by abasing yourself on some TV nerdothon: a clear improvement on the older method of simply killing a celebrity and inheriting the aura). But you cannot become talented without having any talent. Therefore, talent must go … (WAC, xii)

In his 1978 review of Anthony Burgess's *1985*, Amis notes that the final chapter of Part One in Burgess's novel is entitled 'The Death of Love'. Amis quotes Burgess here as saying that Orwell's *1984* is 'Not prophecy so much as a testimony of despair … a personal despair of being able to love.' According to this reading, Orwell's dystopian novel concerns its author's inability to 'love the workers' or find 'sexual love as a passable alternative' (WAC, 118). For Amis, Burgess's novel displays a similar inability to connect love with 'the workers', despite its fictional schools teaching only Trade Union history and its characters speaking 'Worker's English'. Both novels, projecting themselves into the 1980s from previous decades, end up representing a 'failure of love'. This inevitably informs a consideration of *London Fields*, a novel published in 1989 but set in 1999, and which Amis tells the reader in his author's Note was at one stage to be called 'The Death of Love'. This idea remains strong in the published book: 'Perhaps love was dying, was already dead. One more catastrophe. The death of God was possibly survivable in the end. But if love was going out with God … [Amis's ellipsis]' (LF, 132). Even on the tennis court, 'Dink says *nothing* instead of *love*. Fifteen-nothing. Nothing thirty. Even on the tennis court love has gone; even on the tennis court love has been replaced by nothing' (LF, 184). What Amis seems to mean by the death of love is more than just late twentieth-century cynicism and selfishness, it is the threat of extinction:

and now the twentieth century had come along and after several try-outs and test-drives it put together an astonishing new offer: death for everybody. Death for everybody, by hemlock or hardware. If you imagined *love* as a force, not established and not immutable, patched together by all best intentions, kindness, forgiveness – what does love do about death for everybody? It throws up its hands, and gets weaker, and sickens. It is crowded out by its opposite. Love has at least two opposites. One is hate. One is death … And if love was dead or gone then the self was just self, and had nothing to do all day but work on sex. Oh, and hate. And death.   (LF, 297–8)

This is even worse than it at first seems because, as noted above, nuclear war has already happened in Amis's view: anticipation, anxiety, and suspense is the only experience of nuclear war that everyone will have, so the threat of annihilation's possibility is all that people will ever know of it (EM, 17). Humanity already lives as much with nuclear war as it ever will because nuclear war, like death, is something that can only be experienced in advance: as soon as it actually happens it, and we, will be finished.

The 'death of love' has to happen in personal relationships before it can occur on a global level. In the earlier novel, money was the root of all evil, but in *London Fields* the enemies to love dominating the characters' interactions are sex and class. In this can be traced Amis's connection to the most celebrated twentieth-century English satirist. *London Fields* has much in common with Evelyn Waugh's attack on a corrupt, decadent, aimless society in *Vile Bodies*, a novel which ends with the vision of a cataclysmic war in the future. Also, in a review of *Brideshead Revisited* Amis notes that Evelyn Waugh's fictional women are 'cynical *in the heart*, above all' (WAC, 202). Waugh is perhaps the clearest twentieth-century ancestor of Amis's satires and Nicola Six is a good example of Amis's reinvention of the 'standard' Waugh heroine. Indeed, using *A Handful of Dust* as a model – it is foregrounded as a reference point in *The Information* – it would be possible to see, Keith as John Beaver, Nicola as Brenda Last, and Guy as Tony, not least because at one point Samson Young speculates that in a film version of his narrative Guy would be played by one of those actors 'who do the Evelyn Waugh heroes' (LF, 282). In this light the novel also embroils itself directly with questions of class that the characters rarely appreciate:

> Keith acted in the name of masculinity. He acted also, of course, in the name of *class*. Class! Yes, it's still there ... It would surprise Keith a lot if you told him it was *class* that poisoned his every waking moment. At any rate, subliminally or otherwise, it was class that made Keith enlist a third actor in his dealings with Nicola Six. It was class that made Keith enlist Guy Clinch. Or maybe the murderee [Nicola] did it. Maybe she needed him. Maybe they both needed him, as a kind of fuel.   (LF, 24)

This early passage describes the novel's basic plot, in which Nicola's murder is built towards in the context of the contrasting unrequited emotions she arouses in Keith (lust) and Guy (obsessive infatuation). Yet, neither of these is the murderer. This is a role that is allotted to the narrator by Nicola, such that the two of them are the embodiments of the 'death of love' – she a willing murderee, he a willing suicide. After they have sex, Sam muses: 'We put our clothes back on and went out walking, in the dripping alleys, the dark chambers of the elaborately suffering city. We're the dead ... Hand in hand and arm in arm we totter, through communal fantasy and sorrow, through London fields. We're the dead' (LF, 391). Meant for each other, Samson Young and his plotting Delilah, in a passage that parodies the familiar filmic scenes of inamoratas walking through summer 'fields', stroll the streets of the city in which their zombie-like presence signals not love but a death of love that could finally trigger an already impending destruction.

*   *   *

Amis has surrogate figures in each of his long novels. In a metafictional moment in *Money*, 'Martin Amis' explains his own view of the relationship between authors and narrators to John Self (M, 246–8); in *London Fields* Martin Amis is at least hinted at in the London writer Mark Asprey who uses the same initials again for his pseudonym Marius Appleby; and in *The Information* Amis's literary persona is split between two novelists, the unsuccessful austere stylist Richard Tull and the celebrity pop-philosopher of the zeitgeist Gwyn Barry: 'When we started out I think we both hoped to take the novel somewhere new. I thought the way forward was with style. And complexity. But you saw it was all to do with subject' (Richard sarcastically to Gwyn, I, 113). No character in *The Information* is to be taken as a representative of Amis, but the lifestyle he describes is certainly drawn as much from 'experience' as it is in any of his previous novels. For example, it inevitably reminds the reader of several scenes in this novel when, in his essay 'Zeus and the Garbage', Amis mentions that he does most of his male bonding at his local sports club in Paddington (WAC, 4), and this is reinforced by his anecdote of playing the quiz machine at the Paddington club with his friends Chris and Steve in *Experience* (E, 82).

   The Information is a four-part novel about midlife crisis and the thin line between success and failure, between one writer whose

books are 'something like the missionary position plus simultaneous orgasm' and another whose work is 'clearly minority interest to a disgusting degree' (I, 137). It is also of course a novel
about the ways in which the late twentieth century is, as I discussed in the Introduction, an information age with an information culture driven by information technology down an
information highway. Like money, 'Information' is both a value-
free 'good' and a commodity with which modern life is saturated
in a society where the phrase 'knowledge is power' has become
axiomatic. *The Information*'s twin protagonists are turning forty:
almost identical in age they were born only a day apart. They are
supposed to be best friends: middle-class novelists and ex-Oxford
roommates they appear to have everything in common but their
strongest bond is one of envy and contempt. This is a novel of
would-be literary *schadenfreude* as Richard Tull's mounting desire
to precipitate Gwyn Barry's fall from grace is only matched by the
proliferation of his own self-induced humiliating misfortunes
and dope-induced waking nightmares that there are 'newsflashes
about his most recent failures; panel discussions about his obscu-
rity' (I, 36). The novel's plot is a kind of revenger's tragedy (I, 133)
centred on Richard's 'task': 'a literary endeavour, a quest, an
exaltation – one to which he could sternly commit all his passion
and his power. He was going to fuck Gwyn up' (I, 38).

Instead of the previous long novel's nostalgia for London
Fields, *The Information*'s central metaphoric locale is 'Dogshit
Park' and its Keith Talent figure is a thuggish autodidact and
Catholic virgin called Steve Cousins, whose main job, (un)luckily
for Richard, is to 'fuck people up' (I, 159). Steve is consequently
enlisted by Richard as an ideas-man and occasional accomplice
when Tull plans his various doomed schemes: to send Gwyn on a
textual goose-chase, to get him beaten up, to sleep with Gwyn's
wife, Demeter, to tempt Gwyn into adultery, and to sabotage his
prospect of winning a literary prize pompously called 'the
Profundity Recital'. In the novel's third part, the only one not set
in London, Richard travels to the US for the first time, because he
has been commissioned, at Gwyn's suggestion to his publisher, to
write a profile of his friend and fellow-novelist. Richard sees
this as a superb literary opportunity for character assassination
(I, 404–5). When his attempt to lose Gwyn 'the Profunity Recital'
fails, because the tales of Gwyn's illiberal racial, sexual, and social
attitudes that Richard pours into the ears of the judges in fact

accord with their inner prejudices, Richard's final gambit is to frame Gwyn for plagiarism.

As these plots unravel, Richard's problems multiply while he degenerates physically and mentally: his looks seem to deteriorate rapidly and he continues to sob himself awake at night. He is himself assaulted instead of Gwyn and his novel, *Untitled*, is released by a press called Bold Agenda simply because the publishers want to represent all sections of the community and so arbitrarily select Richard as their 'white author' (I, 387). Met on all sides by failure, Richard pours his creative powers into excuses for his impotence with his wife Gina. They embark on discussions over this as though they were beginning a new relationship (I, 205). Richard's most profitable excuse involves 'the death of the novel' because anxiety over it affects him directly as an artist. This 'death' is personally made plain to the 'marooned modernist' Richard by the fact that almost nobody can actually read one of his novels: those who try are at least subject to double vision and at worst hospitalization. Besides, Richard muses, 'Every sensitive man was allowed a mid-life crisis: when you found out for sure that you were going to die, then you ought to have a crisis about it. If you don't have a mid-life crisis, then that's a mid-life crisis' (I, 207). The culmination of his woes arrives when he returns home to find Gina, in 'revenge' for Richard's own infidelity with his secretary, in bed with Gwyn: she has been playing fantasy-role sex games with him for money (I, 486–7). Richard's vendetta against Gwyn ends here; at the moment he discovers a real reason to hate him.

In *Money*, John Self declares that he has four voices in his head: one concerning money, one fixated on pornography, 'the voice of ageing and weather', and a fourth which has 'the unwelcome lilt of paranoia, of rage and weepiness' (M, 108). By the time of *The Information* these voices are still present in Amis's work but they would have to be listed in reverse order to describe the dominant voices in Richard Tull's head. It is the voice raging against the descent towards the dying of the light that brings on his nightly weeping:

> It seemed to him that all the time he used to spend writing he now spent dying. This was the truth. And it shocked him. It shocked him to see it, naked. Literature wasn't about living. It was about not dying.

Suddenly he knew that writing was about denial.

Suddenly he knew that denial was great. Denial was so great. Denial was the best thing. Denial was even better than *smoking* ...

So book now for the sun and fun of Denial. Denial: the true 'never never' land of all your dreams.   (I, 446–7, 451)

But Richard's dreams are nightmares stalked by 'the information': 'The information is nothing. Nothing: the answer to many of our questions. What will happen to me when I die? What *is* death anyway? Is there anything I can do about that? Of what does the universe primarily consist? What is the measure of our influence within it?' (I, 452). After the death of love in *London Fields* we find that Amis's next big novel is preoccupied with what has replaced 'love' on the tennis courts and beyond: 'nothing'. Which is to say, the death of self rather than the death of love.

The novel's toying with astronomy and cosmology is touched on here. It both places Richard's awareness of his own future demise in perspective and also underlines his decay's meaninglessness and inevitability. Its connection with Richard and with *The Information* is partly explained by Richard to his friend and agent, Gal Aplanalp when he describes his projected study, *The History of Increasing Humiliation*: 'It would be a book accounting for the decline in status and virtue of literary protagonists. First gods, then demi-gods, then kings, then great warriors, great lovers, then burghers and merchants and vicars and doctors and lawyers. Then social realism: you. Then irony: me. Then maniacs and murderers, tramps, mobs, rabble, flotsam, vermin' (I, 129). Richard, who is himself an example of this theory, accounts for this decline by the turning to astronomy: 'The history of astronomy is the history of increasing humiliation. First the geocentric universe, then the heliocentric universe. Then the eccentric universe – the one we're living in. Every century we get smaller' (I, 129). Developing from this, Richard tries to 'solarsystematize his immediate circle': he sees his wife as the Earth, other women as stars and comets, Gwyn as Jupiter, Steve Cousins as Mars, his children as satellites, and himself as Pluto: 'Charon was his art' (I, 230–1). Gwyn similarly represents an egocentric universe: 'in Gwyn's novels, there wasn't much talk of astronomy. There was talk of astrology. And what was astrology? Astrology was the *consecration* of the homocentric universe. Astrology went further than saying that the stars were all about *us*. Astrology said that the stars were all about *me*' (I, 437). Gwyn's panacean success with his practical and pantisocratic novel *Amelior* has been to 'make the universe *feel smaller*' and so counter the psychologically damaging effects on individual egos of scientific discoveries that have increasingly marginalized the Earth and its inhabitants from the centre of everything. Gwyn's reassuring Utopian novel therefore aims at amelioration but Richard sees it simply as denial, or Denial: 'the true "never never" land of all your dreams.'

In a review for the *New Statesman*, Amis refers to Northrop Frye's opinion of the structure of a Dickens novel 'as a conflict between two social groups, the family-orientated "congenial" society ... and the institutionalised "obstructing" society' (WAC, 194). Amis's own novels construct their oppositions in different terms but, as he says of Dickens, the congenial society 'is mostly featureless and uniform' while the obstructing society 'is far more exuberantly imagined, peopled not so much by caricatures as by humours' (WAC, 194). In *London Fields* the congenial society is Guy's affluent leisure-class and the obstructing society is Keith's, centred on the Black Cross pub; in *The Information*'s less polarized dialectic the former is Gwyn's and the latter Richard's, with its connections to the world of Steve Cousins. Amis has a penchant for splitting society into two groups, and noting the same attempt in others. In his autobiography he acknowledges the view expressed by a character in his father's 1960 novel *Take a Girl Like You* that the greatest human division is 'between the attractive and the unattractive' (E, 245), while at the same time noting Nabokov's belief that the best way to divide people is between insomniacs and those who fall asleep easily. In *London Fields* Amis again refers to Nabokov's division but the narrator comments that, for him at least, insomnia beats dreaming (LF, 303). *The Information* begins with Richard Tull crying in his sleep, with the narrator's opening comment stating: 'Cities at night, I feel, contain men who cry in their sleep and then say Nothing. It's nothing. Just sad dreams' (I, 9). These are the sad dreams that bring 'the information' to Richard, the connections between his midlife failures and his inevitable death: 'He was being *informed* – the information came at night, to inhume him' (I, 150). Yet, Richard, whose second novel bore the title *Dreams Don't Mean Anything*, is incapable of turning information into (self-)knowledge, beyond the creeping awareness that life is a journey from 'Narcissus to

Philoctetes' (I, 197): from Richard's feeling of youthful attractiveness at Oxford to his current belief that he smells of shit. His response is to become his 'friend's' nightmare, to attempt to exorcise his own demons by transferring them to Gwyn: 'He wants to do to Gwyn what Gwyn has done to him. He wants to assassinate his sleep. He wants to inform the sleeping man; an I for an I' (I, 91). Richard's hatred of Gwyn appears to be fuelled by the way the other writer's enormous success, literary immortality, underlines his own ephemerality: 'the reason our bodies weep and seep in the night, because we're half dead too, and we don't know how or why' (I, 365).

In conclusion, it is interesting to place Amis's criticism alongside his fiction one last time. In his review of Anthony Burgess's *Earthly Powers*, Amis explains: 'There are two kinds of long novel. Long novels of the first kind are short novels that go on for a long time. ... Long novels of the second kind, on the other hand, are long because they have to be, earning their amplitude by the complexity of the demands they make on writer and reader alike' (WAC, 121). Oddly, Amis's own long novels fit equally well into both categories. For the purposes of their plots, their characters, or their treatment of ideas, they need not be as long as they are, but they do need to be for the force of their humour and pathos, the intensity of their much-imitated inimitable style, and the bite of their unrelenting satire.

References and Further Reading

Martin Amis, *Money* (M), Harmondsworth, Penguin, 1985.
——, *London Fields* (LF), Harmondsworth: Penguin, 1990.
——, *Time's Arrow* (TA), London: Jonathan Cape, 1991.
——, *The Information* (I), London: Flamingo, 1996.
——, *Einstein's Monsters* (EM), Harmondsworth: Penguin, 1988.
——, *Experience* (E), London: Jonathan Cape, 2000.
——, *The War Against Cliché* (WAC), London: Vintage, 2002.
John A. Dern, *Martians, Monsters and Madonna: Fiction and Form in the World of Martin Amis*, New York: Peter Lang AG, 2000.
James Diedrick, *Understanding Martin Amis*, Columbia: South Carolina Press, 1995.
——, 'The Fiction of Martin Amis' in *Contemporary British Fiction*, edited by Richard J. Lane, Rod Mengham, and Philip Tew, Cambridge: Polity, 2003, 239–55.
John Haffenden, *Novelists in Interview*, London: Methuen, 1985, 1–24.
Elaine Showalter, 'Ladlit' in *On Modern British Fiction*, edited by Zachary Leader, Oxford: Oxford University Press, 2002.

David Thomson, 'Martin Amis', in *British Novelists Since 1960*, Second Series, edited by Merritt Moseley, *The Dictionary of Literary Biography*, Volume 194, Detroit: Gale, 1998, 7–19.

Richard Todd, *Consuming Fiction: The Booker Prize and Fiction in Britain Today*, London: Bloomsbury, 1996.

Nicolas Tredell (ed.), *The Fiction of Martin Amis*, Cambridge: Icon, 2000.

James Wood, 'Martin Amis: The English Imprisonment', *The Broken Estate*, London: Pimlico, 2000, 186–99.

Web Reading

Key website: http://martinamis.albion.edu/

Interview: http://www.altx.com/interviews/martin.amis.html

2

Pat Barker: In the Shadow of Monstrosities

2.1. Literary History

A writer whose work circles around themes of gender and sexuality, class and history, war and violence, Pat Barker (b.1943) was raised by her grandmother after her father was killed in action during the Second World War. She lived her early life on Teesside, went to school in Stockton, and came to full-time writing after studying international history at the London School of Economics and working as a teacher. In 1983 the Book Marketing Council named her as one of the 20 'Best Young British Novelists', though she had only then published one novel. Barker has said that she is very interested in myths about sexuality and in attitudes towards the socially marginalized, particularly women. She openly questions the effect stereotyping has on women fighting against an ineffective and hierarchized public welfare system which treats them as inferior citizens.

Encouraged to draw on her own experience in her writing by Angela Carter, another novelist deeply interested in the myths surrounding sexuality, Barker set her first novel, *Union Street* (1982), in a closed north-eastern community ruled over by a matriarchal figure. It tells seven linked stories of female working-class experience and already establishes Barker's spare writing style, characterized by down-to-earth humour and unsentimental pathos. The sense of community suggested by the title is largely a thing of the past in the narrative as there is little impression of a shared life. Barker implies the need for a new female working-class unity by having Kelly Brown, the 13-year-old girl who is raped in the opening chapter, comfort the old and dying Alice

Bell at the close of the book. Her second novel was *Blow Your House Down* (1984), a four-part narrative about street prostitutes terrorized by a serial killer in a northern industrial town. It was adapted for the stage by Sarah Daniels in 1994.

The Century's Daughter (1986), republished as *Liza's England*, focusses on working-class women's experience and the changes in social(ist) attitudes over the twentieth century. It views history through the character of Liza Jarrett Wright, a woman born in the first minute of 1900. Liza tells her story to a gay social worker assisting working-class children, Steven, who counters her optimism with a belief that atomized individuals are now growing up without hope or a social conscience. A member of the Labour Party, Liza stresses the importance of community and loyalty but ends the novel fatally assaulted by youths, in an attack that typifies the view that the sense of a shared life Liza experienced growing up in terraced housing has been eroded in the 1980s by Thatcherism and tower-block living.

The Man Who Wasn't There (1989) is the story of a fatherless teenager growing up in the 1950s. The novel considers masculinity in the light of its representations in war films and stories, connecting the novel with the three books that followed it: *Regeneration* (1991), *The Eye in the Door* (1993), and *The Ghost Road* (1995). Set in 1917–18, these three books comprise the *Regeneration Trilogy*, a wide-ranging study of the effects of war on individuals in terms of responsibility and identity. The trilogy is historically and geographically differentiated from Barker's earlier novels but is connected to them by an interest in violence and trauma. Though the story is told from several viewpoints, the books' principal character is the disaffected and déclassé Billy Prior, a sexually promiscuous soldier treated by W. H. R. Rivers (1864–1922) at Craiglockhart War Hospital, the famous psychiatric clinic which only serves as a partial sanctuary from the trenches: 'Craiglockhart frightened him more than the front had ever done' (R, 63). While Prior is fictional, Rivers is one of many real-life figures in the novels, including the poets Robert Graves, Siegfried Sassoon, and Wilfred Owen.

Rivers had been an anthropologist before the war but, with a medical degree, turned to medicine and psychiatry, joining the army in 1915. *Regeneration* takes Rivers's relationship with Sassoon at Craiglockhart as its centre, but the subsequent two novels focus on Rivers and especially Prior, who is finally killed alongside Wilfred Owen by the Sambre-Oise canal at the conclusion of the trilogy, days before the end of the war. *The Eye in the Door* follows Prior after his release from Craiglockhart. He becomes a Ministry of Munitions spy and is detailed to investigate a family he grew up with in Salford called the Ropers who have been linked to anti-war protests. Prior's split allegiances are signalled by the epigraph from Stevenson's *The Strange Case of Dr Jekyll and Mr Hyde* (cf. ED, 134 and 142), but so is a deeper ambivalence within Prior and also divisions of socialism, gender, and sexuality within a nation supposedly fighting a collective war. Prior's duality is figured by his blank spells or 'fugue states', which can last hours and about which he can remember nothing (in psychiatry the term fugue refers to a dreamlike altered state of consciousness, lasting from a few hours to several days, during which a person like Prior loses his memory of his previous life and often wanders away from home). During these blackouts Prior's 'hidden' character surfaces and he becomes indistinguishable from the figures he despises, such as Lionel Spragge, an Intelligence informer who receives a bonus for each objector caught (it is suggestive of a deep interest in doubled identities that Barker's later novels *Border Crossing* and *Double Vision* also contain characters with this sense of duality). When Sassoon is reintroduced in this novel, the theme embraces him also through his position as both soldier and objector: 'I survive out there by being two people, sometimes I even manage to be both of them in one evening … my Jekyll and Hyde performance' (ED, 229). For Rivers, this evidence of a dual personality confirms what he believes to be a necessary manifestation of the mental conflicts created by war: 'most of us survive by cultivating internal divisions' (ED, 233). The feeling is underlined by Rivers's own experience of being a different person in Cambridge from the one he became in the Pacific before the war: 'It was his Melanesian self he preferred, but his attempts to integrate that self into his way of life in England had produced nothing but frustration and misery. Perhaps, contrary to what he usually supposed, duality was the stable state; the attempt at integration, dangerous' (ED, 235).

Each character in *The Eye in the Door* feels as though he or she is 'being *watched* all the time' (ED, 36), and Prior's first attack leaves him with the sensation of 'being naked, high up on a ledge, somewhere, in full light, with beneath him only jeering voices and millions of eyes' (ED, 26). The book's title (see ED, 40) refers both to the surveillance world at the centre of the narrative and to the book's concern with a world composed of 'different sides' (such as objector/collaborator, heterosexual/homosexual, friend/enemy, male/female, upper/lower class) in which Prior mostly has 'A foot on either side of the fence' (ED, 111). In *The Ghost Road* the sense of difference is broadened by extended flashbacks to Rivers's time in Melanesia, uncovering differences between East and West as well as similarities between 'savage' and 'civilised', especially contrasting the 'headhunters' of the islands with both the soldiers and psychiatrists of Europe: 'without [head-hunting] life lost almost all its zest. This was a people perishing from the absence of war … the island's population was less than half what it had been in Rinambesi's youth' (GR, 207). The arch rationalist Rivers is forced by Sassoon's declaration of seeing war apparitions to recall his own experience of ghosts in the culturally and topographically disorienting Melanesian landscape; an experience he cannot rationalize away as 'mass hypnosis' (GR, 188). Attempting to cure his patients of their psychic phantom limbs, Rivers is obliged to recognize that the belief that the dead haunt the living is not simply a primitive superstition or an emotional disorder but an integral and perhaps necessary part of human responses to loss, grief, and trauma. Barker peppers the trilogy with ghostly presences and visions of the dead, drawing a parallel between these hauntings and the twentieth century's fascination with memory and recovered histories, whose provenance Barker appears to locate in the agony and upheaval of 1914–18.

Another World (1998), which knits the present together with the past, is the story of a Newcastle family's confrontations with the legacies of history, in which Barker again uses the First World War as a major reference point despite the novel's contemporary setting. The family is composed of Fran and her son Gareth, Nick and his daughter Miranda, plus the couple's infant son Jasper. They also have a new baby on the way. While the family build their uneasy relationships in the present, spectres from the past push in on them because of the history of their new home: Lob's Hill, once the residence of the wealthy Fanshawe family. Rumours of ghosts and tales of murder are brought to life in their minds by the uncovering of a drawing of the Fanshawes beneath the wallpaper in the family's living room. The portrait shows 'Victorian paterfamilias, wife and children: two sons, a daughter'

(AW, 40). Staring at the picture the family has collectively uncovered by its scraping, Miranda declares ' "It's us", but her stepmother demurs: "No, it isn't. ... *She's* not pregnant" (AW, 41). Throughout the remainder of the book, the threat of repetition hovers close to the family: Gareth and Miranda both at times come close to killing Jasper, as the Fanshawe infant was supposedly killed by its siblings. Nick's 'last impression, before he drifts off to sleep, is that the portrait has risen to the surface of its own volition, that it would have been impossible to keep it hidden any longer, rather as a mass of rotting vegetation, long submerged, will rise to the surface of a pond' (AW, 43). Barker is not interested in suggesting that the past will be enacted again, but that its presence will remain into the future, informing and shaping people's interpretations of themselves and their identities.

Running alongside the narrative of Lob's Hill is the story of Nick's visits to see his grandfather, Geordie, a 101-year old First World War veteran who believes his cancer is a consequence of a bayonet wound – an 80-year old injury that has come back to kill him. Geordie is haunted by the distant past, and particularly his part in the death of his brother in the War: a fact that shapes his dying Mephistophelian words: 'I am in hell.' But this is not the message of the novel, in which supposedly distinct or juxtaposed unities, such as hate and love, death and life, are brought together and interlaced like Fran's and Nick's families. The book overall suggests the proximity of the past to the present, the presence of history behind a layer of wallpaper or a shut door: 'As a small boy [Nick] was always aware of another world on the other side of the door in the hall' (AW, 52). Perhaps unsatisfied that reviews of the *Regeneration Trilogy* had failed to realize that she was not writing 'historical fiction', Barker decided with *Another World* to show more explicitly the connections between the early- and the late-twentieth century, and especially the importance of the First World War. As one character remarks in *Another World*: 'there's quite a lot of evidence to suggest that traumatic memories are stored in a different part of the brain from normal memories, and that's what makes them so incredibly persistent' (AW, 85). For Barker, the key fact of the First World War is that it remains in the collective memory as a persistent traumatic experience that has been insufficiently addressed or acknowledged.

Barker's next novel, *Border Crossing* (2001), returns to territory often traversed in her 1990s fiction. The book explores the different ways in which contemporary society centralizes therapy and self-analysis but often with superficial if not deleterious effects. Tom Seymour is a professional psychotherapist who explains that research shows 'the talking cure' to be often more harmful than beneficial in the case of trauma: numbness and grieving are a part of the healing process which therapy can circumvent. The modern fascination with 'talking it over' is touched on in terms of media debate, creative writing classes, and courtrooms: all of which can seem to attempt to categorize behaviour in terms of pathologies and stereotypes with insufficient attention to the circumstances and particularities of individuals. Tom's role as an expert is contextualized by his failing marriage and his 'excessive' grieving for his father who has died two years earlier. The antagonist of the novel is Danny Miller, now Ian Wilkinson, a man who killed an old woman when he was ten years old and who after his release now wishes to enlist the help of Tom, a key witness in the trial.

Border Crossing places the process of transference at its centre and Ian attempts through a series of rationalizations and manipulations to situate Tom as the guilty party in Danny's life. Borders between the sides of personality, between feeling and thought, between therapist and client, and between personal loyalty and social responsibility are repeatedly transgressed, leaving Ian's life more fulfilled than Tom's in many ways at the close of the narrative. In preparation for this ending, which ensues from Tom's inability to separate out the personal and the professional in Danny's case, the reader is told near the novel's beginning that Tom 'was used to switching off, to living his life in different compartments. He'd learnt early, in his first few months of practice, that those who take the misery home with them burn out and end up no use to anybody' (BC, 13). Midway through the novel, Tom is given a warning, which he applies to everybody except himself, by the governor's wife at Long Garth, the secure unit where Danny precipitated the dismissal of several members of staff over a period of seven years: 'Danny wasn't breaking the rules. They were. He was very, very good at getting people to step across the invisible border. Lambs to the slaughter' (BC, 168).

Ian, who for his own protection is only nominally no longer Danny, remains a disquieting individual, socially rehabilitated but with depths that Tom has uneasily plumbed. He is competed over by numerous voices participating in the discourses of innocence and guilt, punishment and morality, violence and protection, 'good' and 'evil'. To complicate the easy generalizations that surround an individual like Danny and a case like his, Barker draws parallels between her story and real-life examples, such as Jamie Bulger's murder by two ten-year-olds in 1993, and also the experience of numerous characters within the narrative, including Tom, who himself came close to murder as a 'normal' child (BC, 62–3). Towards the end of the novel, when Tom has discovered Danny seemingly about to set fire to his house, Tom realizes he has allowed himself to become too close to Danny: to care for him though not to trust him. He thinks now that: 'if, at some future time, Danny were to set a fire in which somebody died, his silence on that night would return to haunt him. He knew what he should have done. Only, at that crucial moment, Danny had turned to look at him, and it had not seemed possible to betray him' (BC, 274).

Barker's 2003 novel, *Double Vision*, takes the theme of violence in a new direction, but continues the interest she has shown in her recent work in ambivalence, doubling, and split personalities. It utilizes the theme suggested by its title in many ways, presenting characters who see events after a traumatic experience, or for a second time, or at a distance, or in a backward glance. The narrative centres on the overlapping stories of two people: Stephen Sharkey, a war reporter, and the sculptor Kate Frobisher, the widow of a photographer with whom Stephen worked in Bosnia and elsewhere, and who died in Afghanistan. Kate and Stephen share the narrative, and are each forced to reassess their ideas about safety, violence, and war, as Kate is trapped in a crashed car, and Stephen struggles with his nightmares of Sarajevo. The story includes a scene set at the World Trade centre on 9/11, a violent burglary, and a threatening act of identity appropriation; but the centrepiece is a discussion that Stephen and Kate have about Goya, and which captures the dilemma of war photography: that it seems both obscene and necessary to witness and record atrocities. Their discussion of complicity and responsibility foregrounds once more one of the principal themes running through Barker's work: the insufficiently acknowledged traumatic and far-reaching effects of violence on individuals and communities. The novel's sense of this is signalled by a discussion of Stephen's nephew, who has Asperger's, a form of autism which is explained in this way: 'It's basically a sort of difficulty in seeing people as people. ... So you can't change your perspective and see the situation from another's point of view, because you can't grasp the fact that they have their own internal life, and they might be thinking something different from you' (DV, 83–4). This is essentially the book's post-9/11 comment on violence: that it is less easy when the other's equal internal life is acknowledged. Barker thus finds herself in accord with the points of view put across by Amis and McEwan in September 2001 that I discuss in the Conclusion, but she remains a consistent and distinctive voice in contemporary fiction having become a major chronicler of the effects of war on individuals and communities.

2.2. Themes: Violence and Trauma

> *'I think it's too easy for sensitive types' – Danny's voice oozed contempt –*
> *'to assume that everybody who kills is traumatized by it.'*
>
> (BC, 120)

Barker's novels have a common theme of violence, usually but not always male in origin, but their author seems more interested in how that violence comes to affect people – the victims and those around them than in what provokes aggression or brutality. So, for example, while we learn about the women in *Blow Your House Down*, we get to know almost nothing about the killer, his life, motives, or personality. Barker's apprentice work focusses on close-knit communities and male aggression towards women, questioning the effects this has on women's lives, on self-perceptions, and on society. Her early novels are primarily concerned with northern working-class districts and the factors that threaten communal as well as personal values and perceptions. Barker also puts forward a positive image of community and social networks struggling against an ineffective public welfare system that treats her characters as second-class individuals – a perspective broadened to the treatment of soldiers and protestors in the Great War in the *Regeneration Trilogy*.

By the time of her later work, Barker draws all of society into the picture of a violent culture book-ended by threat and fear:

like everybody else, he lives in the shadows of monstrosities. Peter Sutcliffe's bearded face, the number plate of a house in Cromwell Street, three figures smudged on a video surveillance screen, an older boy taking a toddler by the hand while his companions stride ahead, eager for the atrocity to come.   (AW, 3)

Barker's abiding interest in monstrosity and the monstrous is signalled by the epigraph to *Blow Your House Down*, which begins 'Whoever fights monsters should see to it that in the process he does not become a monster.' This caution against meeting violence with a knee-jerk reaction of further violence is couched in terms of a recognition that demonizing others is frequently an externalization of anxieties created by fissures within understanding and knowledge.

This is expanded upon in the *Regeneration Trilogy*: 'You must be wary of filling the gaps in your memory with … with monsters. I think we all tend to do it. As soon as we're left with a blank, we start projecting out worst fears on to it' (ED, 139). Billy Prior picks up on this later in the same novel: 'The gaps in his memory were increasing both in length and frequency, and they terrified him. Like the undiscovered territory on medieval maps, Rivers said. *Where unknown, there place monsters*. But a better analogy, because closer to his own experience, was No Man's Land' (ED, 176). This theme returns in the third volume in Prior's diary: 'We are Craiglockhart's success stories. *Look at us*. We don't remember, we don't feel, we don't think. … By any proper civilized standard (but what does *that* mean *now*?) we are objects of horror' (GR, 200).

In the trilogy, 'horror' is in many ways a matter of trauma, of coming to terms with disturbing memories but blanking out recollections of the past ('Suppose time can slow down. Suppose it's not an ever rolling stream, but something altogether more viscous and unpredictable, like blood. Suppose it coagulates around terrible events, clots over them, stops the flow' (AW, 271)). As the past and the present co-exist in the mind, for Barker the violent and peaceful sides to the individual sit alongside one another in the same person, represented by the frequent use of doubles, reflections, and masks in her books: in *The Eye in the Door* Rivers glimpses the 'other Prior' associated with aggression and power: 'He looked quite different, suddenly: keen, alert, cold, observant, detached, manipulative, ruthless' (ED, 76).

Rivers observes that 'In the fugue state (though it was more than that) Prior had claimed to feel no pain and no fear, to have been born in a shell-hole, to have no father. Presumably *no* relationships that pre-dated that abnormal birth' (ED, 245). This links with the moment in *Regeneration* when Prior tells Rivers about his father: 'Oh, yes, he's very likeable. Outside the house. I've seen him use my mother as a football. ... When I was too little to do anything about it' (R, 61). But Rivers is also haunted by questions of male violence and gender difference: he remembers being disturbed as a child by an adult saying that Charles Dodgson (Lewis Carroll) prefers girls to boys. To his question 'why?' the young Rivers is told: 'Boys are rough and nasty. And they fight' (GR, 32). Much of Rivers's adult professional life is subsequently spent dealing with this phenomenon, though it is Wilfred Owen, the poet of pity, who is best able to make the link between fear and violence and incomprehension: 'You say we kill the Beast', Owen said slowly. 'I say we fight because men lost their bearings in the night' (GR, 144).

Barker gives a religious perspective to the sufferings of the war in the trilogy by linking the perennial fear of gas attacks to the repeated asthmatic problems of the characters, all of them likened to Christ and the circumstances of his death. In *Regeneration*, Prior initiates this theme: ' "The same mind now orders men to be punished by tying them to a limber." Prior stretched his arms out. "Like this. Field punishment No. 1. Crucifixion." ... Either the position, or his anger, constricted his breathing. He brought his arms down sharply and rounded his shoulders. Rivers waited for the spasm to pass' (R, 67). Prior's difficulty in breathing is associated with this form of torture, which also, through the image of Christ's passion, invokes the suffering passivity of the soldiers in the trenches. Burns asks Rivers if he knows what Christ died of: 'Suffocation. Ultimately the position makes it impossible to go on inflating the lungs' (R, 183) (cf. the discussion of Sassoon's poem 'The Redeemer' (R, 82)).

In *Blow Your House Down*, Barker also plays with Christian themes. She draws on the fact that the Yorkshire Ripper believed himself to be tasked by God to kill prostitutes:

> From heaven he came and sought her
> To be his holy bride
> With his own blood he bought her
> And for her life he died.
>
> (BH, 55)

This hymn is begun by Kath, a victim, and completed by her murderer. The brutal manner of Kath's death is implicitly compared

to the poultry production line: 'a line of live chickens fastened to
a conveyor belt by their legs. They jerked past. At the end of the
line a man hit them with something to stun them and another
man chopped off their heads' (BH, 33). After her death, Kath is
taken to the police mortuary and laid out like the chickens at the
factory, in whose shadow the prostitutes solicit: 'Kath Robson lies
on a marble slab. She has been stared at, poked, prodded, measured, photographed, the contents of her stomach analysed, the
secrets of every orifice laid bare. Now, gutted, filleted and par-
celled up again, she is left alone' (BH, 71). Not least because the
police use the prostitutes as bait (p. 88), Kath is seen as a sacrificial victim, like Christ (both experience a death unlike sleep, p. 71
and p. 160), but it is only in Part Four of the book that Barker's
chicken imagery is fully aligned with Christian symbolism. When
Maggie, the final victim of violence in the novel, enters a church
(Christ's holy bride in Kath's song), she finds two images of Jesus.
The first shows Christ 'in his majesty', but the second, tucked
away in a tiny chapel, is a 'chicken Christ':

> There were marks all over his skin, from the flogging, she sup-
> posed, and here and there a thorn had escaped from the crown
> and embedded itself in the flesh of hip or breast. She had seen
> such marks before. They were like, no, *were*, the marks left
> when the spine of a feather is pulled out … The chicken Christ
> on his cross might claim her as his own, but the risen Christ,
> Christ in majesty, pain sloughed off behind him like an out-
> worn skin, had nothing to say.   (BH, 160)

The scene is echoed in Barker's fiction in *Double Vision* twenty
years later when Kate Frobisher sees, 'Christ in Majesty, surrounded by concentric circles of apostles, angels, prophets, patriarchs, and saints. At the moment she hated all representations of
Christ, impartially and with great venom' (DV, 28). This is early
in the novel when Kate has barely begun her own statue of Christ
and when she cannot see a future beyond the suffering she has
felt through Ben's death and her own car accident. In *Blow Your
House Down*, it is Christ's suffering, not his risen glory, that connects with Maggie's experience and offers a possible image with
which she can identify. It is only after she has also witnessed the
violence of nature, its killing so different from that of the chicken
factory or the windswept urban streets, that she can return to her

husband and appreciate the force that Barker offers to compensate for, if never eradicate, violence: love. It is love's unexpected appearance at the end of the story when Maggie's husband tends her ageing, abused body that points up its absence in all of the heterosexual relationships earlier in the novel.

Underlining the importance of Christian imagery, of passion and compassion, in Barker's work, from the early novels through the trilogy to her latest novel, *Double Vision* includes Kate's own paradigm of suffering: an imposing and confrontational sculpture of Christ. Her aim is to defamiliarize the images of pain and violence that people see all around them everyday – whether in a place such as a church or through a medium like television – thus drawing attention to the abiding conviction of Barker's work: the need to reverse the desensitizing effects of over-familiarity on our responses to violence and its effects.

2.3. Key Works: *Blow Your House Down, Regeneration*

By its title, *Blow Your House Down* prompts the reader to think about the story of the three little pigs (in its English variant, the written versions of the folk tale go back at least to James Orchard Halliwell's *Nursery Rhymes and Nursery Tales*, c.1843). In early renditions, the two pigs who build their fragile houses are eaten by the wolf that blows them down, while the third pig, in a house of stone or brick, is protected. The third pig in turn gets to eat the wolf who arrives down the chimney into a waiting cooking pot. Barker's novel is divided into four parts and the reader has to consider the relationship the book has to the three-part structure of the tale. Arguably, the first two parts, ending in murder, correspond to the two little pigs eaten by the wolf, while the third sees the prostitutes fighting back – one of them kills a man she takes to be 'a wolf/man'. Part four, Maggie's story, appears to reach beyond this binary division between preyed upon pigs and rapacious wolves, women as victims and men as violent assailants – exemplified in the 1970s radical feminist slogan 'All men are rapists'.

Barker's standpoint in the novel is summarized by its Nietzschean epigraph from *Beyond Good and Evil* quoted above: 'Whoever fights monsters should see to it that in the process he does not become a monster. And when you look long into an abyss the abyss also looks into you.' The women in the novel fight against the 'monster' or wolf of the story, but Barker widens her narrative in such a way that the reader understands how the division between victim and victimizer is socially and economically determined, and fuelled by a fear that can poison all relationships, not just abusive ones. Barker connects what happens on the streets with what happens in the home, what affects society with what affects the individual, and the world of the narrative with the world of the reader. It is only in the last part of the story that one woman finds that after staring into the 'abyss ... at her feet' she can see a way out of the circle of violence by identifying with the sufferer and not the avenger.

Blow Your House Down is based on the murders of Peter Sutcliffe, the 'Yorkshire Ripper', as are a number of other recent works, such as David Peace's novel *Nineteen Eighty*, Gordon Burn's psycho-investigation *Somebody's Husband, Somebody's Son*, and Blake Morrison's long poem 'The Ballad of the Yorkshire Ripper'. Sutcliffe brutally murdered (at least) thirteen women, most of who were prostitutes, in northern England between 1975 and 1981; an ex-gravedigger, his shadowy presence resurfaces in the menacing figure of Peter Wingrave in *Double Vision*.

Part one of *Blow Your House Down*, narrated in the third person and largely focussed on a single-parent who turns to prostitution, Brenda, leads up to the ferocious and explicitly described murder of Kath, a woman alone; part two, also told in the third person but including a wider circle of Audrey, Elaine, and Jean as well as Brenda, culminates in Carol's murder, Jean's partner; part three ends with Jean, its narrator, going missing after she has killed a man, who may or may not be the murderer; part four returns to third-person narration and moves away from a focus on the women of the earlier parts who have turned to prostitution, to discuss a fellow chicken-factory worker Maggie, a woman attacked by an unknown assailant and who subsequently becomes estranged 'from man' (BH, 164). It is part four of the novel that forces the reader to make comparisons or connections between the murder and other men as well as the prostitutes and other women, just as it widens the circle of violence and hate so that the reader realizes that the book is not only about murder but about cruelty in many forms.

The book utilizes some key images that recur in Barker's later novels. For example, Barker spent her first seven years growing up on a chicken farm and in *Blow Your House Down* chickens (e.g. BH, 65, 140/1) represent the victims of violence, delivered along the factory belt by women workers, while 'killing's for the men' (BH, 34); in *Regeneration* the Rivers family have a chicken farm (R, 150) and there is also a scene focussed on killing chickens in *Border Crossing* (e.g. BC, 239–41)). Opposed to these birds are the starlings in *Blow Your House Down* (e.g. BH, 111, 170) who, high above, are 'blown across the sky like scraps of burnt paper' (BH, 163), and who appear to usher in the nighttime world of the city. It is also apparent that Barker employs the image of the fox's rabbit-kill in *Blow Your House Down* to compare nature's killing to humans' in a way that presages and answers Danny's question in *Border Crossing* (BC, 43): 'Do you think it's different, killing a rabbit and killing a person?' By contrast Maggie is able to separate natural violence from social cruelty and gain a different perspective on what happens in the city by viewing it from the country. In its use of symbolism, *Blow Your House Down* also concentrates heavily on the senses, especially sight (colours, eyes, and shadows are repeatedly mentioned), sound (silence and the whistling wind), and smell (as well as the pungency of the fox and the chickens, Barker puns on the murderer's smell of violets/violence).

The attitude to prostitution put forward in the book is largely concerned with the causal factors of economic necessity and poor social welfare – it is a logical conclusion of working-class gender relations in a time of mass unemployment: 'they went on about being married, but when you got right down to it, past the white weddings and the romance and all that, what they *really* thought was: if you're getting on your back for a fella, he ought to pay' (BH, 30; cf. the comment in chapter two of Angela Carter's *Nights at the Circus*: 'What is marriage but prostitution to one man instead of many?'). In Barker's community, where the social services construe marriage economically as legal prostitution, men are either absent, infantilized, or both ('you and your bloody mother. Least little thing goes wrong you're running round there for a bit of titty' (BH, 6)). Meanwhile the police prey upon the women, using them as bait and considering sexual abuse of them a perk (BH, 42).

The novel develops in two ways from its initial portrayal of victims on the one side and abusers on the other. First, it presents the women's strength in community and numbers, flocking together like the starlings (most novels have one protagonist but

Blow Your House Down has a cast of many), and second in its conclusion with the reconciliation between Maggie and her husband,
Bill. When Maggie is attacked she finds herself potentially joining
the conveyor belt of female victims of male violence, but then
realizes that 'evil' is not only genderless but can be anywhere on
any day:

> across her mind's eye moved a line of faces, all women, young,
> old, fat, thin, smiling, serious. She knew who they were: she'd
> seen them in the papers, as everybody had, but then it had just
> been a story, something that happened to somebody else,
> always to somebody else. But now it was real because it had
> happened to her. The image faded and was replaced by a line
> of chickens waiting to be killed. In each eye the same passive
> uncomprehending terror. Mrs Bulmer's voice went on, and on.
> You thought evil was simple. No, more than that, you *made* it
> simple, you froze it into a single shape, the shape of a man
> waiting in the shadows. But it wasn't simple. This woman, this
> wheezy middle-aged woman, with her corrugated-iron hair
> and her glasses that flashed when she looked sideways to see
> how you were taking it, she knew what she was doing. And
> she was enjoying it. You couldn't put evil into a single, recog-
> nizable shape.   (BH, 155–6)

Maggie's importance is to manage to look into this abyss and not
turn monstrous. The redemptive conclusion of the novel picks up
the comparison between women on the streets, at risk of attack
from men, and slaughtered chickens in the factory production
line. Maggie is described in ways that liken her to one of the factory chickens, with puckered skin and thin legs, as Bill washes her
down until he reaches 'her feet which he cradled, one by one, in
his lap' (BH, 169). No words can be said to break the silence, but
Bill's Christ-like gesture enables Maggie to reach out her hand for
his (though Maggie is not one of the prostitutes, she is linked to
them in small ways, such as the attack on her and the repeated
phrase 'Maggie May, why have you gone away', which is derived
from an old Liverpool seaman's song about a prostitute).

Ending on this scene underscores the novel's emphasis on the
ineffability of violence but also the silent acts of love that heal.
Barker tenders no solutions other than to offer love, not violence
in opposition to a barbarous world, but the question that remains

hanging over the narrative is the single word Maggie speaks after her attack: 'Why?' (BH, 159). It is an echo of the response that Jean's victim had to her: 'Then his mouth opened, it opened very wide and he was gasping and gurgling and trying to speak ... one single word: Why?' (BH, 132). Barker suggests that a caring vigilance is necessary in society as well as a caring compassionate response to the effects of violence. But she also seeks to persuade the reader that a political system that makes women economically dependent on men, and that also devalues male feelings of self-worth by depriving them of socially useful work, institutionalizes conditions that foster violence.

*   *   *

The *Regeneration Trilogy* gradually expands from a small community, the patients and staff at the Craiglockhart hospital near Edinburgh, to the domestic front in London in the second volume, and finally the war in France itself in *The Ghost Road*, a novel which in its title highlights the preoccupation with spectres of the dead that suffuses the trilogy and underscores Barker's conviction that the Great War haunted the rest of the century. A third-person narrative in four parts, *Regeneration* opens with Sassoon's 'A Soldier's Declaration' of July 1917 entitled 'Finished with the War', and ends with Rivers's final note in Sassoon's file: 'Nov. 26, 1917. Discharged to duty.' In-between these two acts of writing the book concentrates on Rivers's patients at the war hospital and the relationships they form with him, with each other, and with non-patients. Aside from Sassoon, who meets Wilfred Owen and helps him to revise his poems, Rivers's principal patients in the story are Billy Prior and David Burns.

Prior, a 'thin, fair-headed young man of twenty-two', is a new patient to the hospital and is initially unable to speak   even though his nightmares keep his roommate awake (R, 41). He does not remember the latter part of his service in France and believes 'talking' with Rivers will not help him, that only hypnosis will unlock his memory. His experiences, and the discussion of his condition, take the narrative beneath the surface of its interest in individual's rational repugnance for war, to a deeper conflicted level on which lurks a desire for violence and mastery.

Burns's experience is a microcosm of the horror of war: 'He'd been thrown into the air by the explosion of a shell and had landed, head-first, on a German corpse, whose gas-filled belly had ruptured on impact. Before Burns lost consciousness, he'd had time to realize that what filled his nose and mouth was decomposing human flesh' (R, 19). The effect of this on Burns has been to make him physically sick when he recalls the incident, as he does whenever he tries to eat. Burns's trauma is characterized by a desire to 'escape', and one afternoon he sets off on a bus away from the hospital. Resting in the countryside under some trees he notices that 'the tree he stood under was laden with dead animals' (R, 38). Burns takes down the birds and small mammals and arranges them around the tree in a circle, stripping naked to lay down beside them in an act that repeats his experience in no-man's-land: 'It didn't occur to him to move. This was the right place. This was where he had wanted to be' (R, 39). Resonant of scarring and trauma, 'Burns' is of course a reminder of one author, but this character is most reminiscent of Edward Thomas, another poet killed in the Great War – for example, Rivers visits Burns at Aldeburgh (cf. Thomas's 'Adlestrop') where they meet Old Clegg (cf. Thomas's 'Lob') who is to teach Burns flint-knapping. Prior and Burns are contrasting victims of war, the former driven by repressed forces compelling him to act ruthlessly, the latter disabled by unconscious fears from which his mind cannot escape (which is to say, they respectively exhibit psychotic and neurotic tendencies).

The novel's title derives from Rivers's interest in the regeneration of nerves after injury (R, 46), and Barker expands the study to mental damage but also brings to the fore the conflict between generations that the war made manifest. This is most sharply brought out in the metaphor of Abraham and Isaac, which is referred to on several occasions. Reminiscent of Maggie's experience in the church scene in *Blow Your House Down*, while on leave Rivers looks at a church stained glass window depicting the preparations for the divinely decreed sacrifice. He considers it, '*The* bargain ... on which all patriarchal societies are founded' – and indeed the story of fathers sacrificing sons proves to have a Melanesian parallel for Rivers in *The Ghost Road* (GR, 102–3). Rivers describes the bargain thus: 'If you, who are young and strong, will obey me, who am old and weak, even to the extent of being prepared to sacrifice your life, then in the course of time you will peacefully inherit, and be able to exact the same obedience from your sons' (R, 149). Rivers considers the bargain has been broken because the inheritors are being slaughtered on service in France while the older generation attend church services at home. Rivers also sees this difference between generations in Freudian terms as Oedipal conflict, a perspective accentuated by Sassoon's allusion to the patricide Richard Dadd (R, 34), and by Rivers's (and others') perception that his patients see him as a father figure (R, 65). To an extent, Rivers becomes the model father that the soldiers have for the most part lacked, both at home and at the front – a caring male in contrast to other callous patriarchs or abusing men-in-power. When Rivers goes on leave because he is on the verge of a breakdown himself, Sassoon thinks: 'He'd joked once or twice to Rivers about his being his father confessor, but only now, faced with this second abandonment, did he realize how completely Rivers had come to take his father's place' (R, 145).

Rivers is portrayed as an unconventional and progressive thinker. Unlike Dr. Yealland, whose electric shock treatments are witnessed by Rivers near the conclusion of *Regeneration*, Rivers believes in empathy and analysis as the best as well as the most humane way of helping his patients. This belief stems in large part from his experience as an anthropologist on the Solomon Islands, where he sees 'the *Great White God* de-throned'. This is when he appreciates, through cultural difference, that British moral standards and social codes are neither superior nor preferable to those of the Melanesians (R, 242). The sexual freedoms and communal identity of the islanders contrast sharply with the isolated and restricted lives Rivers sees in England.

Rivers is similarly accepting of the different sexualities of his patients. This may appear simply part of his liberalism but Barker in interview has hinted at something further: 'I think, you see, that Rivers is homosexual, too. I think that he is in love with Sassoon' (Perry, 56). The book hints at this but its concern with 'the love that dare not speak its name' is central to its exploration of mutism and stammers, emotional repression and denial: 'neurasthenic stammers arise from the same kind of conflict as mutism, a conflict between wanting to speak and knowing that w-what you've got to say is not acceptable' (R, 97). All kinds of repression, sexual, social, and personal, are unearthed in the novel, foregrounding the elements of the time that were unexplored by a society defending its ideals of masculinity. Historically significant homosexual figures are mentioned in passing, from

Edward Carpenter to Oscar Wilde and Robert Ross, while nearly all the book's main relationships involving real people, like Graves and Sassoon, Rivers and Henry Head, are underscored by sexual intimacy. Also, though Prior's bisexuality is only made apparent in the second novel, from the start he repeatedly uses sexual remarks or innuendoes to unnerve Rivers, as when he replies to the doctor's statement that he should look at Prior's chest with: 'Your room or mine?' (R, 61). Rivers's views on the construction of gender are also uncommon for the period, indicated by his reaction to being called a 'male mother' by Prior: 'He distrusted the implication that nurturing, even when done by a man, remains female, as if the ability were in some way borrowed, or even stolen, from women – a sort of moral equivalent of the *couvades*. If that were true, then there was very little hope' (R, 107).

For Rivers, whose interest in Freud's work is unusual in Britain at this time, the soldiers' neurosis is a symptom of gender constructions: the tension between their received notions of masculinity and their experience of the trenches, where men brought up on a diet of *Boys' Own* adventure stories now find they are required not to express themselves through fighting or exploration but to crouch in dugouts, passively waiting in ignorance (R, 107). Indicating a major reason for the book's focus on speech and silence, Rivers believes the soldiers' breakdowns are caused by an inability to express fear and frustration because they have been taught to ignore their feelings: 'They'd been trained to identify emotional repression as the essence of manliness' (R, 48). Rivers later concludes:

> it was prolonged strain, immobility and helplessness that did the damage, and not the sudden shocks or bizarre horrors that the patients themselves were inclined to point to as the explanation for their condition. That would help to account for the greater prevalence of anxiety neuroses and hysterical disorders in women in peacetime, since their relatively more confined lives gave them fewer opportunities of reacting to stress in active and constructive ways. (R, 222)

This is a possible explanation for Sassoon's protest that opens the trilogy: his recklessness has earned him the sobriquet 'Mad Jack' (R, 11), and Rivers believes Sassoon simply 'can't bear to be safe' (S, 36). Sassoon's reasons for opposing the war are not religious or pacific: 'I just don't think our war aims – *whatever they may be* – justify this level of slaughter' (R, 13). It is Rivers's job to persuade Sassoon that he is wrong (R, 15), yet it is Rivers whose attitude to the war seems to change as he gradually comes to see that his principles, and the evidence of the war's effect on the soldiers he sees, should put him on Sassoon's side (e.g. R, 115–16). Sassoon's views do not change as significantly but he is prevailed upon to see his situation differently. For Graves, Sassoon should return to the war because he has signed up for a job he must see through (R, 23), but Sassoon is more swayed by the argument that as a platoon commander he should not desert his fellow soldiers and that it would be ignominious for him to sit out the war in safety while his comrades died (S, 36). If he were to do so, Sassoon would become one of the non-combatants he professes to 'hate' because of what he sees as their callous and complacent attitude towards the suffering of those at the front – and so he returns to look after his men, a motive he later comes to see as naïve in *The Eye in the Door* (ED, 229–30).

Sassoon's conflict of principles – the seemingly antithetical beliefs that he should oppose the war yet also lead and support his men – is mirrored in Rivers's feelings about his own job: 'Recently almost all his dreams had centred on conflicts arising from his treatment of particular patients. In advising them to remember the traumatic events that had led to their being sent here, he was, in effect, inflicting pain, and doing so in pursuit of a treatment that he knew to be still largely experimental' (R, 47). Rivers has to ask himself how much suffering is justified in the pursuit of the patient's cure, just as Sassoon questions how much suffering and what methods are justified in the pursuit of victory. For Rivers, Burns's case is one in which 'the pain involved in insisting on the method would be too great' (R, 47). He is again confronted by this issue towards the end of the book when Yealland treats Callan's muteness with electric shocks. In stark contrast to Rivers's approach to Prior's inability to speak at Craiglockhart, where the emphasis is on listening and empathizing, Yealland tells Rivers 'The last thing these patients need is a sympathetic audience' (R, 228), and then tells his patient: '*You must speak, but I shall not listen to anything you have to say*' (R, 231).

Where Yealland's attitude mirrors the war authorities' response to soldiers in general and Sassoon in particular, Rivers's internal conflicts issue in his unconscious accusing him of muting

Sassoon:

> Only one man was being silenced in the way the dream indicated. He told himself that the accusation was unjust. It was Sassoon's decision to abandon the protest, not his. But that didn't work. He knew the extent of his own influence. … and felt that he was having to appeal against conviction in a courtroom where he himself had been both judge and jury.   (R, 239)

The *Regeneration Trilogy* is Barker's major achievement. In it, she most fully expresses the sense of ambivalence and duality that runs through her fiction as consistently as it runs through the figure of Prior, a man whose in-betweeness is expressed in everything from his sexuality and his class position to his fugue states of mind – and Prior also evinces ambivalence to the war. While Owen and Sassoon have been reductively positioned as anti-war poets who represented a turn in Western attitudes towards a range of issues from patriotism to violence, Barker demonstrates that they, and people throughout the rest of the twentieth century, had far more complex and conflicted feelings. In her mature novels, Barker asks for a fuller understanding of the psychological underpinnings of sexual desire and a better appreciation of the constructions and myths of femininity and masculinity in the context of a range of historical factors including nationalism, feminism, and class division. She also asks the reader to step back from simple denunciations of war and aggression to understand the social, political, and economic circumstances that underpin individual and collective action.

References and Further Reading

Pat Barker, *Blow Your House Down* (BH), London: Virago, 1984.
——— , *Regeneration* (R), Harmondsworth: Penguin, 1997.
——— , *The Eye in the Door* (ED), Harmondsworth: Penguin, 1994.
——— , *The Ghost Road* (GR), Harmondsworth: Penguin, 1996.
——— , *Another World* (AW), Harmondsworth: Penguin, 1999.
——— , *Border Crossing* (BC), Harmondsworth: Penguin, 2002.
——— , *Double Vision* (DV), London: Hamish Hamilton, 2003.
John Brannigan, 'Pat Barker's *Regenerartion* Trilogy' in *Contemporary British Fiction* edited by Richard J. Lane, Rod Mengham, and Philip Tew, Cambridge: Polity, 2003, 13–26.

——, *Orwell to the Present: Literature in England 1945–2000*, London: Palgrave, 2003.

Margaretta Jolly, 'After Feminism: Pat Barker, Penelope Lively and the Contemporary Novel' in *British Culture of the Postwar: An Introduction to Literature and Society 1945–1999*, edited by Alistair Davies and Alan Sinfield, London: Routledge, 2000, 58–82.

Catherine Lanone 'Scattering the Seed of Abraham: The Motif of Sacrifice in Pat Barker's *Regeneration* and *The Ghost Road*', *Literature and Theology*, 13:3, September 1999, 259–68.

Sharon Monteith, *Pat Barker*, Tavistock: Northcote, 2002.

Ankhi Mukherjee, 'Stammering to Story: Neurosis and Narration in Pat Barker's *Regeneration*', *Critique*, 43:1, Fall 2001, 49–62.

Donna Perry, 'Pat Barker' in *Backtalk: Women Writers Speak Out*, New Brunswick: Rutgers UP, 1992, 43–61.

Karin Westman, *Pat Barker's Regeneration*, London: Continuum, 2001.

Web Reading

http://www.mtmercy.edu/classes/barkerbib.htm

http://www.freud.org.uk/warneuroses.html

3

Julian Barnes: 'A Mixture of Genres'

3.1. Literary History

Julian Barnes (b. 1946), who also publishes detective fiction under the pseudonym Dan Kavanagh, has written nine novels under his own name. He is best known for self-reflexive writing that mixes fiction with other forms, such as history, memoir, and the polemical essay. He has also written more conventional novels, which have generally been accorded far less critical attention. His first book, *Metroland* (1980), is a story in three parts set in different periods in the life of Christopher Lloyd; appropriately, it follows the relationship of its protagonist with three people: his wife Marion, his French lover Annick, and his school friend Toni. In the first, semi-autobiographical part, set in 1963, Toni and Christopher are suburban London adolescents contemptuous of the banality of the English middle classes and enamoured of the main ingredients of Bohemian life: art, free sex, and all things French. Part two sees Christopher studying in France during the May 1968 riots, though he confesses he is more interested in sampling Gallic passion and Parisian charm than in politics. In the final part, set back in commuter-train metro land in 1977, Christopher is making a go of the suburban married life he and Toni professed to despise as teenagers while Toni has remained wedded to the ideals of their youth. The narrative moves gently and unsentimentally towards its conclusion that, caught between the unexciting but satisfying domesticity he has with Marion and the superficially attractive but ultimately hollow hedonism of Toni, Christopher has 'grown up' while his emotionally arrested friend has not. Though *Metroland* is observant and funny, it is perhaps primarily the fact that the story is narrated by Christopher that allows Barnes to resist the accusations of smugness and priggishness that have been aimed at the novel. Overall, Barnes's first novel is a contemplative book that affirms 'normality' and resists the Larkinesque temptation to believe that 'life' lies somewhere else – beyond suburbia, at political riots, in leading a Bohemian existence.

Before She Met Me (1982) is a darkly comic study in jealousy and obsession. The Othello (B, 172) of the novel is Graham Hendrick, a man who was loyal for 15 years to his first wife, but has now divorced and re-married. Though his second wife is faithful to him Graham finds he is compelled to collect and catalogue all the information he can find about her many previous lovers. This is initiated by watching love scenes in the films she made when she was a minor actress, Ann Mears. An attack on the view that the sexual revolution of the 1960s was uniformly liberating, the novel, which Barnes considers his funniest, ends with Graham brutally murdering the close friend who introduced him to Ann, and was one of her lovers, before committing suicide. The humour derives from the sardonic wit with which Barnes charts Graham's gradual descent into killing from his initial security: 'The first time Graham Hendrick watched his wife commit adultery he didn't mind at all. He even found himself chuckling' (B, 9).

Often described as a Francophile, Barnes read modern languages at University and has introduced his next novel by saying, 'I had always wanted to do something about Flaubert, but I knew I did not want to write any sort of biography or any sort of work of criticism' (*Cercles*, 256). A commission to write a guide to French writers' houses eventually gave rise to this next book: 'an upside down novel, a novel in which there was an infrastructure of fiction and very strong elements of non fiction, sometimes whole chapters which were nothing but arranged facts. It was a challenge as to how strong and authentic you can make a narrative where you aren't having anything invented in it' (*Cercles*, 259). In *Flaubert's Parrot* (1984) much turns out to be invented, but there is nothing deliberately untrue about Flaubert. This upside down novel consists of three tales: that of Geoffrey Braithwaite, retired doctor, and amateur Flaubert scholar, that of his dead wife, who cuckolded Braithwaite, and that of Flaubert and his parrot. It is simultaneously a work of criticism, a groundbreaking fiction, and an exploration in (auto)biography. The book won Barnes an international reputation, making him as well known in France and the US as in Britain. From a novelist with two respectable but minor novels he suddenly became known as a literary celebrity and an exemplary postmodernist author. The latter at least was partly because *Flaubert's Parrot* alludes to contemporary literary theory: 'We no longer believe that language and reality "match up" so congruently – indeed we probably think that words give birth to things as much as things give birth to words' (F, 88). But Braithwaite himself 'hates critics': a few pages after he has mocked Roland Barthes' list of the things he likes (F, 84), he rails against 'contemporary critics' – like Barthes – who 'pompously reclassify all novels and plays and poems as texts – the author to the guillotine!' (F, 88).

Delighted with the success of *Flaubert's Parrot*, Barnes was disappointed but amused by critics' expectations that he would follow it with a similar book, which he imagined would be entitled something like '*Victor Hugo's Dachshund*'. *Staring at the Sun* (1987) is in fact nothing like his previous novel, but it does have as its heroine a woman called Jean Sarjeant, whose name playfully echoes that of the male hero of Victor Hugo's *Les Miserables*: Jean Valjean. The book spans Jean's life from her birth in 1922 to a plane ride she takes in 2021, on which she sees the sun set twice. The metaphor of the book's title is that human beings have to stare courageously at the fact of a godless universe: stoically face life as chaotic and death as final without the consolations offered by religion. It is a book significantly marked by nothing remarkable and this seems to echo its theme, suggesting that, like Chris in *Metroland*, most individuals reach maturity by accepting their ordinariness and the absence in their lives of either providence or great drama.

A History of the World in 10½ Chapters (1989) is an imaginative exploration of human theories and stories about 'history' in its widest sense, drawing on annals, autobiography, biography, chronicle, memoirs, dreams, public records, family sagas, and other kinds of individual or collective self-representation. The book's very form questions the idea that the past's passage into the future is linear and progressive, asserting that while history makes humans, humans also make history – through story as much as action. It includes the theory that the past is always repeated (most clearly in 'Three Simple Stories'); the belief that history is cyclical (particularly in 'A Dream'); the biblical view of history (in 'The Stowaway'); the concept of fate and also the Christian faith in history as providential (in 'The Mountain' and 'Project Ararat'); the conviction that existence on earth is governed by science, technology, and their relationship with the Gaia hypothesis (in 'The Survivor' where a human catastrophe leads to an imbalance in Nature); and the many arguments that history is fundamentally embroiled in the processes of evolution and the survival of the fittest (perhaps most clearly in 'The Wars of Religion', but it is also in a story such as 'The Visitors'). Above all the book is fascinated by the transformation, through mythology, art, and the imagination, of the events of the past into different stories, memories, and versions of history.

Talking it Over (1991) and *Love, etc.* (2000) form a pair of novels centred on the relationships between three characters, who are also the principal narrators, taking turns to tell aspects of the story from their own point of view: Stuart, Gillian, and Oliver. Stuart and Oliver are unlikely school friends who, like Chris and Toni in *Metroland*, have developed a close but uneasy relationship into adulthood. In the first novel Stuart and Gillian marry and the unfolding story follows the loquacious and erudite Oliver's growing obsession with Gillian, who eventually leaves Stuart for his best friend. The sequel throws this process into reverse as the practical and dogmatic Stuart tries to win Gillian back; it concludes with Gillian still married to Oliver, but pregnant by Stuart. Each of the three characters muses over the possible futures they have, with or without each other. An ending that resists closure is made more open by the characters' appeals to the reader to choose: Oliver asks which of his three plans 'you' would prefer; Stuart asks whether 'you' think Gillian could come to love him again; and Gillian asks if 'you' think Stuart still loves her now. A final few lines are delivered by Mme Wyatt, who answers noncommittally for the reader: 'Don't ask me anything. Something will happen. Or nothing' (L, 250). Like *A History of the World in $10\frac{1}{2}$ Chapters, Talking it Over* and *Love, etc.* are an exploration of perspective, parallax, and the power of will both to influence others and to deceive the self. Singly and together, the novels constitute a semi-parodic three-way talking cure at the end of which everyone is certainly older but no one is perhaps wiser.

The Porcupine (1992) appeared first in Bulgarian and was only later released in its original English. It is the story of an East European country moving from communism to liberal democracy, and is based more on Bulgarian history than that of any other country. Its human story centres on the overthrown Party leader Petkanov, who is brought to trial, prosecuted by the ambitious and aggrieved Solinsky, and finally convicted of mass murder. In formal terms, *The Porcupine* is the most straightforward of Barnes's books and seems almost pointedly to confound critics' expectations: it is political, realist, and serious; yet, it also displays the characteristics of Barnes's other works. Which is to say it remains sceptical of idealism and refuses either to see events from one side or to take comfort from political or religious rhetoric. The sense persists of an uncommitted, slightly detached, and there-fore seemingly well-balanced authorial presence: one that detects traces of sound reason and logic in the justifications offered by Petkanov and sees Solinsky as someone with both power and also history, rather than morality, on his side. Barnes is in no wise a simple reactionary but is predisposed to see the arguments on both sides, and put them to the reader, asking like Gillian and Stuart: 'what do you think?' (L, 242–50).

Barnes's next novel, *England, England* (1998), explores the rela-tionship between heritage and commercialism, history and exploitation, imitation and reality. It is a fantasy, but one that has many recent echoes and real-life parallels. For example, in 2001, a £155m makeover of Stonehenge was announced: developers set about building a tunnel to send underground the traffic that roared along beside the site and they also undertook to build a full-size replica of the stones to put on display, so protecting the originals from further damage. The imitation site, beside the real one, was to be turned into a theme park with buggies and a visitor centre where before there was just an 'uncommercialised' pile of stones. In *England, England* a powerful businessman plans to turn the Isle of Wight into a colossal theme park so that tourists will not have to traipse from Dover to London to Stratford-on-Avon to Chester. Asked about his choice of location, Barnes said in interview with the *Daily Telegraph* that the Isle of Wight 'was one of the first places in Great Britain to be perverted by becoming a tourist destination. It was a rather undeveloped, old-fashioned, quite primitive offshore island until sunbathing became fashion-able. Queen Victoria and Tennyson went there and that did for it. Sea-bathing became all the rage. The traditional industries of smuggling and boat-building lost out to tourism.' In Barnes's novel, the Isle of Wight becomes 'England, England', importing all the main cultural–commercial aspects of the mainland, which is itself transformed into 'Anglia', a backward nation which gradually regresses into its own past, finally becoming a rural country dominated by Celtic culture and pagan ceremonies.

Barnes's entrepreneurial figure, reminiscent of the media magnate Robert Maxwell, is Sir Jack Pitman, whose surname suggests shorthand Englishness and Britain's decrepit mining industry. Sir Jack's business blueprint includes a list, compiled from surveys, of the 'Fifty Quintessences of Englishness'. These stretch from the royal family, double-decker buses, thatched cottages, and cream teas to bad underwear, phlegm, and flagellation. Partly because of its context in a novel, Barnes's checklist of English characteristics, personalities, and achievements is an ironic dig at nostalgia, commerce, and mass tourism. Among the quintessences, past glories overshadow such present-day banalities as 'whingeing', while the list records the traditional English vices of emotional frigidity, snobbery, hypocrisy, and perfidy. The focus of the items is on pre-1960 if not Olde England. It is England in aspic, disabled by its past, backward- rather than forward-looking, assembling a populist past for consumer entertainment. Barnes has said that there is no point in English novelists trying to write in imitation of the great American novel: for a small, post-imperial country different themes and styles are needed, which might include those of *England, England*, whose tongue-in-cheek ironies could be said to evince Englishness as much as Barnes's list of quintessences. The book's title plays with a range of references, but it also alludes to D. H. Lawrence's short story 'England, My England' (1922) and A. G. MacDonell's novel *England, Their England* (1933), but pointedly lacks any possessive pronoun.

Barnes has also written two volumes of loosely connected short stories. One is focussed on the relationship between England and France, *Cross Channel* (1996), and the other ranges over a number of themes, such as ageing and death, that striate Barnes's work, *The Lemon Table* (2004). His articles as London correspondent for the *New Yorker* have been assembled as *Letters from London* (1995) and he has published a collection of essays on French literature and culture: *Something to Declare* (2002). He has also edited Alphonse Daudet's *In the Land of Pain*, produced a book of culinary essays called *The Pedant in the Kitchen*, and written the introductions to several works by other authors, ranging from Clive James's *Reliable Essays* to Aristotle's *The Nicomachean Ethics*.

3.2. Themes: Art and History

> *We can study files for decades, but every so often we are tempted to throw*
> *up our hands and declare that history is merely another literary genre: the*
> *past is autobiographical fiction pretending to be a parliamentary report.*
>   (F, 90)

Barnes is sometimes considered a postmodernist writer because
his fiction rarely either conforms to the model of the realist
novel or concerns itself with a scrutiny of consciousness in the
manner of modernist writing. He has been said to stretch the
bounds of fiction in his novels but it has just as often been suggested that he is an essayist rather than a novelist and his experimental books do not question the bounds of the novel but fall
outside them.

With regard to his own practice, Barnes rarely discusses fictional technique in his novels, except through Braithwaite's med-
itations in *Flaubert's Parrot*, and instead uses painting and other
kinds of imaginative and imitative art to discuss indirectly the
function of writing, as well as to address wider issues of aesthetics and criticism that are common to a range of cultural practices.
This goes from the debates between Toni and Chris in *Metroland*
through to the imitative world created by Jack Pitman in *England,
England*. Chris explains that his and Toni's reason for constantly
visiting the National Gallery in London is because they agreed
that 'Art was the most important thing in life' (M, 29). The boys
consider it rewarding and ameliorative: 'It made people not just
fitter for friendship and more civilized ... but *better* – kinder,
wiser, nicer, more peaceful, more active, more sensitive. If it did-
n't what good was it?' (M, 29). Their 'constructive loafing' is
exemplified by studying the ways in which people are 'in some
way improved' when they see works of art in the Gallery.

The belief in the supremacy of art is reinforced by Geoffrey
Braithwaite quoting Flaubert: 'Superior to everything is – Art'
(F, 108); yet the idea that art is the most important thing 'in life' is
partly paradoxical because in Barnes's books art and life are often
contrasted: 'Books are where things are explained to you; life is
where things aren't' (F, 168). This partly expresses the attraction
of art – there is its beauty but its intellectual value lies in its
attempt to make sense of the world. This is also the argument of
the 'Shipwreck' chapter of *A History of the World*, but in *Flaubert's*

Parrot the differences between life and art are brought out in Braithwaite's attempt not just to understand his own life but that of the nineteenth-century writer who famously claimed that the life of novelists has nothing to do with their writing.

Braithwaite asks early on: 'Is the writer much more than a sophisticated parrot?' (F, 18), and there are many intimations in *Flaubert's Parrot* that the reader cannot reliably get to 'know' the writer any better than Braithwaite can get to 'know' which of many parrots was the Loulou of Flaubert's *Un Coeur Simple*. 'How do you compare two parrots, one already idealized by memory and metaphor, the other a squawking intruder? My initial response was that the second seemed less authentic than the first. Mainly because it had a more benign air' (F, 21). Braithwaite goes on to say: 'The writer's voice – what makes you think it can be located that easily? Such was the rebuke offered by the second parrot' (F, 22). So, though the novel's facts about the French author are not in dispute even the first image of Flaubert encountered in the book is potentially misleading: 'The statue isn't the original one', Braithwaite laconically assures us (F, 11).

Biography is ultimately considered a string of words designed to encompass the writer just as a fish net is a tool to catch fish; but, argues Braithwaite, a fish net can be logically deemed a collection of holes tied together with string: and so can a biography (F, 38; cf. Barnes use of the metaphor in interview, *Cercles*, 263). This description also fits well with Barnes's view of history. 'History isn't what happened. History is just what historians tell us. There was a pattern, a plan, a movement, expansion, the march of democracy; it is a tapestry, a flow of events, a complex narrative, connected, explicable' (H, 242). Historiography is a narrative composed of connections, threads that reach across the gaps in knowledge and understanding where most of the past falls through the net. History emerges for Barnes as a kind of tapestry, a text(ile) woven out of other texts and strands of memory.

But what are his books' objections to the ways in which history is understood? They seem to focus on gaps: what falls through history's net: 'How do we seize the past? How do we seize the foreign past? We read, we learn, we ask, we remember, we are humble; and then a casual detail shifts everything' (F, 90). For Braithwaite, it is only distance, the passage of time that enables us to feel we are able to understand history: 'So how do we seize the past? As it recedes, does it come into focus? Some think so. We know more, we discover extra documents, we use infra-red light to pierce erasures in the correspondence, and we are free of contemporary prejudice; so we understand better. Is that it? I wonder' (F, 100).

Braithwaite's scepticism seems to be based on the view that distance enables us to understand history better only because with the passing of time some events and perspectives are forgotten while others, those that fit our theory of history, remain: 'what a curious vanity it is of the present to expect the past to suck up to it' (F, 130). So theories that fit our present beliefs arise to turn history into a process, a force, a pattern, but Barnes is sceptical: 'And does history repeat itself, the first time as tragedy, the second time as farce? No, that's too grand, too considered a process. History just burps, and we taste again that raw-onion sandwich it swallowed centuries ago' (H, 241).

In Barnes' *History of the World*, what we find throughout the book is a number of parallels, between occurrences of boats, beetles, and behemoths. The reason for this is not because history has a number of parallels, but because the past is habitually perceived in a certain way – stories lead on to other stories and human beings always look for patterns, for systems, for explanations. 'History', this suggests, is a way of constructing reality, of explaining what happens, of tracing patterns in events, of creating a form, a narrative structure, from what has happened in the world.

Barnes has said that against history bearing down on us we can put three things: religion, art, and love. Religion, he thinks, is not true, art does not satisfy everyone, and so love is the final 'fall-back position' (Moseley, 120). History does not give us truth, it just finds things out (H, 242), whereas 'love and truth: that's the vital connection' (H, 240, 245). For Barnes, and this is in many ways the story of Braithwaite's explorations in biography too, 'The history of the world becomes brutally self-important without love' (H, 240). History is therefore seen as impersonal; it leaves out the most important human elements – faith, art, love – and its march of progress, power, and politics leaves many casualties: 'when love fails, we should blame the history of the world. If only it had left us alone, we could have been happy' (H, 246).

3.3. Key Works: *Flaubert's Parrot, A History of the World in 10½ Chapters*

Flaubert's Parrot has been received as a French novel in many ways – one that is concerned with Flaubert in its form as much as in its content. One critic, Terrence Rafferty, has said that it is 'a modernist text with a nineteenth-century heart, a French novel with English lucidity and tact' (Moseley, 90). It perhaps has a parallel with a work that has been described as the best French novel in the English language: Ford Madox Ford's modernist masterpiece *The Good Soldier*. The narrator of that novel, Dowell, says at one point: 'I don't know that analysis of my own psychology matters at all to this story.' Yet the reader concludes that it matters more than anything else. Similarly, Braithwaite (partly echoing Flaubert) says: 'Nothing much about my character matters' (F, 96). Both narrators seem to be telling a story in which their own involvement is peripheral, and yet they are the mediators, organizers, constructors, and arrangers of the stories they tell. No one else would have told the story like this, and Braithwaite's psychology, like Dowell's, matters not because he is the 'author' of the text but because he is its 'narrator', a voice and device used by the author.

As a narrative, *Flaubert's Parrot* contains an extremely unusual range of narrative types: apocrypha, autobiography, bestiary, biography, chronology, criticism, dialogue, dictionary, essay, exam, guide, and manifesto. This is one way in which Barnes challenges the homogeneous formal approach of conventional history, when in fact 'Nature is always a mixture of genres' (F, 134). Barnes's many prose genres taken together question definitions of fact and fiction, history and story, truth and opinion, and the method of the novel stands in stark contrast to Braithwaite's quest to find the 'real' Flaubert's parrot: a search that broadens out from one candidate to a whole roomful. The question of verisimilitude in fiction is implicitly questioned in the novel, as art has a different relationship with reality from history's. Broadly speaking, from Barnes's perspective, this might be summarized as: history aims at a factual truth whereas fiction aims at an emotional one. One of the ways in which Barnes brings fiction to bear on history and biography is to suggest that emotional and factual truths have much in common – both have to convince and persuade the reader that they are in some sense 'correct'. Yet, what is deemed 'correct', emotionally or historically, is far more a matter of socially agreed opinion, of what Foucault calls being 'in the true', than it is of absolute truth. *Flaubert's Parrot* repeatedly exposes 'fact' as opinion and 'truth' as dominant viewpoint by assembling perspectives and versions, claims and counter-claims: all of which, like the colour of Emma Bovary's eyes, depend upon the light in which you view them, or, like Piggy's attempt to make fire in *Lord of the Flies*, depend upon the lens you use (F, 76).

Though the book appears to undercut all knowledge, its argument seems to emerge as something else: the more we know the more ignorant we realize we are, and the more ignorant we realize we are the less deceived we become. This is not a regressive argument but one that affirms the importance of the pursuit of knowledge while recognizing the impossibility of ever being either impartial or simply 'correct' about an event. It is for Barnes a matter of fallibility, complexity, and relativity. In Braithwaite's first chronology, Flaubert dies 'full of honour, widely loved and working hard to the end' (F, 27); in the second he dies 'Impoverished, lonely, and exhausted' (F, 31); and in the third a middle position is expressed by the author himself: 'If [the book] is to appear next winter, I haven't a minute to lose between now and then. But there are moments when I'm so tired that I feel I'm liquefying like an old Camembert' (F, 37). This plurality of perspectives is matched by the three versions Braithwaite gives of his relationship with his wife (F, 162): 'I loved her; we were happy; I miss her' (F, 161); 'She didn't love me; we were unhappy; I miss her' (F, 161); 'We were happy; we were unhappy; we were happy enough' (F, 165). The implication is that there are always at least three versions, as in *Talking it Over* and *Love etc*.

Braithwaite's love for the dead wife who deceived him (Ellen Braithwaite was not Emma Bovary, but there are similarities beyond their initials) is now channelled into a love for someone whose vices and faults are both fascinating and harmless to him: 'perhaps love for a writer is the purest, the steadiest form of love' (F, 127). But the drawback is that this love is based not on experiencing life with someone but on books:

> My wife: someone I feel I understand less well than a foreign writer dead for a hundred years. Is this an aberration, or is it normal? Books say: she did this because. Life says: she did this. ... I'm not surprised some people prefer books. Books

make sense of life. The only problem is the lives they make sense of are other people's lives, never your own.   (F, 168)

If Braithwaite cannot even get to know which is Flaubert's parrot then the simplest facts concerning a writer who thought the author's life of no consequence to the work are cast into doubt: ' "The artist must manage to make posterity believe that he never existed" Flaubert said' (F, 86). In one of his supposed letters, now burned, Flaubert asked Juliet Herbert: 'If anyone ever asks you what my letters contained, or what my life was like, please lie to them. Or rather … just tell them what it is you think they want to hear' (F, 48). By extension, the 'truth' and reliability of Braithwaite's narrative and life are thrown into question. Doubts cloud even the clearest-seeming facts: Flaubert's death is considered by some to be suicide; Ellen Braithwaite's suicide could be considered her husband's murder (F, 168, 181).

When Braithwaite begins to tell the story of his wife, he says: 'This is a pure story, whatever you may think' (F, 160). This may mean 'pure story' in the sense of unadulterated story and it may also be a comment on adultery. Hardy subtitled *Tess of the D'Urbervilles* 'a pure woman' because he wanted to counter the attacks that would be made on her for her sexual history. Braithwaite seems to be doing the same for Ellen – 'whatever you may think'.

Ultimately, in *Flaubert's Parrot* perspective is everything because individuals' perspectives are usually of more importance to them than 'truth'. Over this point, Braithwaite is deeply con-flicted. On the one hand he agrees with Christopher Ricks: 'If you don't know what's true, or what's meant to be true, then the value of what isn't true, or isn't meant to be true is diminished' (F, 77). This relates to his attempt to find out the truth about Flaubert's parrot. On the other hand, he seems to express no disquiet when, at the end of one series of anecdotes, this time about Flaubert's relationship with dogs, he concludes: 'What happened to the truth is not recorded' (F, 65). This appeals more to a side to Braithwaite that critics sometimes overlook, a side that is at ease with Keatsian negative capability, as when Braithwaite says he dislikes coincidences and all that they might intimate of a 'cosmic plan': 'I prefer to feel that things are chaotic, free-wheeling, per-manently as well as temporarily crazy – to feel the certainty of human ignorance, brutality and folly' (F, 66). Yet Braithwaite's own writing is full of coincidences, of connections, lists, parallels, similarities, related anecdotes, and the ironies beloved of Flaubert – and these, rather than 'truths', are what the human mind seems to seek out, to delight in spotting.

Flaubert's Parrot is therefore partly a train-spotter's guide to Flaubert (and Barnes train-spotters will notice an intertextual reference to *Metroland*, which Braithwaite reads and finds a mistake in (F, 93)). Yet this is of more importance to the form of the novel than its content, despite the inclusion of a 'train-spotters' chapter; which is to say that Braithwaite likes to accumulate details, argue about trivia and, above all, compile lists. Alongside the chronologies, the catalogues of dogs, trains, and parrots, Braithwaite even provides his list of ten kinds of novel that should be banned (F, 98–9), yet all of his interest in Flaubert ultimately seems to be a way to defer or avoid talking about his own life and especially his wife. Like Flaubert, Braithwaite puts his obsessive work before his life, as train-spotters are supposed to do. When he mentions Ellen, he starts to talk about her and then breaks off: 'I remember ... but I'll keep that for another time' (F, 76) and 'My wife ... Not now, not now' (F, 105). Here lies the human aspect to a novel which has been accused of amounting to little more than verbal and intellectual gymnastics. Barnes himself has said that *Flaubert's Parrot* is perhaps above all 'a novel about a man whose inability to express his grief and his love ... is transposed into an obsessive desire to recount to you the reader everything he knows and has found out about Gustave Flaubert, love for whom has been a more reliable constant in his life than has been love for Ellen' (*Cercles*, 262). While Braithwaite weaves a net of facts and details about the comparatively trivial subject of Flaubert's parrot, the important subject of his relationship with his wife, and his love for her, slips through the holes.

*   *   *

The past is a distant, receding coastline, and we are all in the same boat. Along the stern rail there is a line of telescopes; each brings the shore into focus at a given distance ... our normal activity [is] scurrying from one telescope to another, seeing the sharpness fade in one, waiting for the blur to clear in another. And when the blur does clear, we imagine that we have made it do so all by ourselves.

(F, 101)

Alongside *Flaubert's Parrot*, *A History of the World in 10½ Chapters* is Barnes's most experimental book. It lies self-consciously between a novel and a collection of interlinked short stories, some of whose principal connections are: the Ark, wine, woodworm, the beetle and the Behemoth, hallucinations/dreams, the end of the world, segregation and survival, and the human fetish for the number seven (a number to which half again is added to reach 10½). The seeds of all of these motifs are sown in the first chapter and returned to throughout the book, but the most prominent theme is that of the journey. All of the ten full chapters in *A History of the World* contain expeditions or odysseys: a holiday cruise, worms transported in wood, a survival boat, a raft, a Victorian expedition to find Noah's Ark, people trapped aboard the Titanic, within a whale, or on the liner *St. Louis*, a film crew journeying upstream, a space ship, and a dream of going to heaven. Even the 'half chapter' contains its reference to this theme in its observation that, 'Trusting virgins were told that love was the promised land, an ark on which two might escape the Flood' (H, 231). The theme of the journey, by land, sea or air, is there to suggest the passages of life and time, but love is the element missing from the history of the world as it was from Braithwaite's chronicles of Flaubert. The stories in *A History of the World* do not appear in chronological order but follow a trajectory from Genesis through to Heaven, covering banal events and significant moments in religion, politics, evolutionary theory, space exploration, and human mythology.

The final story, 'The Dream', underlines the book's concern with repetition. It is a mythical tale of sempiternal return, of the recurring dream and the endless iterations suggested by the concept of eternity. Its argument appears to be that any timeless Heaven we can envisage, however perfect, will become tedious to earthly human beings. There are no new inventions, discoveries or stories, simply the possibilities of living as oneself forever in a vast but unchanging paradise without a future to bring newness into the world. The chapter affirms the inevitability on earth of each mortal generation repeating humanity's past, but in their own way – with variation; whereas, in Heaven the same existence is elongated forever, experiencing all of life's variety, but then still having an eternity to 'survive', in the sense of endure. Presented as a Utopian vision that becomes a nightmare, 'The Dream' asserts the importance for human beings of both a struggle against possible failure and a belief in endings – intimating that the release that death offers is preferable to an eternal life. Even a 'Groundhog Day' should end, and allow time to continue, once it has been perfected. The story seems to be outside of history and yet its fundamental premise is that this Heaven is like earth, only tuned up to a perfection of which humans can only dream. Which is to say that it is entirely bound up with history; history provides the only templates for human visions of paradise. It is not a critique of 'Heaven' but of the human ability to imagine utopia.

By contrast, Barnes's opening chapter focusses on humans' imagining of their origins. 'The Stowaway' concentrates on the diluvian moment of the destruction of the first fallen paradise on earth and the birth of history. It uses the account of the Flood from Genesis (8:4) as a starting point for all existing life on the planet: a primal narrative of survival, of debates between story and history, religion and science, human and animal perspectives, authorized and alternative versions. It initiates the image of extinction and (un)natural selection that runs through the remaining chapters in its focus on the woodworm and the Behemoth; it also suggests humanity's inability to see different sides to events and also people's propensity for intoxication and delusion. These are the elements of history: 'We make up a story to cover the facts we don't know or can't accept; we keep a few true facts and spin a new story round them. Our panic and our pain are only eased by soothing fabulation; we call it history' (H, 242, echoing 109). In effect, 'The Stowaway' takes a founding myth of human, largely Western, belief, and suggests that the only narrative of it we have, the word of God passed down through Moses, is not a single, true account but an interested, partial one. A different narrator, an unofficial, even fugitive one, gives a widely diverging account from the same starting material. Barnes also sets up his narrating woodworm as the one character who appears throughout the stories. Mocking those critics who would assert that a long piece of prose fiction without at least one character consistently featuring throughout is not a novel, Barnes inserts this bookworm as a figure who pops up intermittently as though eating its way through the course of human histor(iograph)y.

'The Visitors' also focusses on competing viewpoints. As in the first chapter, this story involves the separation of 'the clean from the unclean' (H, 44), but now the selection involves not animals but humans. The leader of The Black Thunder group announces that he will inform the passengers 'what is happening. How they are mixed up in history. What that history is' (H, 51). Our guide, Franklin Hughes, makes a deal with the hijackers to tell the passengers about this history in exchange for their agreement to relegate his girlfriend in their list of executions. To the audience on the cruise ship, including his girlfriend, Hughes appears a collaborator, such that when the American Special Forces raid the ship: 'Neither the leader nor the second-in-command survived, so there remained no witness to corroborate Franklin Hughes's story of the bargain he had struck with the Arabs' (H, 58). In the face of what appears to be the evidence, Hughes's version is assumed to be another self-interested oration and even his girlfriend, 'who had become Irish for a few hours without realizing it', never speaks to him again.

'The Stowaway' is a first-person account by the uninvited woodworm who is literally not-wanted-on-voyage, while 'The Visitors' is a third-person narration focalized through Hughes. Pointing up Barnes's perennial interest in form, each subsequent story is narrated or presented differently. 'The Wars of Religion' takes the form of a translation of legal argument and debate: sixteenth-century court submissions, petitions, and records. Religion is still to the fore, as the church authorities argue over the 'interference' of woodworm in human history, and, creating a connection with the first story, the woodworms are at one point considered an abomination because they could not have been allowed on the Ark. The chapter concentrates upon that which supposedly separates humans from animals, 'discourse of reason', and proceeds to explore the abuses to which the faculty of logic can be put, creating facts, arguments, and historical beliefs that are both ludicrous and erroneous. It seems to justify the viewpoint of the woodworm who narrates 'The Stowaway':

> we don't deny, of course, your cleverness, your considerable potential. But you are, as yet, at an early stage of your development. We, for instance, are always ourselves: that is what it means to be evolved. ... You aren't too good with the truth, either, your species. You keep forgetting things, or you pretend to. ... It surprises you that guns kill, that money corrupts, that snow falls in winter. Such naïvety can be charming; alas, it can also be perilous. (H, 28–9)

To a degree this is a matter of 'truth' opposed to 'fabulation', which is central to 'The Survivor'. Here, two competing accounts of reality and sanity vie with one another in the asterisk-separated sections that make up much of the story. Kath Ferris decides that she has herself unconsciously invented her rescue to cope with her situation: 'The mind got carried away, she found herself repeating. Everything was connected, the weapons and the nightmares. That's why they'd had to break the cycle. Start making things simple again. Begin at the beginning. People said you couldn't turn the clock back, but you could. The future was in the past' (H, 104). The doctors' version of events is different: they maintain that Kath was found off Darwin, going round in circles in her boat, and hallucinating: 'You mustn't fool yourself. ... We've got to look at things how they are; we can't rely on fabulation any more. It's the only way we'll survive' (H, 111). The human hope of rescue and drive for survival becomes the subject of 'Shipwreck', which develops into a meditation on the processes and choices involved in turning life, or more particularly tragedy, into art. The chapter itself is also concerned with a prominent postmodernist device, ekphrasis: the verbal representation of visual representation. The second half of the chapter offers perspectives on Géricault's 1819 painting popularly known as 'The Raft of the Medusa'. This inquiry opens with the rhetorical sentence, 'How do you turn catastrophe into art?' (H, 125). The answer to the question of why, if not how, is offered by the narrator:

> We have to understand it, of course, this catastrophe; to understand it, we have to imagine it, so we need the imaginative arts. But we also need to justify it and forgive it, this catastrophe, however minimally. Why did it happen, this mad act of Nature, this crazed human moment? Well, at least it produced art. Perhaps, in the end, that's what catastrophe is *for*.   (H, 125)

The succeeding discussion is reminiscent of *Flaubert's Parrot*: it contains three responses to the actual painting, preceded by eight alternative moments the painter might have chosen, with eight accompanying notes explaining the pros and cons of each possibility, none of which Géricault selected: 'the painting which survives is the one that outlives its own story. Religion decays, the icon remains; a narrative is forgotten, yet its representation still magnetizes' (H, 133). Barnes's narrator, in discussing the painting, provides a justification for the novel that lies before the reader: 'We are all lost at sea, washed between hope and despair, hailing something that may never come to rescue us. Catastrophe has become art; but this is no reducing process. It is freeing, enlarging, explaining' (H, 137). Those familiar with Barnes's fiction will remember that such is also the view Chris and Toni would have subscribed to in their perambulations around the national gallery in *Metroland*.

In 'The Mountain' the question of the nature and value of art is raised again: a father admires the 'progress' he sees embodied in 10 000 feet of mobile canvas unwinding the story of the Medusa's shipwreck in a series of episodes in Marshall's Marine Peristrephic Panorama. By contrast, his daughter feels Géricault's painting 'though static contained for her much motion and lighting and, in its own way, music – indeed, in some fashion it contained more of these things that did the vulgar Panorama' (H, 145–6). While her dying father deems Genesis to contain nothing more substantial than 'the Myth of the Deluge', Miss Ferguson believes in the 'reality' of Noah's Ark; she also considers her father's inability to see beauty in Géricault's painting to be paralleled by his failure to recognize God's 'eternal design and its essential goodness' when the 'proof of this plan and of this benevolence lay manifest in Nature, which was provided by god for Man's enjoyment' (H, 147). Miss Ferguson sets off to find the Ark but the important thing for her is that her pilgrimage is a result of God-given human free choice: 'There always appear to be two explanations of everything. That is why we have been given free will, in order that we may choose the correct one. My father failed to comprehend that his explanations were based as much upon faith as mine. Faith in nothing' (H, 154). This is in fact an example of Pascal's wager, a rational argument for religious faith: since the individual does not know for certain whether or not God exists, it is logical to believe, because the possible consequences are salvation or mere self-deception, whereas the consequences of not believing in God's existence are damnation if he does and oblivion if he doesn't.

'Three Simple Stories' are about survival, repetition, and the mythic potential of narrative. Each story parallels its 'factual' roots with 'fictional' ones: the fabrications of a Titanic survivor who may have dressed as a woman to be one of the first into the lifeboats and then farcically repeated this costumed exit on the set of a film of the disaster, *A Night to Remember*; Jonah and his three nights in the whale (plus a conflation of Melville's 'Bartleby the

Scrivener' and *Moby Dick*); Christ's time in the Wilderness of forty days and forty nights, the duration of the *St. Louis*'s passengers' ordeal (H, 188). 'Project Ararat', exemplifies the conclusion of the first tale in 'Three Simple Stories: 'Marx's elaboration of Hegel: history repeats itself, the first time as tragedy, the second time as farce' (H, 175). Also, where Miss Ferguson's story in 'The Mountain' ended in tragedy with her death on Ararat, Spike Tiggler's ends in farce as he believes the remains he finds on the mountain are actually Noah's, when what he in fact discovers are the remnants of Miss Ferguson. The story concludes with Tiggler deciding to launch a second Project Ararat. Significantly, however, the chapter starts and ends in the second person, inserting the reader, positioned on an island ferry, into the narrative in a way that brings to mind a comment on history from *Flaubert's Parrot*: 'Does the world progress? Or does it merely shuttle back and forth like a ferry?' (F, 105). The dominant suggestion is that history repeats itself, as in 'Upstream', loosely based on the 1986-film *The Mission*, where the conceited Euro-American film actors believe that they can determine the difference between truth and make-believe, unlike the Amazonian 'primitive Indians' whom they, like the long-dead Jesuit missionaries the actors are pretending to be, try to persuade to accept their way of thinking.

Barnes's half chapter, 'Parenthesis', suggests that it is an aside or interruption in the text. It appears as an argument placed in brackets to show it is a digression from, or rather a different slant on, the apparent thesis of the book. Its purpose is to assert the importance of the personal within the long narrative of history and to reassert a belief in perspectival relativity. This shorter piece is not a story so much as a meditation that points out that history can be seen in terms of evolution, biological determinism, political struggle, and so forth, but from a human perspective the only point of life is love in its many forms.

Finally, it is important to remember that Barnes's novel is not *the* history but *a* history of the world. It has been criticized for being nothing of the sort but Barnes's retorts to his objectors are incorporated in the novel itself, which implies that historiography is always partial and selective: it is not complete and comprehensive but fragmentary, told from a point of view, and subject to the author's theories and prejudices as well as the narrative features of story-telling. Indeed, *A History of the World* contains its own commentary: 'The history of the world? Just voices echoing in the dark; images that burn for a few centuries and then fade; stories, old stories that sometimes seem to overlap; strange links, impertinent connections' (H, 242).

Of all the novelists discussed in this book, Barnes is perhaps the one most concerned with the variety of forms of the novel. Though the tone and colour of his writing is always recognizable, there is no way of telling what kind of fictional experiment will feature in any new book. Each one sets its own parameters and challenges for the writer and the reader, which may be why many reviewers find Barnes easy to admire but too cerebral and indeed reserved to love.

References and Further Reading

Julian Barnes, *Metroland* (M), London: Robin Clark, 1981.

——, *Before She Met Me* (B), London: Picador, 1986.

——, *Flaubert's Parrot* (F), London: Picador, 1985.

——, *A History of the World in* $10\frac{1}{2}$ *Chapters* (H), London: Jonathan Cape, 1989.

——, *Love, etc.* (L), London: Jonathan Cape, 2000.

Jackie Buxton, 'Julian Barnes's Theses on History (in $10\frac{1}{2}$ Chapters)', *Contemporary Literature*, 41:1, 2000, 56–86.

Steven Connor, *The English Novel in History: 1950–1995*, London: Routledge, 1996.

Andrzej Gasiorek, 'Postmodernism and the Problem of History: Julian Barnes', *Post-War British Fiction: Realism and After*, London: Edward Arnold, 1995, 158–65.

David Leon Higdon, 'Unconfessed Confessions': The Narrators of Graham Swift and Julian Barnes, *The British and Irish Novel Since 1960*, edited by James Acheson, London: Macmillan, 1991, 174–91.

Merritt Moseley, *Understanding Julian Barnes*, Columbia: University of South Carolina Press, 1997.

Matthew Pateman, *Julian Barnes*, Plymouth: Northcote House, 2002.

Lars Ole Sauerberg, *Intercultural Voices in Contemporary British Literature*, London: Palgrave, 2001.

James B. Scott, 'Parrot as Paradigms: Infinite Deferral of Meaning in *Flaubert's Parrot*', *Ariel: A Review of International English Literature*, 21:3. 1990, 58–68.

Richard Todd, *Consuming Fiction: The Booker Prize and Fiction in Britain Today*, London: Bloomsbury, 1996.

Web Reading

http://www.identitytheory.com/people/birnbaum8.html

'Julian Barnes in Conversation', *Cercles*, 4, 2002, 255–69, www.cercles.com.

http://www.salon.com/weekly/interview960513.html

4

Angela Carter: The Demythologizing Business

4.1. Literary History

In *A History of the World in 10½ Chapters*, Julian Barnes uses the phrase: 'Myth will become reality' (181). This is a sentiment that sits at the heart of Angela Carter's (1940–92) writings, the most well known of which are nine novels and four collections of short fiction – though these represent only a part of her published work. Carter also authored children's stories, poetry, radio plays, and film and television scripts. She additionally wrote several introductions, including that to the Virago edition of *Jane Eyre*, and translated or edited a number of works, notably the first and second *Virago Book of Fairy Tales*. Most importantly for interpretations of her fiction, she published volumes of selected writings, *Nothing Sacred* (1982) and *Expletives Deleted* (1992), and an 'exercise in cultural history', *The Sadeian Woman* (1979). All of Carter's work can be considered part of the same project to demythologize the naturalized fictions surrounding gender and sexuality. Hermione Lee has identified Carter 'with a feminism which employs anti-patriarchal satire, Gothic fantasy, and the subversive rewriting of familiar myths and stories, to embody alternative, Utopian recommendations for human behaviour' (Sage ed., 310).

Carter's early work, which is in the main expressionist in contrast to her later mannerist style (Haffenden, 91), includes the novels set in her University town, known as the 'Bristol Trilogy': *Shadow Dance* (1966), *Several Perceptions* (1968), and *Love* (1971). Carter revised *Love* in 1987, and added an *Afterword*. Unusually, the *Afterword* begins by addressing the reader in the manner of an authorial discussion of the genesis of the novel and its characters – 'the pure, perfect products of those days of social mobility and sexual licence' (L, 113) – but quickly changes into an extension of the book's narrative into the 1980s. In this coda, Carter drags her children of the sixties towards middle age, weaving their lives with cultural touchstones of the intervening years, such as the film *Paris, Texas* and the work of the photographer Robert Mapplethorpe. The gesture towards completion, by cursorily sketching a projected future for characters whose lives at a moment in time have been carefully drawn seems to echo the conclusion to numerous nineteenth-century novels but Carter's breaking of the fictional frame illustrates both that she has few pretensions to satisfy the reader's curiosity about the characters' fate and that she is more interested in drawing attention to the changes of the sixteen years between the two editions: 'I'm more benign, the world is far bleaker' (L, 113).

The novels in the Bristol Trilogy are also connected by their focalization through male characters, in stark contrast to Carter's other two early novels: *The Magic Toyshop* (1967) and *Heroes and Villains* (1969) which focus on female protagonists. The later book is 'a discussion of the theories of Jean-Jacques Rousseau' (Haffenden, 95) in a narrative that crosses the gothic novel with post-apocalyptic sci-fi. *Heroes and Villains* is set in a ruined future where society has divided into groups: the professors, soldiers, and workers on the one hand, the 'savages' on the other. Its heroine is Marianne, a professor's daughter who romanticizes the life of the tribal world outside the confines of her own ordered, prosaic world, where she lives in a white, steel and concrete tower. A projection of the polarized sensibilities of the 1960s, the book's trajectory takes Marianne from her father's rule to subjection in a tribe presided over by a beautiful Barbarian, Jewel, and a renegade Professor, Donally. Triumphing over patriarchy in its many forms, and anticipating some of Carter's later short-story heroines, Marianne ends the narrative, when the two leaders are dead, by declaring, 'I'll be the tiger lady and rule them with a rod of iron' (HV, 150).

Though *The Magic Toyshop* was published before 1970, it is seen as a key text, and a watershed, in Carter's work. Consequently, it is worth describing in some detail here. At the start of the novel, three orphaned children, Melanie, Jonathon, and Victoria, are taken in by their maternal uncle, a toy maker and puppeteer called Philip Flower who lives with his mute wife Margaret and her two brothers Francie and Finn Jowle. The claustrophobic narrative concerns the power relations involved in the English paterfamilias's rule over the three Irish Catholic Jowles and the three children of his sister and her despised academic husband. While Philip takes Jonathon as his apprentice and Margaret fosters the infant Victoria, Melanie is befriended by Finn, the prime target of Philip's violent rages. The puppet master's manipulation of those he has made financially dependent is exemplified in his Boxing Day theatrical performance of the Greek myth of Leda and the swan. In front of the other members of the household, Philip pulls the strings of Zeus, the God turned bird, while Melanie plays the part of the raped girl. In a narrative bristling with references to Genesis, particularly the story of Noah and the Garden of Eden, the rebellions against this south London Jehovah take two forms: Francie and Margaret are involved in an incestuous relationship; Finn smashes and buries the swan beside a broken statue of Queen Victoria on park wasteland. When Philip suddenly returns to the house to find these two heresies late one winter afternoon, 'at the most British time of the day and year' (MT, 196), Finn is so startled he drops a cigarette which sets fire to the house. In the meantime, the three Irish siblings have resolved to confront their tormentor and wrest their freedom from him at any cost.

The liberty won by the Jowles' defiance is symbolized by Margaret's finding her voice at the end of the novel when she needs to warn the others of Philip's return: 'Catastrophe had freed her tongue ... she found her old voice again the day she was freed' (MT, 197). Finn and Melanie escape through the roof and down into the garden while Francie and Margaret remain to defy Philip in person. Watching the patriarch's house burn, Melanie and Finn stand like Milton's Adam and Eve about to leave for a new world, facing each other in a 'wild surmise', an allusion to the end of Keats's famous poem about spectacular discovery, 'On First Looking into Chapman's Homer.' Discovery is not the conclusion to the novel only but also to its central theme, the adolescent Melanie's recognition of her corporeal, sexual self, described in the book's opening lines, with their quotation from Donne's *Elegies*: 'The summer she was fifteen, Melanie discovered she was made of flesh and blood, O, my America, my new found land. She embarked on a tranced voyage, exploring the whole of herself, clambering her own mountain ranges, penetrating the moist richness of her secret valleys, a physiological Cortez, da Gama or Mungo Park' (MT, 1). Thus, as early as 1967, Carter was affirming the importance of the body in women's reclamation of their identities from the male gaze, and this was to occupy a central position in her fiction, as it was in feminism, throughout the 1970s.

Over the next ten years, Carter's new fictions were notably less well received than her previous ones, not least because the two novels published in this time had increased theoretical sophistication and less romantic plotting. Her previous works had frequently used 'outsider' figures, like the barbarians and the Celtic Jowles, as representative of phases through which the principal women in the story might move in order to discover freedoms. The early novels therefore served in many ways merely to expose the male-dominated limits of counter-cultural living, by subjecting the women to abuse, if not death as in *Love*, and leaving those still alive at the end with only a hopeful, unexplored future. Carter's novels of the 1970s, *The Infernal Desire Machines of Doctor Hoffman* (1972) and *The Passion of New Eve* (1977) portrayed somewhat fantastical alternative societies, but without the earlier works' optimistic sense of liberation. For Carter in the 1970s, 'The pleasure principle met the reality principle', as she observes in the 1982-note to a 1967-essay in *Nothing Sacred* (NS, 84). The earlier, less successful novel, is narrated by Desiderio, an agent of the Minister of Determination charged with destroying *Doctor Hoffman's* Marcusian machines, which turn desires normally confined to fantasy into the quotidian reality of a South American capital city. Carter called the book's argument a 'dialectic between reason and passion, which it resolves in favour of reason' (Day, 65). Her next novel, now often considered her best, mounted an even more forceful attack on the gendered constructions of sexual identity, again using fantasy to assert the claims of reason.

The Passion of New Eve exemplifies Carter's interest in myth making. A book she described as her attempt at the Grand European Novel, it recounts the story of Evelyn, an English academic who goes to take up a new job in a holocaust-gothic New York. In America, Evelyn, who is obsessed with a Hollywood actress called Tristessa (an amalgam of screen stars like Louise Brooks, Greta Garbo, and Marlene Dietrich), becomes sexually involved with a young black woman, Leilah, whom he mistreats. Evelyn then leaves for the desert lands where he is twice captured, first by a band of radical feminist Amazons from Beulah, who surgically transform him into a woman, and then by Zero, a 'non-verbal poet' who rapes day by day each of the women in his harem, including the 'new Eve'. When Eve meets Tristessa s/he finds that this embodiment of male fantasy is in fact a man in drag – is literally a male construction of womanhood. The book's interest in the formation of sexualized gender images is pointed up by a comment Carter made in her 1975-essay 'The Wound in the Face': '"The feminine character, and the idea of femininity on which it is modelled, are products of masculine society", says Theodor Adorno. Clearly, a female impersonator knows more about his idea of the character he is mimicking than I do, because it is his very own invention, and has nothing to do with me' (NS, 92). Carter's novel ends with Eve taking a fantastical journey back through Western humanity's mythologized history to the ocean where life began: 'We start from our conclusions. ... At night I go back again to Tristessa's house, that echoing mansion, that hall of mirrors in which my whole life was lived, the glass mausoleum that had been the world and now is smashed' (PN, 191). Unlike several of Carter's early novels, this ending is not a literal liberation into a future freedom and rebirth, but an imagined return to the source: the only point from which history could be rewritten and a new humanity born into reason and not myth: 'Ocean, ocean, mother of mysteries, bear me to the place of birth' (PN, 191).

The Bloody Chamber and Other Stories (1979) redirects Carter's interest in the mythology of sexual relations by turning to folk and fairy tales. She writes in *The Sadeian Woman*, published in the same year:

> Myth deals in false universals, to dull the pain of particular circumstances. In no area is this more true than in that of relations between the sexes. ... and archetypes serve only to confuse the main issue, that relationships between the sexes are determined by history and by the historical fact of the economic dependence of women upon men. This fact is now very largely a fact of the past and, even in the past, was only true for certain social groups and then only at certain periods.   (SW, 5–7)

While the short fictions in *The Bloody Chamber* re-vision a range of tales from 'Snow White' and 'Puss in Boots' to 'Sleeping Beauty' and 'Beauty and the Beast', the title piece of Carter's collection reworks the less well-known story of 'Bluebeard'. What the reworked narratives have in common is an ornate sensual prose style allied to subversive content. According to Patricia Duncker, fairy tales have arisen from two main traditions: the first is the German *Märchen* (derived from the word for news or gossip) and Volksmärchen (meaning 'folk' tale); the second kind are those oral tales appropriated by the French aristocratic tradition known as *contes de fées*, most likely descended from the Countess d'Aulnoy's book of that name, translated into English as *Tales of the Fairys* in 1699. The most famous examples from these countries are the Rhineland stories collected and domesticated by the Brothers Grimm in Germany (1812) and those transcribed from the oral tradition by Perrault in France (*Histoires ou Contes du Temps Passé* (1697)). In both countries, bourgeois authors committed to paper for the first time folk tales handed down from an earlier age, creating a loose canon of didactic stories for children that reflected the values of the aristocracy rather than the peasantry. Duncker explains:

> The term fairy tale is now used to describe both the orally transmitted folk tales and the literary productions of bourgeois and aristocratic writers in the late seventeenth and eighteenth century. This important distinction lies smothered under the blanket term, fairy tale; it is a split which occurred gradually in Europe, coinciding with the invention of childhood and the rise of the bourgeoisie. The classical notion of ... childhood as a time of preparation and initiation into the adult world was not generally held during the Middle Ages . ... Thus a radical current in popular culture was appropriated and contained ..., the tales, trapped in the anthologies by literary archaeologists like the Brothers Grimm, were captured for consumption by an educated audience and finally relegated to the nursery. (224–5)

Carter uses the tools of a male literary tradition to represent both women's attraction and repulsion for patriarchal structures. She thus redeploys the role models of fairy tales, the conventional positions that the stories ask readers to identify with depending on their age and gender: the single man as threatening wolf, the older unmarried woman as wicked witch, the daughter as vulnerable innocent, her father and brothers as rescuers.

Nights at the Circus (1984) and *Wise Children* (1991), Carter's final two novels, self-consciously engage intertextually in a complex and allusive way with the constructed nature of literary and gendered history and mythology, the first book with the realist novel and the second with Shakespeare. Both take the form of comedy, initially opposing the genre of tragedy held superior by the English male tradition but ultimately uniting high and low. Like *The Passion of New Eve*, *Nights at the Circus* engages with mythology and with the fantasy of historical change without fundamental revaluation. By contrast, for Carter it is history alone 'that forged the institutions which create the human nature of the present in the first place. "It's not the human 'soul' that must be forged on the anvil of history but the anvil itself must be changed in order to change humanity"' (NC, 240).

Like all Carter's other work, *Nights at the Circus* is an exploration of ideas in narrative form. Carter described it as a picaresque novel in which 'people have adventures in order to find themselves in places where they can discuss philosophical concepts without distractions' (Haffenden, 87). The plot centres on Fevvers, a woman given the alternatives of being a 'fraud' or a 'freak': an orphan abandoned outside an East End brothel who has now grown up to be a winged trapeze artist. Carter once glossed Fevvers as 'basically Mae West with wings', though Fevvers also owes a lot to the mythological figure of Victory (Haffenden, 88 and 93; NC, 37). The narrative of *Nights at the Circus*, set in 1899, is arranged in three parts. The first centres on an interview given by Fevvers and her foster mother Lizzie to Jack Walser, an American journalist out to expose the feathered aerialist as a fake. In the second part, Fevvers is now a performer in Colonel Kearney's Grand Imperial Tour travelling circus, currently in St. Petersburg. Walser is also there, masquerading as a clown. In part three, the troupe has travelled by train to Siberia, en route to Japan. When the train is blown up, several members of the circus, including Fevvers and Lizzie, are taken prisoner by a band of peasant outlaws who wish to use Fevvers's influence with the Prince of Wales to win them amnesty from the Tsar. Meanwhile, escapees from a Siberian prison who intend to found a lesbian colony but require male sperm have captured Walser, who has lost his memory in the train explosion. When the remainder of the troupe finally meet Walser again he is living with a tribe in thrall to a Shaman. Fevvers expels the Shaman and

Walser's memory returns, but he is sufficiently changed for the couple, unusually for a Carter novel, to end united (as in so many nineteenth-century realist narratives from Austen to Brontë).

Nights at the Circus continues Carter's interest in male designs on women. She noted in interview that 'Fevvers has encounters with three different varieties of the mad scientist, a figure which – as mad scientist/shaman/toymaker/male-authority figure – has remained remarkably consistent, if I may say so, in the particular schema of my novels for the last twenty years' (Haffenden, 88). These three varieties of patriarchy represent appropriations of Fevvers by, respectively: (Christian) science, sexual desire, and mythological cults. The first is represented by Christian Rosencreutz, who desires to gain immortality by acquiring the winged angel's mysterious 'vital spirits' in Berlin; the second by the sexually predatory Grand Duke in St. Petersburg; and the third by the Shaman in Siberia. To locate the book squarely in the 1890s, Carter makes Fevvers (supposedly born from an egg like Helen of Troy was born from the mating of Leda and the swan) into a fantastical 'New Woman', while the socialist and feminist Lizzie is the embodiment of the radical working-class tradition. Their task in the narrative is to turn the 'unhatched' Walser into the 'New Man' with whom Fevvers can enter the 'New Century' (NC, 281). Yet, Walser is to be less a lover than the journalist turned 'amanuensis of all those whose tales we've yet to tell him, the histories of those women who would otherwise go down nameless and forgotten, erased from history, as if they had never been, so that he, too, will put his poor shoulder to the wheel and help to give the world a little turn into the new era that begins tomorrow' (NC, 285). *Nights at the Circus* tells a Victorian story through a twentieth-century lens and Carter's next novel continues many of its double-voiced preoccupations into this 'new era'.

Wise Children is the story of two families told by Dora Chance, who says: 'in the course of assembling notes towards my own autobiography, [I] have inadvertently become the chronicler of all the Hazards' (WC, 11). Dora and her sister Nora are illegitimate children of Melchior, the current head of the Hazard clan. The complex narrative, told in the present tense as a direct address to the reader, is composed of Dora's reminiscences as she prepares for an evening party one night in the late 1980s. The party is on 23 April which is thought to be Shakespeare's date of birth but is also the birthday of the novel's principal twins: Melchior and his brother Peregrine are 100 while Dora and Nora are 75. The Hazards are a dynasty of major Shakespearean actors while the Chance twins are captivated by popular entertainment, especially music hall and cinema. Conscious of the way the world sees them – as desirable 'freaks' like Fevvers – Dora and Nora are 'showgirls' from 'the wrong side of the tracks': 'we've always lived on the left-hand side, the side the tourist rarely sees, the *bastard* side of Old Father Thames' (WC, 1). Similarly, the novel attempts to reclaim Shakespeare for 'illegitimacy': for 'low' culture, where Carter believes he belongs.

In addition to *The Bloody Chamber*, Carter's other short-story collections are *Fireworks: Nine Profane Pieces* (1974), conceived when Carter lived in Japan in the early 1970s, *Black Venus* (1985), which includes an important story for *Wise Children* called 'Overture and Incidental Music for *A Midsummer Night's Dream*, and the posthumously published *American Ghosts and Old World Wonders* (1993).

4.2. Themes: Disguise and Carnival

> *[A] figure of whom minds have as yet no conception, who is rising out of mankind, and will have wings and who will renew the world.*
>
> (Apollinaire, quoted in SW, 79)

Carter's work is replete with masks and disguises in their many forms. The eponymous magic toyshop is itself a place of performance but its front room carries for its customers 'a tremendous stock of wild and scarey masks' (MT, 80). The tales of *The Bloody Chamber* are suffused with animal disguise and transformation, and *The Passion of New Eve* presents all human gendered behaviour as role-playing – as though 'the whole world' were the circus or stage of her final two novels, on which I will concentrate in this section. One view of disguise is offered in Carter's early essays:

> Disguise entails duplicity. One passes oneself off as another, who may or may not exist. … Though the disguise is worn as play and not intended to deceive, it does nevertheless give a relaxation from one's own personality and the discovery of maybe unsuspected new selves. One feels free to behave more

freely. This holiday from the persistent self is the perpetual lure of fancy dress. Rosalind in disguise in the Forest of Arden could pretend to be a boy pretending to be a seductress, satis-fying innumerable atavistic desires in the audience of the play. And we are beginning to realize once again what everybody always used to know, that all human contact is profoundly ambiguous. (NS, 86–7)

Acknowledging that ensemble dressing is no less but also no more of a construction than conventional dress, Carter was also aware of its liberatory power: 'Style means the presentation of the self as a three-dimensional art object, to be wondered at and han-dled. And this involves a new attitude to the self which is thus adorned' (NS, 86). In the 1960s, Carter primarily saw disguise as a stylistic tool for self-refashioning. She wrote of heterogeneous costumes: 'All these eclectic fragments, robbed of their symbolic content, fall together to form a new whole, a dramatization of the individual, a personal style' (NS, 86).

Though influenced by Roland Barthes's book of semiological cultural analyses *Mythologies*, Carter's idea of the fusion of dress codes has much in common with the Russian critic Mikhail Bakhtin's theory of language as heteroglossia, as speech acts con-taining a plurality of relations in all statements. Bakhtin argued that all 'utterances' are composed of heterogeneous speech ele-ments taken from multiple discourses (official, religious, scien-tific, colloquial, sexual, and so on), such that every linguistic statement amounts to 'another's speech used in another's lan-guage'. For Carter, all garments, like all speech acts, have a num-ber of associations and meanings, making dress, whether predominantly uniform or motley, open to a diversity of state-ments and interpretations. She describes a hippy girl in:

a Mexican cotton wedding dress (… thus at one swoop turning a garment which in its original environment is an infinitely potent symbol into a piece of decoration); her grandmother's button boots (once designed to show off the small feet and moneyed leisure of an Edwardian middle class who didn't need to work and rarely had to walk); her mother's fox fur (bought to demon-strate her father's status); and her old school beret dug out of the loft because she saw Faye Dunaway in *Bonnie and Clyde* (and a typical role-definition garment changes gear). (NS, 86)

This description can be likened to the clothes worn by the female protagonists in several of Carter's fictions, where the costumes donned by the characters signal either their variance with the dominant males in their regimentals, or self-alienation through conformity to masculine fetishes (e.g. PN, 19). Carter's stories also frequently revolve around characters who cross-dress. In *The Passion of New Eve*, the most desired character is a transvestite. In *Wise Children*, Nora makes the Wildean comment that 'It's every woman's tragedy … that, after a certain age, she looks like a female impersonator' (WC, 192). Yet, Carter does not stop at gender cross-dressing; following on from the anthropomorphic creatures of *The Bloody Chamber*, Fevvers is supposedly a 'genuine bird-woman' (NC, 17). Reminding one of Tristessa, Fevvers perplexes Walser, who has to ask, 'Is she really a man?' (NC, 35). Broadening cross-dressing into areas more commonly addressed in *The Bloody Chamber*, Walser himself is at one point costumed as a human chicken and in Carter's next novel there are 'transvestite poultry' (WC, 116).

Disguise and transformation are therefore not limited to masks and clothes, which are only an aspect to the many forms of self-representation in Carter's work, where both hair and perfume are significantly employed to conceal and dissemble. For example, names are not to be trusted. In *Wise Children* Dora says of the 'Grandma' who gave the twin sisters their name: 'I don't think for one moment that Chance was her name, either. All that I know about her is: she'd arrived at 49 Bard Road on New Year's Day, 1900' (WC, 26 – for the reader of *Nights at the Circus*, the peroxide blonde 'Grandma' might in spirit at least be Fevvers arrived back in London from Siberia (cf. NC, 290)). Like names, fathers are always in doubt. In a family saga where there 'is a persistent history of absent fathers' (WC, 35) almost all of the major characters at one point have their paternity questioned. Indeed, the title of Carter's final novel alludes to this double uncertainty: 'It's a wise child that knows its own father', hissed Peregrine, like the gypsy's warning. 'But wiser yet the father who knows his own child' (WC, 73). As in the plays of Shakespeare, Carter uses twins and illegitimacy in *Wise Children* to explore the constructions of identity. Identities are consequently swapped and doubled throughout the novel, most frequently by Dora and Nora. While for others, the Chance sisters are differentiated by their perfumes, exchanging which enables them to stand in for each other on occasion (e.g. WC, 83), Dora says more than once: 'On our own you wouldn't look at us twice. But, put us together ... ' (WC, 77).

The Chances and the Hazards appear together twice: first, at a West End Shakespearean revue called *What you Will* (the title appears with different punctuation on four other occasions) and then at an interwar Hollywood film of *A Midsummer Night's Dream*, which went so badly wrong it is now considered 'a masterpiece of kitsch' (WC, 111 – the real-life counterpart of this is Max Reinhardt's 1935-film of the play with James Cagney and Mickey Rooney). Hollywood is seen as the ultimate world of 'mad' artifice (Carter is aware that 'wood' is an obsolete word for madness): 'Welcome to the land of Make-Believe! To where the moon shone on Charlie Chaplin every moonlight night. Welcome to Dreamland' (WC, 120). This celluloid world is a fabulous place where nothing is real: 'The wood near Athens covered an entire stage and was so thickly art-directed it came up all black in the rushes, couldn't see a thing, so they sprayed it in parts with silver paint to lighten it up' (WC, 124). Hollywood thus represents the novel in general, where deaths, pregnancies, parents, and lovers are not what they seem. In a novel packed with Shakespearean allusions, quotations, and parallels, the narrative suitably ends with a series of revelations to match those at the end of Shakespeare's plays. These cover the driving forces of comedic renewal: sex, births, and deaths are revealed to be other than they seem. The plot is also as convoluted and steeped in mistaken identity as a renaissance comedy, as when Saskia's revenge on her father and her best friend by incestuously sleeping with the couple's son is foiled because her supposed half-brother Tristram is in fact her cousin: Melchior is not her father, Peregrine is.

One of the most *colourful* characters in this world of representation and misrepresentation is Gorgeous George, who has the world and its British Empire tattooed on his body: 'First of all, Melchior wanted George to get his clothes off, somehow, as a little reminder, according to Melchior, of the essential *Englishness* of Shakespeare, but Peregrine managed to persuade his brother that Bottom was supposed to be a citizen of Athens, Greece, and hence unlikely to sport a map of the British Isles on his pecs, let alone Africa on his abdomen' (WC, 151). This icon of English imperialism ends the book a penniless drunk, to whom Dora gives a 20-pound note, with Shakespeare on the back, for old times' sake. Carter is thus interested in the images of nationality, another of the forms of socially constructed identity, like gender, that she aims to demythologize. So, Dora has been taught to write by her American ex-boyfriend, 'Irish', signalling, as in *The Magic Toyshop*, a Celtic resistance to English imperial patriarchy (the demise of the British Empire is also apparent in *Nights at the Circus*, in touches such as the coffin draped in a Union Jack (NC, 117)). If this trope is charted across the fiction, it emerges that Carter appears perennially concerned with the British empire as an exploitative enterprise founded on ethnicity; not surprisingly, therefore, her late fiction includes several victimized black women whose portrayal opposes patriarchal racism, from Leilah in *The Passion of New Eve* and Jeanne Duval in 'Black Venus' to Tiffany in *Wise Children*.

With regard to genre, Carter complicates the traditional masks of tragedy and comedy in *Wise Children*, reminding the reader: 'Comedy is tragedy that happens to other people' (WC, 213). The dethronement of tragedy from its dramatic pedestal is accomplished in Carter's work by the use of carnival, though Carter is always conscious that a world-turned-upside down does not remain so for long: ' "Life's a carnival", he said. He was an illusionist, remember. "The carnival's got to stop, some time, Perry", I said. "You listen to the news, that'll take the smile off your face" ' (WC, 222). So, when the carnival mood holds sway at Melchior's Lynde court, where a house fire 'unleashed a kind of madness' (NC, 103) of intertextual Shakespearean sex, the topsy-turvy world lasts only as long as it takes the East Sussex fire brigade to put out the flames.

Carnival is a way of subverting orthodoxies and hierarchies, if only temporarily, in opposition to the staples of tragedy, murder, and power: at one point, Dora says, 'I do not wish to talk about the [Second World] war. Suffice to say it was no carnival, not the hostilities. No carnival' (WC, 163). Carter's use of Carnival is thus ambivalent, aware both that it can serve as a safety valve for a ruling system and that its liberating aspects are also controlling ones:

> It's interesting that Bakhtin became very fashionable in the 1980s, during the demise of the particular kind of theory that would have put all kinds of question marks around the whole idea of the carnivalesque. I'm thinking of Marcuse and repressive desublimination, which tells you exactly what carnivals are for. The carnival has to stop. The whole point about the

feast of fools is that things went on as they did before, after it stopped.   (quoted in Gamble, 2001, 184)

Bakhtin's theory of 'carnivalization' in the novel considers the ways in which comedy treats of a world turned upside-down: 'This carnival spirit offers the chance to have a new outlook on the world, to realize the relative nature of all that exists, and to enter a completely new order of things' (RW, 34). His discussion of carnivalized literature emphasizes that the ancient world acknowledged equal status to the serio-comical beside the 'high' genres. Though forms of imaginative writing that emphasized life's serious aspects dominated centuries of Western literature, the defining features of this older and revolutionary kind of writing were to become fundamental to the evolution of the novel. Bakhtin argues that the diverse texts that constitute the genre he terms 'serio-comical', from the work of Rabelais to Cervantes, are bonded by the influence of carnival, where 'all distance between people is suspended, and a special carnival category goes into effect: free and familiar contact among people' (*PDP*, 123). He says that in carnival there is 'a suspension of all hierarchic distinctions and barriers among men and of certain norms and prohibitions of usual life' (*RW*, 15). The carnivalization of modern literature therefore also calls for a place, like the circus or film-theatre for example, that provides 'meeting and contact-points for heterogeneous people' from all walks of life (*PDP*, 128).

Carter's reworking of canonical literature and her employment of scatological imagery thus fits with Bakhtin's description of a system of 'debasings and bringings down to earth, carnivalistic obscenities linked with the reproductive power of the earth and the body, carnivalistic parodies on sacred texts and sayings etc' (*PDP*, 123). So, when Fevvers is hungry, her appetite is Rabelaisian: 'She gorged, she stuffed herself, she spilled gravy on herself, she sucked up peas from the knife … until at last her enormous appetite was satisfied; she wiped her lips on her sleeve and belched' (NC, 22).

Bakhtin maintains that at the centre of carnival 'is the *mock crowning and subsequent decrowning of the carnival king*' (*PDP*, 124). We see this in *Wise Children* in Melchior's beloved symbolic crown, which his father wore in *King Lear* but which has now been replaced with a gold-painted cardboard one (WC, 20), Melchior's desire for which presents him as a 'fool' (WC, 108). We also see this in *Nights at the Circus* in the figure of the circus clowns' leader, Buffo, who is 'the Lord of Misrule' (NC, 175). As Bakhtin observes: 'he who is crowned is the antipode of a real king, a slave or a jester; this act, as it were, opens and sanctifies the inside-out world of carnival' (*PDP*, 124).

So, what is sometimes read as magic realism in Carter's work is perhaps more properly seen in Bakhtinian terms as 'an application of carnivalization to the portrayal of contemporary reality and contemporary everyday life; everyday life is drawn into the carnivalized action of the plot; the ordinary and constant is combined with the extraordinary and changeable' (*PDP*, 158). Like the novel for Carter, carnival for Bakhtin is a way of displaying otherness; both are always changing and are always intertextual. Carnival makes familiar relations strange, as in the traditional fools' days; but Bakhtin deems to be carnivalesque all manifestations of a comparable counter-culture which is popular and democratic, and in opposition to a formal and hierarchical official culture. Not surprisingly, therefore, a sure distinguishing feature of the carnivalesque is laughter, which is never allowed in official celebration, but which for example, provides the end to *Nights at the Circus* in 'the spiralling tornado of Fevvers' laughter' (NC, 295), while *Wise Children* concludes with the carnivalesque credo: 'What a joy it is to dance and sing!' (WC, 232).

Carter's final two novels can thus be seen as carnivalesque celebrations, conducted as comedies but in full awareness that the world rarely remains turned upside down for long.

4.3. Key Works: *The Passion of New Eve* and 'The Bloody Chamber'

> *I'm interested in myths – though I'm much more interested in folklore – just because they are extraordinary lies designed to make people unfree. ... I wrote one anti-mythic novel in 1977, The Passion of New Eve – and I conceived it as a feminist tract about the social creation of femininity, amongst other things – and relaxed into folklore with a book of stories about fairy stories, The Bloody Chamber, in 1979.*
>
> (NFL, 71)

Carter was a deeply knowing and self-conscious writer whose books were very deliberately written as ideas and arguments dressed up in narratives. Significantly influenced by her specialism in medieval literature on her English degree, she once said: 'I do put everything in a novel to be *read* – read the way allegory was intended to be read, the way you are supposed to read *Sir Gawayne and the Grene Knight* – on as many levels as you can comfortably cope with at the time' (Haffenden, 86). Carter's fictions, though they can be appreciated for their own stories, are thus works in which, like allegories, the apparent meanings of the characters and events are used to symbolize another, deeper meaning, which in Carter's work usually involves a commentary on the socialization of relations between the sexes.

The Passion of New Eve, its title redolent of both the Old and New Testaments, reassesses the construction of gender and replaces coherent identities with plural selves, echoing the French philosopher Jean Baudrillard's argument that in a world where gender is a consumer commodity, we are all transvestites. Originally published under a sci-fi imprint, the novel's portrayal of identity parallels theories of the cyborg-self presented in Donna Haraway's work, and of the performative basis of gender expounded in Judith Butler's book *Gender Trouble*. Thus, in its emphasis on the media and the cinema, mirrors, artifice, and myth, *The Passion of New Eve* exemplifies postmodernist scepticism about authenticity and individual choice. It is also a book about the geography of modern existence, where the world, bombarded with images, 'dreams itself American', veering between the desert, where all human action is exposed as artificial, and the city, where violent nomads and guerrilla forces push towards a revolution signalling the imminent end of history; which is the time and place from which, Carter observes, 'our flesh arrives' (SW, 9). In contrast to the possible freedoms offered by the Freudian pleasure principle in her earlier novels, Carter's fiction in the 1970s affirms that:

> Flesh is not an irreducible human universal. Although the erotic relationship may seem to exist freely, on its own terms, among the distorted relationships of a bourgeois society, it is, in fact, the most self-conscious of all human relationships, a direct confrontation of two beings whose actions in the bed are wholly determined by their acts when they are out of it.   (SW, 9)

The major characters in *The Passion of New Eve* are remade, in the images of Earth Mother, Hollywood icon, or ideal woman, all of which Carter sees as dangerous mythologies. Her conviction that identity is a construction is apparent in the proliferation of effigies and dolls, images and mirrors in her novels. She once said in interview: 'Tristessa has set up in the house a waxworks called The Hall of the Immortals, which contains the dead martyrs of Hollywood including Jean Harlow and Judy Garland, and that was supposed to be indicating something quite specific about the nature of illusion and of personality, which Hollywood did and does invent' (Haffenden, 87).

Yet, the American cinema is not the only source of invention. The refashioning of female identity by Mother's desert cult in *The Passion of New Eve* is as pernicious as the representations of femininity purveyed by cinema. In *The Sadeian Woman* Carter writes:

> All the mythic versions of women, from the myth of the redeeming purity of the virgin to that of the healing, reconciling mother, are consolatory nonsenses; and consolatory non-senses seems to me a fair definition of myth, anyway. Mother goddesses are just as silly a notion as father gods. If a revival of these cults gives women emotional satisfaction, it does so at the price of obscuring the real conditions of life. This is why they were invented in the first place. (SW, 5)

The novel thus plays off myth against history, and constructs a complex allegory in which Tristessa and Eve are both Adam and also Eve, while Zero sees himself as a God and Mother equates herself with the Earth goddess, making her daughter Leilah a reincarnation of Adam's first wife Lilith (PN, 174). In Mother's matriarchal Beulah, the Blakean female Eden of illusion and transience, Evelyn is told that 'Myth is more instructive than history' (PN, 68), but near the end of the book a different principle is advocated. Leilah informs Eve that, as the civil war rages, 'History overtook myth. ... Mother tried to take history into her hand but it was too slippery to hold. ... Historicity rendered myth unnecessary' (PN, 172–3).

History emerges as both the source of and the antidote to myth because cultural inventions distract from the 'real conditions of life' but also reveal them.

> Our external symbols must always express the life within us with absolute precision; how could they do otherwise, since

that life has generated them? Therefore we must not blame our poor symbols if they take forms that seem trivial to us or absurd, for the symbols themselves have no control over their fleshly manifestations, however paltry they may be; the nature of our life alone has determined their forms. A critique of these symbols is a critique of our lives.   (PN, 6)

Carter's novel appeared more fully to express the relationship between science and mythology when, 25 years after *The Passion of New Eve* was published, the first cloned human being was announced:

> this Christmas a baby girl was born in America in almost miraculous circumstances and, with heavy-handed significance, she was called Eve, after the first mother of mankind. If it isn't all a fake, she is not a human in the ordinary sense but a clone – the first cloned human baby – and she was created by a company owned by a sect which believes that humans were created by scientists from another planet.   (Minette Marrin, *The Sunday Times* Main Section, 29 December 2002: 15)

For Carter, all individuals are the cloned children of constructed histories, born into social relations that have been created by the dominant forces of one generation and can be recreated by the next. However, she also felt that, as more gender- or race-based myths of human nature proliferate it becomes more urgent, if more difficult, to reason away the stereotypes that serve to circumscribe identities.

*   *   *

'The Bloody Chamber' is narrated in the first person by a 17-year-old bride. Less a rounded character than a symbol of nubile sexuality, she is an unnamed heroine modelled as a cultural stereotype on the male fantasy of the virgin bride: 'The tulle and taffeta bride in her crackling virginal carapace, clasping numinous lilies, the supreme icon of woman as sexual thing and nothing else whatever, survives as part of the potlatch culture at either end of the social scale' (NS, 89–90). The story begins with the girl's night-train journey from Paris to her new husband's home: a castle on the coast. In Paris she has been living in reduced circumstances with her widowed mother and her nanny, the former apprehensive, the latter snobbishly pleased, at the girl's wedding to an old Marquis.

At the castle, following the delayed consummation of the marriage, the Marquis interrupts their honeymoon to go away on business, entrusting the narrator with all the keys. The curious bride visits the one room the Marquis has forbidden her from entering and there discovers a torture chamber containing the embalmed remains of her husband's previous three wives. When the Marquis returns and prepares to add his new bride to the chamber, she is helped by the castle's young blind piano tuner, but finally rescued by her mother.

'The Bloody Chamber' is based on the fairy tale of 'Bluebeard', best known in Charles Perrault's French version from around 1697. Bluebeard is historically identified with Gilles de Rais, a fifteenth-century French nobleman executed for murdering children, whereas the fictional Bluebeard murdered six wives for disobeying his command not to enter a locked room but was killed before he could murder the seventh.

Carter was aware of the different versions of the story and their possible basis in real life, just as she believed that in re-working popular fairy tales she was adding to a genre already based on retelling. Her story also plays with a number of other fairy tales, such as Rapunzel (from Grimms' *Nursery and Household Tales*), Cinderella (about 700 versions of which are known to exist), and Red Riding Hood (in Perrault's version the girl is eaten by the wolf, but in the Grimms' story she is rescued). Yet, Carter parodies various other literary genres in her story, such as the gothic (the remote castle with its dungeon) and the romance (the rescue on a white charger and the rags to riches story involving music, money, and marriage), as well as opera (especially in references to Richard Wagner's opera *Tristan and Isolde*). She also toys with the conventions of realism. 'The Bloody Chamber' begins with the stock characters of a widow and her only daughter living humbly in a Parisian apartment, Carter complicates this stereotype by making the unnamed narrator's mother a kind of adventure hero who has shot tigers and fought Chinese pirates. Immediately, the story incorporates a gender role-reversal to encourage the reader to think about the conventions of certain kinds of narrative, and Carter includes incongruities in the plot that mirror the baroque way in which she blends genres. So, the impoverished lifestyle of the innocent narrator includes a maid, and thus simultaneously evokes the 'charm' of poverty and the 'allure' of wealth. The world of castles and white horses is mixed up with telephone calls from agents in New York – uniting Romantic chivalry with twentieth-century living.

Overall, in Carter's attraction to the polymorphously perverse, the story seems to attempt to tantalize the reader with multiple, seemingly contradictory, forms of narrative pleasures drawn from horror, romance, pornography, and the adventure story. Consequently, much of the fascination of the story centres precisely on the way in which it continues throughout to weave together diverse genres alongside the fairy tale: morality play, revenge tragedy, confessional narrative, Poe-like 'Tale of Mystery', and feminist Bildungsroman. Also, the exaggerated use of rococo description and ornate language draws attention to the artificiality and conventionality of the narrative process. While all the characters, from the housekeeper to the piano tuner, function namelessly as roles (the Marquis is given few words, stripping him of a voice though he is empowered by his wealth and status, while the piano tuner is sightless and so though the narrator is naked can't physically subject her to the male gaze), the story relies heavily on symbolism, much of which anticipates the revelations behind the chamber door, from the recurring motif of the funereal white lilies, to the use of keys, mirrors, and dismembered arms. Carter also indulges in allusive language in the style of Gothic borrowings from medieval Romance, so a bedroom becomes an 'embalming parlour' and the Castle 'a lovely prison'.

Carter's story additionally trades on intertextual allusions to such canonical nineteenth-century poems as Browning's 'My Last Duchess' and Tennyson's 'The Lady of Shalott'. More important is the overarching project of developing rewritten fairy tales, a project which seems to stem from Carter's 1977-translations of Perrault's nursery stories. Carter claimed to be in the 'demythologizing business' (quoted in Gamble, 2001, 10). She said: 'the literary past, the myth and folklore and so on, are a vast repository of outmoded lies'. She also once said that all realist fiction from Jane Austen onwards was a collection of etiquette guides – books on morals and manners that instruct us how to behave. Carter's own fiction thus aims to strip away both the 'lies' and the 'etiquette' from traditional narrative forms. However, we might wonder how Carter's stories subvert orthodoxies if most narratives

merely reinforce them. The first aspect to note is her use of irony;
the way in which all her stories are written tongue-in-cheek, a feature advertised by excessive, hyperbolic descriptions, such as:
'my mother herself had gladly, scandalously, defiantly beggared
herself for love' (BC, 7). A second is her use of the fantastical and
the bizarre to bring together the familiar with the unexpected,
while always mocking the power of fiction to enchant, to draw
the reader into an imaginative identification with the characters.
In 'The Bloody Chamber', she additionally allows the new bride to
tell her own story, making her into an active narrator instead of a
passive character in the story, realigning the reader's perspective.

In all the stories in *The Bloody Chamber*, Carter adopts the form
and many of the plot elements of fairy tale but adapts the roles of
characters. In one story, reworking 'Red Riding Hood', the grandmother becomes the wolf, in another based on the same fairy tale
the young girl and not the wolf is sexually predatory, and, in 'The
Bloody Chamber', the girl's mother becomes the rescuer, not her
father or brother. The mother is portrayed as in every respect the
explorer-hero of *Boy's Own* stories, except of course she is a
woman. 'The Bloody Chamber' ends with mother rescuing
daughter, as though from patriarchy as much as from her mur-
derous husband. Carter thus uses juxtaposition and pastiche to
undermine the authority of traditional stories, re-working some
of the conventions (even clichés) of romantic fiction.

The 'bloody chamber' itself is a locked room in the castle
which her husband forbids the heroine from entering even
though he gives her the key; it is also an image of genitalia (certainly, the vagina after first penetration or during menstruation;
less obviously, the clitoris or penis swollen with blood). The phal-
lic key the Marquis insists that she must not use while he is away
also suggests the key to unlock a chastity belt, illustrating one
way in which Carter multiplies the generic roles that the bride is
meant to take on in the story, where, without a name, she
becomes representative of all past conventional heroines. Her
husband is himself most easily identifiable, after Bluebeard, with
the Marquis de Sade (note the importance for this story of the
French pronunciation of Mar*quis*), a figure who is much debated
in Carter criticism.

Lorna Sage, noting that Carter's *Bloody Chamber* tales were
written while she was re-reading Sade, argues that they constitute
a cruelly self-conscious anatomy of the spell cast on women by

the enchantment of passivity. So, in 'The Bloody Chamber' there are images of cruelty (violent pornography in the marquis's book-case, Moreau's painting of his first wife *Sacrificial Victim* (BC, 20)) and sexual excess ('A dozen husbands impaled a dozen brides while the mewing gulls swung on invisible trapezes in the empty air outside' (BC, 17)). However, Marina Warner in her introduction to Carter's *Second Virago Book of Fairy Tales* thinks that Carter found in Sade 'a liberating teacher of the male–female status quo and made him illuminate the far reaches of women's polymorphous desires' (SFT, x). Arguably, like Sade's binaristic reading of women, as Juliette and Justine, Carter found two possible ways of reading him: as the controlling patriarch and the liberating teacher.

It is in this way that we can understand the end of *The Passion of New Eve*, where Tristessa, the transvestite embodiment of the masculine construction of 'the notion of a woman's being, which is negativity ... the absence of being' (PN, 137), becomes the father of the baby that the man-turned-woman Eve carries with her after she has travelled back through the cave of origins to the point at which history's mythologizing began, and where she finds not the alchemical one prime substance but a multiplicity of possible forms. The stories in *The Bloody Chamber* are themselves variations on the forms of human identity, in distinction from the sexually determined binary positions allotted in most fiction. Their value as a collection is to explore the possibility of alternative gender roles across a spectrum of different stories that in their original written forms offered only stereotypes of female passivity.

References and Further Reading

M. M. Bakhtin, *Problems of Dostoevsky's Poetics* (PDP), translated and edited by Caryl Emerson, Manchester: Manchester University Press, 1984.
——, *Rabelais and his World* (RW), translated by Helene Iswolsky, Bloomington: Indiana University Press, 1984.
Joseph Bristow and Trev Lynn Broughton (eds), *The Infernal Desires of Angela Carter: Fiction, Femininity, Feminism*, London: Longman, 1997.
Angela Carter, *Nothing Sacred* (NS), London: Virago, 1982.
——, *The Magic Toyshop* (MT), London: Virago, 1981.
——, *Heroes and Villains* (HV), Harmondsworth: Penguin, 1981.
——, *Love* (L), Revised Edition, London: Picador, 1988.

Angela Carter, *The Passion of New Eve* (PN), London: Arrow, 1978.
——, *The Bloody Chamber and Other Stories* (BC), Harmondsworth: Penguin, 1981.
——, *The Sadeian Woman* (SW), London: Virago, 1979.
——, *Nights at the Circus* (NC), London: Pan, 1985.
——, *Wise Children* (WC), London: Vintage, 1992.
——, *The Second Virago Book of Fairy Tales* (SFT), edited by Angela Carter, introduced by Marina Warner, London: Virago, 1993.
——, 'Notes From the Front Line' (NFL) in *On Gender and Writing*, edited by Michelene Wandor, London: Pandora, 1983, 69–77.
Aidan Day, *Angela Carter: The Rational Glass*, Manchester: Manchester University Press, 1998.
Robert Eaglestone, 'The Fiction of Angela Carter' in *Contemporary British Fiction* edited by Richard J. Lane, Rod Mengham, and Philip Tew, Cambridge: Polity, 2003, 195–209.
Alison Easton (ed.), *Angela Carter: Contemporary Critical Essays*, London: Macmillan, 2000.
Sarah Gamble, *Angela Carter: Writing from the Front Line*, Edinburgh: Edinburgh University Press, 1997.
—— (ed.), *The Fiction of Angela Carter*, Cambridge: Icon, 2001.
John Haffenden, *Novelists in Interview*, London: Methuen, 1985, 1–24.
Hermione Lee, ' "A Room of One's Own, Or a Bloody Chamber?": Angela Carter and Political Correctness', in *Flesh and the Mirror: Essays on the Art of Angela Carter*, edited by Lorna Sage, London: Virago, 1994, 308–20.
Jago Morrison, *Contemporary Fiction*, London: Routledge, 2003, 155–78.
Linden Peach, *Angela Carter*, London: Macmillan, 1998.
Lorna Sage, *Angela Carter*, Plymouth: Northcote House, 1994.
—— (ed.), *Flesh and the Mirror: Essays on the Art of Angela Carter*, London: Virago, 1994.

Web Reading

http://perso.wanadoo.fr/andrew.milne/
http://www.themodernword.com/scriptorium/carter.html

5
Kazuo Ishiguro: Remain in Dreams

5.1. Literary History

Kazuo Ishiguro (b.1954) has published five novels to date, all concerned with individuals scanning their pasts for clues to their sense of identity, loss, or abandonment. Ishiguro has also produced a handful of short stories and written two plays for television, *A Profile of Arthur J. Mason* and *The Gourmet*, both commissioned in 1982 and both transmitted by Channel 4 in the 1980s. Though some critics have sought to place Ishiguro in a Japanese tradition, he has himself most frequently cited Dostoevsky, Kafka, Dickens, Charlotte Brontë, and above all Chekhov as his major influences.

'A Strange and Sometimes Sadness', a short story Ishiguro wrote in 1980 on the University of East Anglia Creative Writing Masters degree, under the tutelage of Malcolm Bradbury and Angela Carter, was developed into his debut novel *A Pale View of Hills* (1982). The story draws on Ishiguro's strong sense of separation and severance from Japan and centres on the memories of a twice-married Japanese woman living alone in southern England. Etsuko reflects back on the time in the early 1950s when she became a mother in Nagasaki, which was also the town of Ishiguro's birth and which he left at the age of five. Etsuko has a young daughter Niki who has come to stay with her, but her reclusive firstborn child Keiko is now dead, having hanged herself while living isolated in Manchester. The book is a gentle meditation on memory and sublimated pain, which uses fantasy and displacement to reveal indirectly the distress of a woman who has lost her homeland, her husbands, and her elder daughter.

Ishiguro's second novel, *An Artist of the Floating World* (1986), is set wholly in Japan. Ishiguro knew the country only from childhood but decided to rely for his details and imagery on his own memories rather than conduct research. Like his first novel, this book is concerned with Japan shortly after the war, though its aftermath in *An Artist of the Floating World* is present in the memory of war crimes rather than the shadow cast by the atomic bomb that devastated Nagasaki. Ishiguro's second novel moves from the almost exclusively female society of *A Pale View of Hills* to a patriarchal culture in which the narrator Ono reflects in four diary entries on his present fragmented family and his past life as the artist of the title. Ishiguro has said that he wrote his first two novels because he wanted to 'put together all these memories, and all these imaginary ideas I had about this landscape which I called Japan' (Wong, 2).

This emphasis on the ways in which reality is filtered through images and memory also applies well to Ishiguro's most famous and well-received book, *The Remains of the Day* (1989). His third novel is set in July 1956 at the time Britain was on the brink of war with Egypt over the latter's closing of the Suez Canal. The 'Suez Crisis' is generally held to mark Britain's post-war realization that it could no longer assume a dominant role in international affairs nor automatically command the agreement of other world powers, nearly all of who sided with Egypt. Though the crisis is not in fact mentioned in Ishiguro's novel, this is itself both an index of the narrator's refusal to attend to what is going on around him and an example of how history has rendered his traditional views of Englishness anachronistic. The narrator, Stevens, is the butler at Darlington Hall, near Oxford, where he now serves an American called Farraday. Stevens has worked at the house for the majority of his adult life. Most importantly, he was butler at the time the previous owner, Lord Darlington, held secret international conferences from 1923 onwards to seek European peace and stability in the interwar years. Throughout his service, Stevens deferred to Lord Darlington's views, seeing his own role as that of attendant to a great man whose opinions Stevens deemed unquestionable on the grounds that they were those of a well-intentioned gentleman. Now, in the 1950s, when Lord Darlington is dead and thought of by many as a Nazi collaborator, Stevens reflects upon life in the house at the time of these important meetings. Farraday has suggested he take a holiday and Stevens's initial reluctance to do so is overcome by a nostalgic letter from Miss Kenton, the Hall's old housekeeper, who had left to get married many years ago. Miss Kenton is now living in the West Country village of Little Compton, to which Stevens slowly drives in Farraday's impressive Ford and in Lord Darlington's old clothes. The events recounted in Stevens's diary of his journey across England in the present are accompanied by the memories of the past that prey on his mind.

The Remains of the Day was received by most critics as a third 'realist' novel, one in which Ishiguro had perfected his style of restrained, repressed Japanese-English first-person narration. To such readers, Ishiguro's fourth novel came as a shock, but its continuities with the previous work are strong and deep, not least because it explores memory, narration, and the relationship between individual and social identity. *The Unconsoled* (1995) has a number of immediate similarities to *The Remains of the Day*. It is also told over a few days, in what could be considered diary entries, by a man staying away from his home. Both narrators conflate their pasts and their presents in an attempt to come to terms with their lives – each embarks on an inner emotional journey in parallel with their outer exploration. The chief difference is that Stevens in *The Remains of the Day* appears in control of his narrative, whereas Ryder in *The Unconsoled* is more obviously driven by his desires and fears, not least because his narrative seems to be the product of his unconscious.

In *A Pale View of Hills*, one character tells the narrator: 'it's good to take a glance back now and then, it helps keep things in perspective' (PVH, 29–30). Ishiguro's subsequent fiction has continued to explore the truth of this remark, to examine the extent to which looking back is desirable, for perspective and possibly catharsis, and yet disorienting, involving individuals in a world they cannot change except in their imagination. All Ishiguro's narrators are looking for clues to explain how they have become who they are, but it is only in his fifth novel, *When We Were Orphans* (2000), that Ishiguro creates a professional detective as the book's narrator. Like *The Remains of the Day*, the book is divided between its interwar years, with its first six parts stretching from 1930 to 1937, and the 1950s, moving to the London of 1958 in its seventh and final part. Most critics have seen this novel as a hybrid of the styles of *The Unconsoled* and Ishiguro's initial work. Certainly, the first half of *When We Were Orphans* suggests a return to the narrative approach of the early novels, whereas the second half takes its protagonist, Christopher Banks, into a perplexing world more similar to that found in *The Unconsoled* than to anything in Ishiguro's other writing. The novel appears to be Ishiguro's most explicit investigation to date into the ways in which childhood informs later life and yet eludes the adult it affects. Banks's mind is thrown back repeatedly to his friendship in Shanghai with a Japanese boy called Akira and to the detective games they used to play. In the present of the novel, one mystery continues to evade the powers of the famous private investigator: the disappearance of his parents when Banks was ten years old. On his hunt for his mother and father, Banks – whose name evokes the process of shoring up as well as boundaries, investments, and memory banks – finds the past intrudes upon his progress until he becomes lost in a maze of subterranean Shanghai streets where he seems to discover only Akira once more. This may in fact all take place in Banks's mind as he becomes less and less in touch with outside reality: much of the story, as in *The Unconsoled*, appears to be an externalization of the narrator's inner turmoil. Banks's search for his missing parents is entangled with his psychological pursuit of his own identity, and for a resolution to his feelings of abandonment, of being suddenly thrust into an adult world without parental guidance. At more than one point Banks appears to be on the verge of repairing the psychological damage of his desertion in childhood, especially through a possible relationship with Sarah Hemmings, another orphan, but instead his life is marked by repetition. He abandons Sarah (WO, 223–4), as he abandons the orphan he adopts, Jennifer (WO, 149), and as indeed he once abandoned Akira (WO, 100–4), replaying his own abandonment by both his parents and his 'Uncle Philip' (WO, 122). Like Ryder in *The Unconsoled*, Banks unconsciously turns his deepest personal fear into a universal one: 'After all, the whole world's on the brink of catastrophe. What would people think of me if I abandoned them all at this stage?' (WO, 212).

Like Ishiguro's earlier narrators, Banks is more preoccupied with the past than the present. He also is compelled to repeat his own history, searching for answers to questions that will potentially remain with him always, while the other characters seem powerless to help. As Miss Collins says: 'Mr. Ryder, it really would be a great sadness to me if you were to continue making your mistakes over and over. And to think that all the time, I was here, watching you and doing nothing' (U, 147). Yet, the past to which the narrators repeatedly return is in no sense an objective one; not only are their reminiscences subjective, they are refracted through displaced and projected experiences.

5.2. Themes: Narrating Self, Family, and Nation

Narration is by no means a straightforward matter in Ishiguro's books. His five novels to date all use first-person narrators and are all deeply concerned with the act of narration itself: with events seen from one person's fallible and subjective point of view. *A Pale View of Hills* contains a detailed and vividly remembered story that in the end is compromised by the narrator's self-contradictions, just as in *An Artist of the Floating World* Ono's claims to be a war criminal appear to be fabricated. The narratives of Stevens, Ryder, and Banks are similarly not to be trusted, told as they are by individuals who have inordinate emotional and psychological investments in the stories they piece together.

In *The Remains of the Day*, Stevens's narration takes the form of a personal record, whether it is considered to be a diary or an interior monologue, made on his excursion from Oxford to the West Country. The book is arranged as a prologue followed by a series of accounts across six days as Stevens builds up a sense of his present from the juxtaposition of the days' events with remembered pieces of the past. The narration unfolds easily in Stevens's memory and though he apparently remembers events accurately he rarely strikes the reader as understanding their significance. He also hardly ever questions the veracity of his recollections despite the time lapse between hearing discussions and recounting them 30 years later. At one point he says, 'The bedroom doors of Darlington Hall are of a certain thickness and I could by no means hear complete exchanges; consequently, it is hard for me now to recall precisely what I overheard' (RD, 95); yet Stevens reports detailed conversations without acknowledging the vagaries of human memory – in fact, he admits to making a mistake only once (RD, 212). Stevens is less troubled by these concerns, illustrating his lack of self-awareness, than several of Ishiguro's other narrators. Etsuko, for example, admits that 'It is possible that my memory of these events will have grown hazy with time' (PVH, 41), while Banks declares 'it is even possible I have remembered incorrectly' (WO, 68).

Ryder, in *The Unconsoled*, is a narrator whose unreliability is of a different order from Ishiguro's other first-person storytellers. He can overhear conversations that take place out of his earshot; he is not sure whether a woman he meets is his wife; he moves in space and time in ways that seem impossible. In short, his story takes place on another plane of reality from the one on which causation and memory are reliable guides; his situation has most often been compared to that of Kafka's protagonists, especially Joseph K. in *The Trial* – where the associative logic of dreams takes hold of even quotidian events. Ryder, a world-renowned pianist, can in some ways be considered to embody a development of the idea of the 'artist of the floating world'. In Ishiguro's second novel it is deemed necessary 'to wake up artists and introduce them to the real world' (AFW, 172), to awaken them from all their fantasies, which may be Ryder's world of anxious nightmares or Ono's 'night-time world of pleasure, entertainment, and drink' (AFW, 145).

Several of Ishiguro's narrators can be considered in terms of Sartre's understanding of inauthenticity and bad faith, which principally occurs when individuals identify too fully with the role they perform for others. Stevens, who is the prime example, believes that 'A butler of any quality must be seen to *inhabit* his role, utterly and fully' (RD, 169). He criticizes butlers who do not allow their profession to take them over completely: 'For such persons, being a butler is like playing some pantomime role; a small push, a slight stumble, and the façade will drop off to reveal the actor underneath. The great butlers are great by virtue of their ability to inhabit their professional role and inhabit it to the utmost' (RD, 42–3). Stevens thus insists that whenever he is on duty he must be a butler and nothing but a butler, defined in terms of the highest expectations anyone might hold for such a job, which in itself is perhaps unremarkable, except that Stevens's profession is one in which he has almost no 'time off' or private space – and even these areas of his life remain within the house in which he serves. The reader therefore wishes to ask of him the same question Miss Kenton puts: 'why, why, why do you always have to *pretend*?' (RD, 154). The answer from one angle is that it is much easier to do so, to reduce life to professional conduct, than to face the messy decisions and emotional responsibilities of private life.

A gloss on Sartrean philosophy can be useful here:

Human existence, in short, is 'ambiguous', many-sided. Bad faith operates when a person, instead of facing up to his inevitable 'ambiguity', resolves it by ignoring or denying some of the poles between which his existence stands. Such denials are in bad faith, and not simply intellectual errors, because there are bound to be moments of self-awareness when each of the many poles of one's 'ambiguous' existence asserts itself. However dogged, for example, a person's attempt to identify himself with the view that others have of him, there will be 'occasions of failure' when a sense of 'solitude' reminds him of the 'subjectivity' that persists despite his 'objectivity for others'. In this manner, bad faith always involves denial of something which, at times at least, we know to be true of ourselves. (David E. Cooper, *Existentialism*, Oxford: Blackwell, 1990, 119)

In *The Remains of the Day* there are several occasions on which the repressed emotion breaks through and begins to overwhelm Stevens. These are signalled by the remarks of others: 'are you alright there?' asks Mr Cardinal (when Miss Kenton announces that after 14 years alongside Stevens she is now leaving to get married, RD, 220); or by Stevens's own admissions: 'at that moment my heart was breaking' (RD, 239); or by his actions, most obviously when he starts crying (RD, 243).

Ishiguro's three most recent novels, which are also those set entirely outside of Japan, have been criticized for their unrealistic or implausible narrators. However, as much as Angela Carter or Martin Amis, Ishiguro creates a consistent world, which the reader needs to understand rather than assess for its verisimilitude. In his work, Ishiguro explores themes of loss, trauma, dislocation, failure, and memory. A central theme is the narrator's self-deception, while the organization of each novel is that of the narrator's memory and its medium the linguistic labyrinth of the narration itself. A good metaphor for the narrators' investigations into the layers of their own lives occurs at the start of *When We Were Orphans*: 'As I set about opening it, I quickly realized the package had been wrapped in numerous sheets, and my friends would laugh noisily each time I removed one layer, only to be confronted by another. All the signs, then, were that I would find some joke item at the end of it all' (WO, 8).

The title of Ishiguro's most recent novel suggests the importance of children in his stories, of their relationship with their parents, and of the adults' relationships with their childhood selves. So, the narrator of *A Pale View of Hills* is haunted by the suicide of her daughter and her story focusses on the ways in which Etsuko copes with this loss by fixating upon but distorting the past, inventing the childhood fears her friend's daughter Mariko has of a woman who killed herself (PVH, 74), or displacing the present, in her dreams of a little girl at risk playing in the park (PVH, 47, 55). In Ishiguro's second book, it is the conflict between generations that underpins the story of *An Artist of the Floating World*, whose central concerns are with disagreements between parent and child, teacher and pupil. In *The Remains of the Day*, Stevens's relationship with his father is characterized by formality, to the extent that he refers to him simply as 'Father', in the third person, even to his face. This protocol is only breached on the night Stevens senior dies, when his son addresses him twice as 'Father' and twice as 'you' (RD, 97). However, in their short conversation that night, Stevens's attempt to communicate goes no further than this small shift, because each of the four addresses occurs in an almost identical phrase: 'I hope Father is feeling better now'; 'I'm glad Father is feeling so much better'; 'I'm so glad you're feeling better now'; and 'I'm so glad you're feeling better now' again (RD, 97). While his father, aware that he may die soon, attempts to broach the subject of personal feelings by saying 'I hope I've been a good father to you', which he repeats, Stevens is unable to respond beyond making the change from 'Father' to 'you'. Stevens is of course very much like his father, such that the reader might expect them to be close, yet their similarity rests precisely on their austere professionalism. This similarity is also pointed up by Miss Kenton observing that Stevens's room 'resembles a prison cell' (RD, 165), which echoes Stevens's comment on his father's room: 'I recall my impression at the time was of having stepped into a prison cell' (RD, 64).

In the similarity and distance between father and son, the book suggests Oedipal conflict. Stevens, intending to refer to his own professionalism, says ambiguously of the night his father dies: 'For all its sad associations, whenever I recall that evening today, I find I do so with a large sense of triumph' (RD, 110). He similarly has 'a deep feeling of triumph' (RD, 227) when he discharges his duties properly after Miss Kenton's announcement that she is leaving Darlington Hall. This is despite his own belief that, though she has decided to marry, 'Miss Kenton was at that moment crying' (RD, 226–7). Attendant on Lord Darlington, in charge of the other members of the household, Stevens is to a degree so preoccupied with hierarchies and status that he cannot relate in any other way than formally (or competitively) with either his father or Miss Kenton.

The fundamental family group involves three people and consequently, according to both fairy tales and psychoanalysis, triads are central to the individual's understanding of self because they represent the primary mental and usually physical relationship between the child and its parents. Groups of three characters are thus crucial in Ishiguro's novels. In *When We Were Orphans*, the unit of three is there in Banks's early life as an only child with his parents and in his creation of an imitation family with the adopted orphan Jennifer and her nanny Miss Givens. In *The Unconsoled* the narrative is grouped in sets of three characters: Mr and Mrs Hoffman, and their son Stephan; Brodsky, Miss Collins, and Bruno, the beloved dog that stands in for their child; Ryder, Sophie, and her son Boris (or Ryder, Sophie, and her father Gustav, a variant on the parodic familial triangle developed between Stevens, his father, and Miss Kenton). The influence of parents on children is clear in several of the novels: in *The Remains of the Day* Stevens's experience of working while his father lay upstairs dying is a repetition with variation of the time his father had to serve the General he held responsible for the death of his son, Steven's elder brother Leonard (RD, 40–1). Stevens's memory of his father's restraint and fortitude is crucial to his sense of dignity, which he defines as 'not removing one's clothes in public' (RD, 210), in contrast to 'the Continental' who will 'at the slightest provocation, tear off his suit and his shirt and run about screaming' (RD, 43). This is a metaphor for the absolute separation of personal and professional life, to the perpetual restriction of the former, and is tied to a traditional understanding of Anglo-Saxon behaviour, as a great butler is bound 'almost by definition, to be an Englishman' (RD, 43).

Which brings the discussion on to another theme in Ishiguro's work: that of national identity, particularly English rather than Japanese. In *When We Were Orphans* Christopher Banks, brought up in Shanghai surrounded by people who are Chinese, Japanese, German, and American, is told by his 'Uncle Philip' he might grow up 'a bit of a mongrel' when he asks 'How do you suppose one might become more English?' (WO, 76). Banks's question explicitly addresses an issue that runs under the surface of most of Ishiguro's work: the extent to which national characteristics are bred in the bone and/or can be acquired. More importantly perhaps, his question implicitly queries the signs and symbols of shared identity that are as much debated by Ishiguro's critics, often too keen to identify the Japanese qualities of a writer who concerns himself with universal themes, as they are explored in various ways by the novels themselves.

In *The Remains of the Day*, Darlington Hall is partly a metonym for England and its post-war decline. The Hall now has four kept staff, whereas it used to have 17 under Stevens's care, and before that it once had 28. The aristocracy that used to own the Hall has died away and the estate has been taken over by an American. A crucial passage for appreciating Stevens's understanding of what England represents and who represents England occurs early in the novel: 'those of our profession, although we did not see a great deal of the country in the sense of touring the countryside and visiting picturesque sites, did actually "see" more of England than most, placed as we were in houses where the greatest ladies and gentlemen of the land gathered' (RD, 4). Characteristically, Stevens takes the aristocracy to represent not just the nation's people but also the country itself. His idea of Englishness rests on notions of dignity and gentility that are themselves narrowly defined in terms of breeding. His discussion of 'greatness' in a butler (RD, 29) is mirrored by his commentary on greatness in the landscape, characterized by 'calmness' and 'restraint' (RD, 28): 'It is with such men as it is with the English landscape seen at its best as I did this morning: when one encounters them, one simply *knows* one is in the presence of greatness' (RD, 44). It is this idea of 'greatness', an imperial appellation starting to seem anachronistic in the 1950s, that for Stevens defines the country, its landscape, and its gentry. He is consequently much occupied by the question of what makes a 'great' butler. Stevens disagrees with the Hayes Society's view that a great butler has to belong to a 'distinguished household': 'It was made clear, furthermore, that the Society did not regard the houses of businessmen or the "newly rich" as "distinguished", and in my opinion this piece of out-dated thinking crucially undermined any serious authority the Society may have achieved' (RD, 32). Stevens's objection, though it is never stated, is presumably that this criterion would exclude himself, in a Hall now owned by an undistinguished American businessman, and also his father, who served in the home of an industrialist 'for fifteen years at the height of his career' (RD, 37). This is the first suggestion that Stevens's idea of 'greatness' and 'national identity' might change by the end of the novel. It also makes plain the ways in which a sense of self, of the family, and of national identity may be entangled, illustrating the emotional investment the individual has in controlling the narration of the past.

5.3. Key Works: *The Remains of the Day, The Unconsoled*

> *"One had to be guided by the judgement of the true ladies and gentlemen,"* argued the Society, or else *"we may as well adopt the proprieties of Bolshevik Russia".*
>
> (RD, 32)

As Stevens's journey to see Miss Kenton proceeds, his narrative traverses the past on two levels, that of the personal and that of the political. Here, I will look at each in turn, before considering the ways in which they are entwined.

From one angle, *The Remains of the Day* is the story of a man whose dedication to his profession has almost entirely stifled his personal life, though it would be possible to read this differently and argue that because of his extreme social awkwardness, Stevens throws himself into his job to avoid close relationships. Despite daily contact with his father and with a woman who shows signs of caring for him, he is unable to communicate affection for them. It is Stevens's repression that has made him such an efficient butler, someone who is always externally focussed because he unconsciously wishes to avoid internal emotional turmoil. Illustrating his lack of self-knowledge, he argues that this is solely a matter of 'dignity', which 'has to do crucially with a butler's ability not to abandon the professional being he inhabits. Lesser butlers will abandon their professional being for the private one at the least provocation' (RD, 42). For this reason, he thinks of the night in 1923 when he served Lord Darlington and M. Dupont as 'a turning point in my professional development' (RD, 110). There is no sense that Stevens feels the death of his father that night, a personal matter, was as important as his professional decorum, let alone more so.

His unswerving belief in professional dignity also means that Stevens disapproves of the servants at Darlington Hall developing personal relationships, observing that it interferes with their work (RD, 51). When a recently appointed maid, Lisa, runs off with the Hall's second footman, she leaves a long note for Miss Kenton, which Stevens also reads. He remarks that the girl makes no mention of her gratitude to the housekeeper nor expresses any regret at letting the other staff down. All of this throws light on Stevens's failure to embark upon a relationship with Miss Kenton, yet his romantic side is revealed by his memory of the note since there is only one line he attempts to recall: 'we have love and who wants anything else' (RD, 157). This is as revealing as when Miss Kenton finds him with a romantic novel, which he pretends to be reading to improve his vocabulary (RD, 167). His rejection of her attempt at familiarity on this occasion is, he decides, the turning point in their relationship, because Miss Kenton invaded 'the one place in the house where privacy and solitude are guaranteed' (RD, 165). The scene juxtaposes Stevens's interest in a novel about love – which he is perhaps reading to learn 'romance' in the same way that he later tries to acquire skills at 'bantering' from radio shows – with his rejection of the woman who flirts with him, illustrating Stevens's equation of privacy with solitude rather than intimacy.

Stevens's lack of personal charm and social ease is intimated by his attitude towards 'bantering'. On the one hand, he sees this as the key to cultivating an informal manner when called upon to do so by his new employer: 'I have been endeavouring to add this skill to my professional armoury' (RD, 130). On the other hand, the very fact that he considers this a 'professional' matter illustrates his eschewal of a personal life, and his quasi-scientific attempts to acquire repartee seem akin to someone trying to practise spontaneity. It is also significant that Stevens fails until the end of the novel to see that 'banter' is not just oil for easing social situations, but is related to more personal exchanges, such as Farraday's suggestion that Stevens's interest in Miss Kenton is romantic. More crucially, Stevens is at no point able to shift his relationship with his father from a professional to a personal level, epitomized by the missed opportunity to respond to his father's deathbed gesture towards connection when he reveals that he hopes he has been a good parent. Both of these widely different attempts at intimacy leave Stevens embarrassed and powerless to reply. He is similarly unable to sympathize with Miss Kenton when her aunt, to whom she was very close, dies. He neglects to offer his condolences, then decides to defer them, but turns his anxiety over expressing sympathy into criticism of her when they meet later (RD, 177–8). After a life of professional service, he is at a loss how to relate to others in a personal way: 'It is curious how people can build such warmth among themselves so swiftly' (RD, 245). He finally decides that in 'bantering lies the key to human warmth' (RD, 245), and this may be an important insight as he edges towards the final years of his working life, represented by and retold in the six days of his diary.

The political dimension of *The Remains of the Day* can be considered from several perspectives. First, there is the difference between Lord Darlington's gentleman-amateur attempts at diplomacy, which he thinks of as a matter of 'honour' (RD, 103) compared with the American Lewis's 'professionalism'. This is linked to the concept of *noblesse oblige*: the traditional belief that those in a socially privileged class have an obligation to be honourable and generous. The American politician Lewis alludes to the redundancy of this principle in modern life when he says 'All you decent, well-meaning gentleman, let me ask you, have you any idea what sort of place the world is becoming all around you? The days when you could act out of your noble instincts are over. Except you here in Europe don't seem to know it' (RD, 102). This accusation made in the 1920s stresses the crucial importance of the First World War to *The Remains of the Day*. Although Stevens is reminiscing from the time of the Suez Crisis in 1956, implying the novel's emphasis is on the changes wrought by the Second World War and the dismantling of the European Empires, the seeds of this moment were sown over thirty years earlier – the honoured but incompetent General attended by Stevens's father is an example of the simultaneous currency and bankruptcy early in the century of the idea that generals and gentlemen of the aristocracy could assume to know what was best for their nations.

Yet Stevens's choice of faith in this idea, with his choice to subsume all of his personal desires to serving Lord Darlington, is not a totally blind one. It is a choice of aristocracy over democracy, as his discussion with Harry Smith makes clear, even though the deferential position he regards as reflected glory makes him a willing vassal. Smith says 'there's no dignity to be had in being a slave. That's what we fought for ... you're born free and you're born free so that you can express your opinion freely. ... That's what dignity's really about' (RD, 186). Stevens only comes to understand this view at the close of his narrative: 'Lord Darlington ... chose a certain path in life, it proved to be a misguided one, but there, he chose it, he can say that at least ... I can't even say I made my own mistakes ... what dignity is there in that?' (RD, 243).

By contrast with Smith, Stevens believes that in serving Lord Darlington he had been performing a public service just as he believes Lord Darlington had been. He divides his generation of butlers from the previous one by arguing that his peers concern themselves with the 'moral status' of their employers whereas their elders were concerned simply with titles and ancestry (RD, 114). In this sense, Stevens can be said to have believed in Lord Darlington and to have served him for 35 years for this reason. Hence, in contrast to his earlier belief that 'my chief satisfaction derives from what I achieved during those years, and I am today nothing but proud and grateful to have been given such a privilege' (RD, 126), there is his deep feeling at the end of the novel of having wasted his life when he starts to accept the general opinion of Lord Darlington as at best misguided – a realization his professional life has been based on misplaced trust that immediately follows his understanding that he spurned the opportunity of a private life with Miss Kenton.

The major reference point the reader is reminded of in Stevens's misguided loyalty is that of the individuals who chose to follow Hitler. *The Remains of the Day* asks: to what extent did those who appeased or followed the Nazis believe they were doing good and to what extent could any individual abrogate moral responsibility by following the orders of their 'superiors' – which was the argument given by several German officers indicted for war crimes at the 1945–46 trials at Nuremberg, the setting of Nazi rallies in the 1930s and in particular of anti-Semitic decrees in 1935 (cf. RD, 137). There is a parallel here with Stevens's behaviour over the Jewish maids who are sacked because Lord Darlington has come under the influence of anti-Semites. At the time, because it is his duty to obey Lord Darlington unquestioningly, Stevens expresses no qualms to Miss Kenton over the dismissals, but he does do so when Lord Darlington comes to regret the decision (RD, 153). Like defendants at the Nuremberg trials, Stevens says he thinks the sackings were wrong but followed his orders out of a sense of loyalty and duty. He tells his accuser, Miss Kenton: 'His Lordship has made his decision and there is nothing for you and I to debate over' (RD, 148). Stevens emerges as someone who has followed the views of others for so long, he is a stranger to his own emotions and opinions.

* * *

I dreamt that I woke up. It's the oldest dream of all, and I've just had it.
(Julian Barnes, *A History of the World in*
$10\frac{1}{2}$ *Chapters*, 283 and 309)

Like *The Remains of the Day*, *The Unconsoled* can be read as the story of a man whose dedication to professional excellence has over-restricted his personal life. Its protagonist, Ryder, is another individual like Stevens whose formality may be suggested by the fact that he never reveals his first name. Ryder is a renowned concert pianist on a European tour who arrives in an unnamed city whose inhabitants are insistent that he intervenes in their cultural life, social disputes, and personal problems.

However, Ishiguro has said that in this novel he is interested in the 'language of dreams' and the narrative is radically indeterminable in almost every way. It is quite possible to discuss what happens in *The Unconsoled* as though its events were of the same nature as those in the earlier novels, yet provisos have to be placed on any reading of the text because its incidents and construction are either part of a dream or akin to those of a dream. The reader must therefore consider what the psychological meaning of the book's events might be for the dreamer, if we take this to be Ryder (whose name combines the first syllable of writer and the second of reader). While for Ishiguro 'Writing is a kind of consolation or a therapy', it is this kind of consolation that Ryder, the writer/reader, dreamer and analyst, is unable to find (cf. Wong, 6).

The Unconsoled, perhaps even to a greater degree than Ishiguro's other novels, is concerned with the emotional and psychological life of its narrator. The dreamlike quality of the narration is signalled by its structure. The book's title in itself seems to be a variant on 'the unconscious'. The story is divided into four parts and all except the first part begin with awakenings: 'I was woken' (U, 155), 'I awoke' (U, 293) and again 'I awoke' (U, 413). The first part, by contrast, begins with Ryder's arrival in the unnamed city. He checks into his hotel, is taken up to his room and slides 'into a deep and exhausted sleep' (U, 17). It is the second chapter that begins with an awakening: 'When I was roused' (U, 18), suggesting perhaps that the four parts are waking dreams, with the book's first chapter as a kind of introduction. Yet, in the first chapter Ryder awakens just as he is drifting off into sleep, and it is here that he has his first inexplicable experience:

> something suddenly made me open my eyes again and stare up at the ceiling. I went on scrutinizing the ceiling for some time, then sat up on the bed and looked around, the sense of recognition growing stronger by the second. The room I was now in, I realised, was the very room that had served as my bedroom during the two years my parents and I had lived at my aunt's house on the borders of England and Wales.   (U, 16)

This is the reader's initial hint that the stressed and wearied Ryder is entering into an interior world where everything around him is filtered through his own memories. He returns to the recollected state of a scared child listening to his parents rowing and this sense of impotent anxiety is added to the stress he has already experienced arriving in a city where he has no idea what his itinerary is, but knows that a great number of things are expected of him. In these opening pages, everything necessary for the dreamwork of the rest of the novel is told to Ryder. He has met Gustav and heard of the 'Porters' Dance', he has heard of Sophie and Boris, who are later transformed into his family. He has met Miss Stratmann and discussed his demanding schedule, of which he can recall nothing. Even small occurrences later in the book have been seeded in this opening, such as Boris's obsession with his number-nine toy footballer, which has been suggested by the man next to Ryder on the plane (U, 15). Ryder has also heard mention of Brodsky, Hoffman, Christoff, the Citizens' Mutual support Group, the Civic Arts Institute, the Old Town, 'our societies, the local media' (U, 11), the city councillors, and how 'people here believe you to be not only the world's finest living pianist, but perhaps the very greatest of the century' (U, 11). He is told that the preparations for 'Thursday night' are putting people 'under unusual pressure' (U, 3). In addition to this concert on Thursday, Ryder has 'two rather important social functions' and he hopes that 'no one was offended' by being left out of his schedule

(U, 11). These are the characters and details that are then blended in Ryder's unconscious, together with mixed memories of his peripatetic English childhood and his old friends, to form the dreamscapes of the rest of the novel, where his imagination runs riot with the professional and personal insecurities hidden underneath his fame and success. The dream tools of condensation and displacement work upon scraps of information and past experience to weave together new forms, evident in examples ranging from Ryder's transference of his parents' rows to fierce arguments he has with Sophie in front of 'their son' Boris, to his watching a version of *2001: A Space Odyssey* with Clint Eastwood and Yul Brynner (U, 93,100). In other words, Ryder is allowed to do more freely than any other narrator what Ishiguro himself does when writing, putting together a narrative 'out of little scraps, out of memories, out of speculation, out of imagination' (Mesher, 146). All the people Ryder meets/dreams in the rest of the novel seem to be projections of his fears and desires concerning his past and the present visit, which is why he can attend a formal dinner in his dressing gown, can expose himself to the unconcerned guests, and can later be praised for the speech he never gave. In *The Unconsoled* Ishiguro found a method through which to present his narrator's unconscious processes more forcefully than in his earlier novels where the protagonists' emotional world was always mediated by a conscious mind. As Ryder says at the beginning of the story, in words that could equally apply to Ishiguro: 'This discovery – that the blemish that had always threatened to undermine my imaginary world could in fact be incorporated into it – had been of some excitement for me' (U, 16).

The Unconsoled is Ishiguro's most explicit treatment of creative misremembering and the anxiety the individual pours into trying to come to terms with the past – and it may be for this reason that Ryder shares his name with the elegiac narrator of Evelyn Waugh's *Brideshead Revisited*. Having spent his career to date exploring the mechanisms of emotional repression, Ishiguro has said in interview that he is now interested in exploring their opposite in a way of writing 'that somehow takes on board some of the post-Freudian tensions in life – that comes not from buckling up, not from being unable to express yourself, but from just being pulled left, right, and centre by possible role models and urges, by a sense that you're missing out' (Shaffer, 14). It remains to be seen if this comes to fruition, but it may result in a new voice emerging from a writer who has investigated more fully than other British novelists of his generation the impact of the past on the operations and influences of the unconscious mind.

References and Further Reading

Malcolm Bradbury, 'The Floating World', *No, Not Bloomsbury*, London: Arena, 1989, 363–6.

Steven Connor, *The English Novel in History: 1950–1995*, London: Routledge, 1996, 104–112.

Laura Hall, 'New Nations, New Selves: The Novels of Timothy Mo and Kazuo Ishiguro' in *Other Britain, Other British*, edited by A. Robert Lee, London: Pluto, 1995, 90–110.

Kazuo Ishiguro, *A Pale View of Hills* (PVH), New York: Vintage, 1990.

———, *An Artist of the Floating World* (AFW), London: Faber, 1987.

———, *The Remains of the Day* (RD), London: Faber, 1989.

———, *The Unconsoled* (U), London: Faber, 1996.

———, *When We Were Orphans* (WO), London: Faber, 2001.

Bruce King, 'The New Internationalism: Shiva Naipaul, Salman Rushdie, Buchi Emecheta, Timothy Mo and Kazuo Ishiguro' in *The British and Irish Novel Since 1960*, edited by James Acheson, London: Macmillan, 1991, 192–212.

Barry Lewis, *Kazuo Ishiguro*, Manchester: Manchester University Press, 2000.

John P. McCombe, 'The End of (Anthony) Eden: Ishiguro's *The Remains of the Day* and Mid-Century Anglo-American Tensions', *Twentieth-Century Literature*, 48:1, Spring 2002, 177–97.

D. Mesher, 'Kazuo Ishiguro', in *British Novelists Since 1960*, Second Series, edited by Merritt Moseley, *The Dictionary of Literary Biography*, Volume 194, Detroit: Gale, 1998, 145–53.

Brian W. Shaffer, 'An Interview with Kazuo Ishiguro', *Contemporary Literature*, 42:1, Spring 2001, 1–14.

Cynthia F. Wong, *Kazuo Ishiguro*, Plymouth: Northcote House, 2000.

Mark Wormald, 'Kazuo Ishiguro and the Work of Art' in *Contemporary British Fiction* edited by Richard J. Lane, Rod Mengham, and Philip Tew, Cambridge: Polity, 2003, 226–38.

Web Reading

http://65.107.211.208/uk/ishiguro/ishiguroov.html

http://www.geocities.com/Athens/Ithaca/1828/Kazuo_Ishiguro.htm

http://www.utc.edu/~engldept/booker/ishiguro.htm

6

Hanif Kureishi: In Black and White

6.1. Literary History

A restless and versatile writer, Hanif Kureishi (b.1954) has worked as widely as any leading British novelist. He began his career as a playwright, has published extensively as an essayist, is an Oscar-nominated screenwriter, and has written radio plays and collections of short stories as well as novels. In common with the narrators of both *The Buddha of Suburbia* and *Intimacy*, Kureishi has a British mother and an Indian father – who came to England from Bombay at the time of India's partition in 1947 while most of his large family went to live in Karachi. The only Asian boy at his school, Kureishi found himself caught between the working-class life of his friends in Bromley and the privileged background of his father's family in Pakistan. He later studied philosophy at King's College, London, while at the same time working at the Royal Court Theatre, where he first had a play performed in 1976.

Kureishi's early dramatic works are chiefly interesting in terms of their mapping out of themes that dominate his novels and filmscripts; also, the major influences on his plays, Chekhov and Strindberg, are important figures behind his fiction too. *Borderline* (1981), researched in the Asian community in Southall, and developed in the theatre with the Joint Stock company, explores the forces impacting on Indians in post-Imperial Britain: the violence and abuse they suffer from whites on the one hand and the cross-generational tensions between an Asian and a Western life on the other. *Birds of Passage* (1983) tells the story of a lower middle-class family who have to sell their house to a former

Asian lodger. Though it touches on prostitution and family conflict, it is at heart a study of the effects of the recession on people in Britain in the early 1980s. *Outskirts* (1981), probably Kureishi's most successful early play, concerns two schoolfriends, Bob and Del, who have drifted apart over the course of a dozen years but are united by the adolescence they spent together, hanging out on local waste ground. Del, now a teacher, is still haunted by the attack they thoughtlessly made on an Asian when they were teenagers, while Bob, who has leanings towards the racist National Front party, is unemployed and listless. To a degree, the play represents Kureishi's own ambivalent attitude to his schoolfriends and his intense desire to escape a routine future living in the suburbs.

The idea of a lost friendship between two schoolfriends implicated in the racial animus of the times re-emerges in Kureishi's first filmscript, for Stephen Frears's *My Beautiful Laundrette* (1985). It was this film, in traditional terms a rites-of-passage story, which brought Kureishi both a mainstream audience and high critical acclaim. The film utilizes character types from the earlier plays: the amoral Asian business entrepreneur from *Birds of Passage*, the reunited schoolfriends from *Outskirts*, the sexually precocious, Westernized Asian woman from *Borderline*. Set in South London, Kureishi's script addresses racial and gender stereotypes in its depiction of a sexual relationship between two boys, one Pakistani and one white, which also becomes the commercial basis for the film's central Thatcherite entrepreneurial dream: the successful renovation of a laundrette, ambiguously christened 'Powders'.

Sammy and Rosie Get Laid (1988), again directed by Frears, is a more explicit dissection of the troubles within Thatcher's Britain. The film concerns the return of a politician to see his son Sammy, a young Pakistani accountant in London. Sammy lives in Brixton with Rosie, an English woman. Rosie, Sammy, and Sammy's father each have sexual encounters in episodes that are interleaved with scenes of riots, drug-dealing and promiscuity: all so very different from the Imperial metropolis that Sammy's father remembers. In terms of Kureishi's output, the film stands as a further but more violent assault on the anatomy of 1980s Britain begun in *My Beautiful Laundrette* and concluded in Kureishi's next filmscript, *London Kills Me* (1991). Also directed by Kureishi, *London Kills Me* deals with homelessness and drug-abuse in the capital of England, which Kureishi once damned as 'an intolerant, racist, homophobic, narrow-minded, authoritarian rat hole.' Based on the dealer Glynn Roberts, the main character, Clint, lives in a squat above a Sufi center with his drug-posse friends Muffdiver and Sylvie. The narrative is driven by Clint's attempt to get a job as a waiter, for which he needs a pair of smart shoes. Covering a weekend in the lives of these friends, the familiar Kureishi storyline explores the forces pulling Clint in each direction: towards drugs and continued homelessness or towards employment and respectability.

Kureishi's first novel, *The Buddha of Suburbia* (1990), is in many ways autobiographical, as is much of his work, in outline at least. Kureishi has described the novel's source material as 'south London in the 1970s, growing up as a "semi-Asian" kid; pop, fashion, drugs, sexuality' (DS, 18). Largely because the narrator Karim, like Kureishi, was born in England of mixed parents, the subject of hybridity is a constant presence in the book. Karim explains his 'almost English' and 'semi-Asian' position on the first page: 'I am an Englishman born and bred, almost .... Englishman I am (though not proud of it), from the London suburbs and going somewhere. Perhaps it is the odd mixture of continents and blood, of here and there, of belonging and not, that makes me restless and easily bored' (BS, 3). This immediately introduces the main themes of the novel, which is concerned with questions of belonging, relocation, and identity. The major tone of the book is irony: Kureishi says: 'Irony is the modern mode, a way of commenting on bleakness and cruelty without falling into dourness and didacticism' (RS, 43). *The Buddha* emerges as a story in the Western tradition of *Candide* (Karim is given a copy early on), a narrative of growing understanding and awareness. Critical reviews on the one hand put Karim in the category of picaresque heroes like those of Richard Wright, James Baldwin, and Ralph Ellison (all of whom Kureishi read avidly), while others saw him in terms of English serio-comic heroes such as those of H. G. Wells, Angus Wilson, or Kingsley Amis.

In Kureishi's second novel, *The Black Album* (1995), the leading character is Shahid Hasan, a student fascinated by literature and pop music. Shahid is also, as Kureishi had been, an aspiring author engaged in writing a novel about his early life. The story traces Shahid's first months at a London college to which he has come to study under a young radical lecturer, Deedee Osgood.

The narrative develops two strands. On the one hand, Shahid begins an affair with Deedee, a white liberal academic who believes strongly in education and freedom of expression. The two discuss issues of black history and contemporary culture, take drugs, attend raves, and explore each other's sexual preferences. On the other hand, Shahid finds himself making friends with a group of Muslim students who are actively involved in the local community, publishing, protecting, and proselytizing against white supremacy. These perspectives are brought together when the students burn a copy of Salman Rushdie's *The Satanic Verses*, although the book's title itself is not explicitly mentioned. Deedee tries to stop the arsonists and defends the book on the grounds of free speech. In turn, the Muslim students speak out against Western society and promiscuity, accusing Deedee of attacking minorities and of racist censorship. The novel is broadly sympathetic to both positions but clearly ends in a celebration of the importance of adventure, imagination, and pleasure alongside responsibility and radical politics. Shahid discovers himself agreeing with his friends when he is with them but finding the world more subtle and suggestive at other times. *The Black Album* concludes with Shahid and Deedee affirming that their relationship should continue 'until it stops being fun'.

Since *The Black Album*, Kureishi has published three collections of short stories and two novels, as well as written filmscripts, and his first play since 1983, *Sleep With Me* (1999). One of the short stories of *Love in a Blue Time* (1997), 'My Son the Fanatic', has also been filmed for the BBC. This story more closely echoes the themes of Kureishi's early work than the majority of his publications after *The Black Album*. 'My Son the Fanatic' returns to some of his second novel's themes while again exploring father–son relationships, like *The Buddha of Suburbia*. The story focusses on Parvez, a Punjabi taxi driver in England who becomes concerned by the eccentric behaviour of his son Ali. When confronted, Ali accuses his father of being 'too implicated in Western civilization': eating pork, drinking alcohol, and mixing with prostitutes. Ali becomes more and more trenchant in his views and declares he will work with 'poor Muslims who were struggling to maintain their purity in the face of corruption'. The story ends with Parvez physically assaulting Ali at prayer after the boy has offended Bettina, his father's prostitute friend. Ali responds by asking, 'So, who's the fanatic now?' The conflict between Western and

Muslim values results in intolerance and violence, with Kureishi demonstrating once more how opposed principles in a family with roots in two cultures can tear loved ones apart.

Intimacy (1998), whose themes are reworked in the play *Sleep With Me*, proved to be a controversial novella because the separation from his partner described by its candid but self-centred narrator paralleled events in Kureishi's own life. 'Hurting someone is an act of reluctant intimacy' says the narrator (I, 4), Jay, whose story begins with him dispassionately watching his family move about their business while he reviews in his mind the fact that he is about to leave them. Jay's partner Susan is seen by him as a hard and charmless woman but in the narrative she appears quite different and *Intimacy*, though most often read as a simple confessional, teases away repeatedly at the separation between perception and reality, the complexity of human emotions, and the tensions created by alternative impressions. It is a study in simultaneous bad faith and authenticity, about the contradictions and self-delusions involved in trying to be true to oneself while deceiving others. This tension places Jay in the category of Kureishi's other ironically presented and intentionally flawed narrators in many of the short stories, characters symptomatic of the times. As Jay says: 'I am of a generation that believes in satisfying itself' (I, 79).

In 'Strangers When We Meet', the first and longest story of Kureishi's next book, *Midnight All Day* (1999), the narrator Rob alludes to *Intimacy* when he says he has 'been reading an account by a contemporary author of his break up with his partner. It is restless, and, probably because it rings true, has been taken exception to' (MAD, 47–8). 'Strangers When We Meet' is set in two time frames, the first telling the story of the illicit affair between the narrator, Rob, and a married woman, Florence, who has offered him advice over his burgeoning career as an actor. Their plan to meet in a village by the sea is turned upside down when Florence's dependable but unimaginative husband decides to accompany her on holiday. As the three characters, staying in adjacent rooms, prowl around each other, Rob's mounting frustration leads him first to sleep with the hotel barmaid and then to leave altogether. In the second part, when the ex-lovers meet again many years into the future it is revealed that Florence in fact invited her husband on holiday, because the security he offered was more important to her than the gamble of a possible future with Rob. Now, their roles are in some ways reversed, as it is she who needs advice as she takes up acting but Rob who comes to appreciate the importance of Florence's relationship with her husband (the film of Kuresishi's *Intimacy* also draws heavily on this story).

Midnight All Day continues to mark a shift in emphasis in Kureishi's work from the concerns of youth in the first novels to those of middle age – a balance between the two is only struck in his next novel. Kureishi also refers less and less to the colour or ethnicity of his characters, as though this is of far less importance to him now than their personal relationships. Also, though there are still comic set-pieces, most absurdly in 'The Penis', about a porn star whose celebrated appendage literally takes on a life of its own, most of Kureishi's short stories reflect the sombre tone of their titles. The stories are generally concerned with the middle-class and mid-life crises, focussed on adult relationships and infidelities but also on questions of masculinity and men's role in the care of children.

This last aspect to Kureishi's recent writing is central to his next novel. *Gabriel's Gift* (2001) moves on a generation from *The Buddha of Suburbia*. Gabriel Bunch is a 15-year-old from North London with three gifts: he has 'hallucinations' and can communicate with his dead twin brother Archie, he has a range of artistic talents and interests from fine art to film, and he has a painting: a present from the pop star Lester Jones, whose character, with his one blue eye and his one brown eye, seems to be based on David Bowie.

Gabriel's other ability, which is less explicitly treated as a gift in the novel, is to keep his parents together after their separation, such that, at the end of *Gabriel's Gift* as at the end of *The Buddha of Suburbia*, the novel's central parent-figures agree to get married (GG, 177). Gabriel's father, Rex, is an aging rocker: an ex-bassist who takes up music teaching as the only way to survive when he leaves the family home. Gabriel's mother, Christine, is a waitress and an ex-clothes maker whose heroine is the designer Vivienne Westwood. Her discontent manifests itself in the artistry of her suffering, which ranges from interminable silence to immensely forceful volleys of criticism: 'Whichever method she selected was guaranteed to ensure that her "common-law" husband and son felt it was them – bad guilty men, both – who had strangled and stifled her' (GG, 6). Both parents consider the 1960s, when they were young and on the periphery of fame, to be a golden age, which Christine is trying to move on from and Rex is trying to get back to. Since his heyday, Rex has also played for a year with *The Buddha of Suburbia*'s Charlie Hero, who appears with Karim in the second half of the novel. Karim is 'fresh out of the clinic. He's in that big film with all the sand – I can't remember what it's called.' (GG, 122: an in-reference to the film *The English Patient* (1996), which features Naveen Andrews, who played Karim in the BBC serial adaptation of *Buddha*). Karim now has a son Haroon and is getting married; and, as Bowie did for *The Buddha of Suburbia*, Lester Jones is 'laying some stoical music on [Karim's] new film' (GG, 125). The other people in Gabriel's like are Zak, co-filmmaker and emblematic 'divorce "go-between" ' (GG, 65), and Hannah, a somewhat crudely drawn east European au pair.

The book's trajectory is more that of a learning curve for Gabriel's parents than for the adolescent Gabriel, whose only shift is from the reference to his day at school on the first page to his entry into his intended future career as a filmmaker on the last. It is Rex and Christine who have to come to terms with the end of their youth, with the loss of one of their children, with the gifts they actually have rather than their pipe dreams of another life. At one point, Gabriel makes two copies of the painting Lester has given him. These imitations, symbolic of false lives, are each taken for the real thing by his parents. One disappears with Gabriel's dad to be sold to pay debts. The other is taken and hung up at work by his mother for people to admire her reflected glory. Both these appropriated paintings are in fact fakes; Gabriel retains the original picture to the end of the novel when the three of them are brought back together in a happy ending that sees the counterfeit paintings and lives abandoned for the reality of their love for each other. This achieved, Gabriel can end the novel beginning on his film, which signals the start of new artistic endeavours.

In 2002 Kureishi published a third collection of short stories largely concerned with middle-age reflection and melancholy, *The Body*, which moves further into the realms of mid-life crisis in its preoccupations with love, work, and parenthood. Of the eight pieces, the title story is the most substantial. It offers a contemporary take on the age-old desire for youth: Adam, a writer in his sixties has an illegal transplant which installs his brain in a much younger body, in which he temporarily enjoys a life of sex and drugs before succumbing to incipient feelings of existential weightlessness and finally of entrapment. Reviewers again chose to read the stories of flawed masculinity and tentative paternal role-models through the lens of autobiography, seeing in them expressions of Kureishi's own attempts to come to terms with age. Kureishi's recent work has paired him again with Roger Michell, the director of the TV adaptation of *Buddha*, to make *The Mother* (2003), a provocative film about a widow in her sixties who begins a passionate affair with a younger man. This was followed by a play, *When the Night Begins*, in 2004, about a widowed woman who returns home to confront the stepfather who abused her.

6.2. Themes: Nationality, Ethnicity, and Rock 'n' Roll

Kureishi's early work is fundamentally concerned with identity and frequently considered to be autobiographical. He has said in his essay 'The Rainbow Sign' that the derision heaped on Pakistanis in England led him, like Karim, to deny that side to his self. His characters are defined by the intersection of their race, class, culture, and sexuality. Alongside these factors, Kureishi places contemporary attitudes to politics and religion.

In Kureishi's first novel, Karim is a hybrid in almost all things: race, sex, and sub/urban identity. However, this is frequently reflected back to him as a handicap. As he embarks on his acting career, the first theatre director he meets, Shadwell, wants him to play Mowgli in an adaptation of Kipling's *The Jungle Book*. He says to Karim: '[Eva's] trying to protect you from your destiny, which is to be a half-caste in England. That must be complicated for you to accept – belonging nowhere, wanted nowhere' (BS, 141).

The book takes this traditional logic and inverts it, arguing that hybridity means doubleness not homelessness, addition not division. A journey from a sense of duplicity to one of doubling also describes the narrative curve of the novel. At its start, on the one hand, Karim wants to be English and not at all Indian. Only near the end of the novel will he acknowledge that he has any connections with Indian culture. On the other hand, Karim will not be allowed to be English throughout the book. He is therefore constantly denying and denied a position as English or Indian, but it takes most of the course of the book for him to realize that these are not mutually exclusive and he can be part of an ethnicity that is both English and Indian. Throughout the novel, Karim is constantly asked to 'be Indian': by his schoolteachers; by racist abuse in the streets; by radical theatre directors. These can to a degree be characterized as the positions of the political right and left. The right feeds off a notion of Englishness which excludes the culture of everyone except a minority of Anglo-Saxon people, whether in England or abroad. Just as the generic term 'man' is held to include 'woman' but also renders women invisible, the term 'English' in theory includes those whose identity it renders invisible through its construction of Englishness: the working-class, women, migrants. It is also significant, completing the book's cross section of British society, that the suburban liberals in Kent also want Karim to be Indian – because it is their shortest route to the India that they want to experience in Bromley. In this sense, India is portrayed as a spiritual experience rather than a country. The Chiselhurst couple, Carl and Marianne, epitomise this attitude with their sandalwood buddhas and josticks, arguing that there are 'two sorts of people in the world – those who have been to India and those who haven't' (BS, 30). This of course, would make Karim one of the others, because he has never been to India.

Similar pressures to be Indian are pressed on Karim's father, Haroon, who is enshrined as the Buddha of suburbia, though he has not been to India for almost 30 years, and on Karim's friend Jamila, who is required by her parents to be a dutiful Muslim daughter. The notion of a hybrid identity, of Karim as a black English person, is constantly denied – on the one hand by those who want to have a racial underclass they can abuse and on the other by those who want to have an authentic 'native' of whom they can approve. When he develops his improvized character for Pyke, the second theatre director he meets, Karim says: 'At night, at home, I was working on Changez's shambolic walk and crippled hand, and on the accent, which I knew would sound, to white ears, funny and characteristic of India' (BS, 188–9).

It is only at the end of the book that Karim thinks he has spent his life rejecting a part of his identity, ignoring the fact that Indians are 'his people'. He says:

Partly I blamed Dad for this. After all, like Anwar, for most of his life he'd never shown any interest in going back to India.

He was always honest about this: he preferred England in
every way ... . He wasn't proud of his past, but he wasn't
unproud of it either; it just existed, and there wasn't any point
in fetishizing it, as some liberals and Asian radicals like to do.
(BS, 212–13)

In a way this is Karim's learning curve as he learns to appreciate
that his identity is dual or plural: 'I did feel, looking at those
strange creatures now – the Indians – that in some way these were
my people, and that I'd spent my life denying or avoiding that
fact ... as if I'd been colluding with my enemies, those whites
who wanted Indians to be like them' (BS, 212). At the same time,
Karim realizes that he does not have the kind of 'Indian' identity
that is most wanted by those around him – one rooted not in
England but India. He says: 'If I wanted the additional personality bonus of an Indian past, I would have to create it' (BS, 213).
The importance of acting as a metaphor enters here as Karim is
inventing an Indian past for himself at the same time as inventing
a character for his stage performance.

Karim's experience in some ways mirrors that of Kureishi:
'From the start I tried to deny my Pakistani self. I was ashamed.
It was a curse and I wanted to get rid of it. I wanted to be like
everyone else. I read with understanding a story in a newspaper
about a black boy who, when he noticed that burnt skin turned
white, jumped into a bath of boiling water' (RS, 9). Yet,
Englishness as a part of Karim's identity is also important in the
book, and once more this echoes the experience of Kuresihi, who
says that in Pakistan, 'anti-British remarks made me feel patriotic,
though I only felt patriotic when I was away from England' (RS, 17).
Being English in Karachi is a different phenomenon from being
English in England.

The Buddha of Suburbia first presents the reader with England as
a place radically different from the kind of country imagined in
the colonies. Haroon arrives in England in the 1940s:

Dad was amazed and heartened by the sight of the British in
England .... He'd never seen the English in poverty, as
roadsweepers, dustmen, shopkeepers and barmen. He'd never
seen an Englishman stuffing bread into his mouth with his
fingers, and no one had told him that the English didn't wash
regularly because the water was so cold – if they had water at

all. And when Dad tried to discuss Byron in local pubs no one warned him that not every Englishman could read or that they didn't necessarily want tutoring by an Indian.   (BS, 25)

When Haroon's friends Anwar and Princess Jeeta come to England they expect to be treated with respect, especially because of their education and family background. Instead they seem to find that in England in the 1950s there is no differentiation made between migrants; as the non-white ex-colonized, they are automatically consigned to the lowest social class.

In contrast to this, Kureishi has repeatedly pointed out that the cross-fertilization of nationality and ethnicity has been producing new identities

> I'm British, as I wrote in *The Rainbow Sign*. Just like Karim in the *Buddha*. But being British is a new thing now. It involves people with names like Kureishi or Ishiguro or Rushdie, where it didn't before. And we're all British too .... But most of the critics in England don't understand that. So there isn't any understanding of Britain being a multicultural place. They think that I'm, let's say, a regional writer or writing in a sort of subgenre. They think writers like [me] are on the edges. We are still marginalized culturally .... They don't see that the world is now hybrid.   (Kaleta, 7)

Karim's hybridity is evidenced in the way he takes apart all either/or choices: he says that choosing between men and women would be like choosing between the Beatles and the Stones. Karim is 'an Englishman born and bred, almost' and he is constantly both abused and valued for his difference. He is called curryface and shitface, and openly abused or threatened in the street, while Shadwell, is appalled that Karim has never been to India and cannot speak Urdu or Punjabi. To combat these assumptions over physical identity – located in skin colour, gender, of sexuality – Kureishi employs irony. When Karim is asked by Pyke to come up with a black character – 'someone from your background' – he thinks: 'I didn't known anyone black. I'd been at school with a Nigerian. But I wouldn't know where to find him' (BS, 170). Similarly, Karim uses parody as a way of subverting orthodoxies and stereotypes. At the last performances of *The Jungle Book* he plays with the theatregoers' expectations about his character's Indianness: 'I sent up the accent and made the audience laugh by suddenly relapsing into cockney' (BS, 158).

The contemporary setting of each of Kureishi's first two novels is integral to their narratives, from the late 1960s and the 1970s of *The Buddha of Suburbia* to the late 1980s of *The Black Album*. Most significantly, *Buddha* ends on the night Margaret Thatcher came to power in 1979, and *The Black Album* develops against the backdrop of the Rushdie Affair ten years later. *Buddha* begins in the era of 'Powellism', when Duncan Sandys, an ex-Secretary of State for the commonwealth and colonies (1960–64) was able to say about 1967 Britain: 'The breeding of millions of half-caste children would merely produce a generation of misfits and create national tension' (RS, 11). However, Enoch Powell stands as the pre-eminent figure of the Right against immigration and for Englishness in a restricted, exclusivist sense. In 1965, Powell, though with little chance of winning, stood for the Conservative Party leadership. In 1968, he made his infamous 'rivers of blood' speech, which predicted mass rioting if immigration was not stopped. Three years later, Powell's repeated calls for a massive repatriation scheme ended in the Immigration Bill which denied the right of Commonwealth workers to settle in Britain. It was not until November 1972 that Britain put a Race Relations Act, however feeble, into force and Powell's influence started slowly to decline, though this was replaced by the more trenchant opposition mounted by the National Front.

Diametrically opposed in many ways to the judgements and promulgations of the New Right are the freedoms and promiscuities advocated by rock 'n' roll. Kureishi's other early passion in life alongside literature was music, and he has edited, with Jon Savage, *The Faber Book of Pop* (1995). It was a concern with radical politics and the state of the nation that first drew Kureishi to drama in the late 1970s but he also felt that, unlike the novel, contemporary theatre aspired to be like pop music. He says in the introduction to *Outskirts and Other Plays*: 'A festival of "happenings" and new plays by performance-oriented groups was called "Come Together" after a Beatles song. And dozens of young people were working in this "alternative" or "fringe" theatre. The plays ... used nudity, insult, music, audience participation and comedy'.

Mirroring this, both Karim in *Buddha* and Shahid in *The Black Album* are surrounded by musical reference points. Similarly, in

Intimacy Jay sits in his room contemplating his life and its sound-track: 'I run my hand down the CDs piled on every available surface. Classical, of all periods, with dark Beethoven my god; jazz, mostly of the fifties; blues, rock 'n' roll and pop, with the emphasis on the mid-sixties and early seventies. A lot of punk. It was the hatred, I think, that appealed. It is great music but you wouldn't want to listen to it' (I, 58).

Kureishi's interest in music as a guide through life continues across his short stories and into *Gabriel's Gift*. One character in that novel declares: 'Who do we have to turn to these days for spiritual guidance? Not the priests, politicians or scientists. There are only artists left to believe in. So: I am a supergroupie' (GG, 161). Gabriel has imbibed the musical taste of his parents, who denigrate modern 'beeb-beeb' music beside the guitars of Hendrix, Clapton, and Keith Richards, though classical composers from Mahler to Steve Reich also get a place in the roll call of the book's musical touchstones. In this world 'God's favourite album' is and always will be *Sergeant Pepper's Lonely Hearts Club Band* and Gabriel's father's favourite phrase is 'One day in the sixties' (GG, 29). Rex declares that by the 1990s pop music has become a fashion-driven youth cult: 'In my opinion, pop nowadays is panto for young people and paedophiles' (GG, 137). But it is only by putting the past in perspective that Rex is able to move forward, to understand that there is both respect and a living to be made by passing on his knowledge to the new music makers. At one point, they are listening to Hendrix in a bar: ' "This was all I wanted," said Dad. "To make a noise like that and have people listen to it thirty years later" ' (GG, 141). Yet, pop music seems to mean more in Kureishi's fiction as an index of life growing up in the 1960s and 1970s than as a profession. In *Gabriel's Gift*, Gabriel's dad has played in bands since he was 14, the most well known of which was Leather Pigs with Lester Jones, and is known by Gabriel's mother as 'Johnny-about-to-be-famous': 'Dad was smart enough to know that by his age you had either become successful, rich and pursued by lawyers, stalkers and the press, or you found something else to do; "something else" was the end' (GG, 26). It is consequently the father more than the son in *Gabriel's Gift*, where in *The Buddha of Suburbia* it was more the son than the father, who comes of age and realizes that he has a connection with others: Rex may have missed his chance for self-fulfilment and celebrity but his son's generation will have the opportunity to succeed where he failed.

6.3. Key Works: *The Buddha of Suburbia, The Black Album*

While parallels can be drawn between author and narrator in many of Kureishi's novels, readers are not meant to sympathize too much with the protagonists. For example, Karim debates with himself the rights and wrongs of using Changez as his character after Changez has asked him to promise not to. Karim decides it is the first moral dilemma he has ever had to face – yet, the next time we read about him at rehearsal he has taken Changez's character as his model. Similarly, at the book's ending Karim has criticized his socialist friend Terry for taking a screen role as a police officer but Karim ends by accepting the Asian-stereotype part of a shopkeeper's son in a soap opera.

Karim can be seen as a picaresque hero moving through suburbs and cities, from Bromley to New York, encountering characters who are themselves to an extent stereotyped, if only ironically. They are figures who represent features of national and ethnic identity as much as they might be seen as rounded individuals. His father, Haroon, is therefore presented paradoxically as a British civil Servant and part-time Oriental mystic. His idea on coming to England had been to follow the path of Gandhi and Nehru: 'Dad would return to India as a qualified and polished English gentleman lawyer and an accomplished ballroom dancer' (BS, 24). Instead, Haroon becomes a Greater London guru who never returns to India. Karim parodies the way in which his father is supposed to be a spiritual guide, by observing that he cannot even find his way around Beckenham. The stereotype of the Indian mystic, a spiritual leader without a concern for practicality, is obvious here. Haroon, who has spent his life becoming 'more of an Englishman' (BS, 21), now exaggerates his accent and manner to seem more Indian when he is cast in the role of Buddha. (Karim goes through the same transformation when he is asked to change his accent and manner to play Mowgli.)

Karim's mother is, by contrast, a caricature of lower-middle-class British reserve and sensual denial who meets her calm and unemotional equivalent in Jimmy, the pale, earnest Englishman. In stark contrast, Karim's prospective step-mother, Eva, is initially presented as the archetypal avant-garde Bohemian character of the late 1960s: someone who latches on to Eastern culture as an extension of her rejection of parochial middle-class values and of her search for the unconventional and the creative.

However, she is more ambitious than her counter-cultural opinions suggest: Eva is one of the characters who move with the times, like her similarly rebellious son Charlie, and are seen to be constantly tuning in to the latest fashions and fads.

Charlie is the object of Karim's desire for most of the book. For a period, this fixation is transferred to Eleanor. Both represent a kind of ideal for Karim as both are quintessentially English in a way that Karim finds attractive and impressive. Charlie, a kind of cold and ambitious but beautiful youth rebel abhors Englishness but later admits that he is selling his national identity in America, though it is now a caricature of Englishness based on a false Cockney accent. Charlie is an opportunist, who literally jumps on the punk band wagon and later moves to America because he will be better off: 'England's decrepit. No one believes in anything. Here [in America] it's money and success. But people are motivated. They do things. England's a nice place if you're rich, but otherwise it's a fucking swamp of prejudice, class confusion, the whole thing' (BS, 256). In distinction from this, Eleanor represents English power and Imperial privilege. Karim puts it this way: 'we pursued English roses as we pursued England; by possessing these prizes, this kindness and beauty, we stared defiantly into the eye of the Empire and all its self-regard ... We became part of England and yet proudly stood outside it' (BS, 227). Karim's theory here is reminiscent of Frantz Fanon's view of the colonized's search for a position in the colonizer's domination. In *Black Skin, White Masks* Fanon argues that it is through sexual possession that a transference of identity can be accomplished, by gaining possession of someone who exemplifies the elite group from which one is excluded. It is again, something that Karim has to move beyond by the end of the book in recognizing his self-worth. Fanon also avers the need for recognizing and reclaiming one's own history. Karim does the same in his sudden realization that his relationship with Eleanor has been based on his own self-denial: he spends all his time with Eleanor discussing her family, friends, and problems while his own history, in terms of race and class, has been deemed uninteresting. It is emblematic of the book's use of colonial role-playing in post-imperial Britain that Eleanor chooses to play a memsahib of the Raj as her character in Pyke's play, while Karim is encouraged to play someone 'black'.

The person Karim eventually turns to for developing his role is Changez. In the novel's comic plot Changez plays the traditional role of the 'innocent' or fool. On the one hand, Changez, who has been reading novels featuring Sherlock Holmes and the Saint (BS, 83), does not understand the society he has landed in. He is devoted to the idea of loyalty (though not fidelity) within marriage, and does not see the sexual and racial tensions around him. He is shocked and confused when Karim assumes that Jamila is having a lesbian affair; because Changez thought that his wife and her friend Joanna were just sharing the same room. Also, Changez is made an innocent abroad when he declares: 'how much he liked English people, how polite and considerate they were ... They don't try to do you down like the Indians do' (BS, 223). On the next page, Jamila rings up Karim because Changez has been attacked by a National Front gang. Yet, because Changez is the 'innocent fool' character he is also the kindest and most giving person in the novel. Though he does not understand the machinations of the more sophisticated world around him, he is the least aggressive or vindictive person in the novel. Consequently, like Lenny in Steinbeck's *Of Mice and Men* he is also the gentle giant who ends up unwittingly killing.

Lastly, Jamila is the character most sure of who she is and what she wants to achieve. This can be best illustrated by the ending of the book. The last chapter has Karim back in England. He goes to see Terry who tells him: 'England's had it. It's coming apart. Resistance has brought it to a standstill. The Government were defeated in the vote last night. There'll be an election .... It's either us or the rise of the Right' (BS, 258). Terry is correct, and the novel closes with the dawning of the age of the New Right's dominance. It is 1979 and the end of the Labour government. The chapter progresses with this imminent change hanging over the story, and it finishes on the night of the election that brings the Conservatives to power. Generally, the characters are oblivious of this – Karim celebrates his new job in a soap opera, which will bring him money and celebrity; Haroon and Eva, the progressive Bohemian couple, announce they are going to marry; and even London has changed: 'Everyone was smartly dressed, and the men had short hair, white shirts and baggy trousers held up by braces' (BS, 270). In the midst of these widespread changes in personal and national political fashions, only Jamila continues to stick by her principles: to live in a squat, conduct a lesbian relationship, raise a child outside of her marriage, and spend the last day and evening, when Karim and the others are celebrating their own successes at a restaurant, campaigning for the Labour party.

*   *   *

In ways similar to Kureishi's first novel, *The Black Album* is concerned with syncretism: black and white, high and popular culture, Tory national and Labour local government, liberals and fundamentalists. The novel takes its title from a rare album by Prince – made in the face of accusations that he was losing touch with his black musical roots – whose title plays on that of the Beatles record popularly known as *The White Album*. These two cultural reference points, which for Kureishi can represent the best of white and black pop music, in one sense delimit Shahid's experience in the novel. Throughout the narrative, Shahid oscillates between the two sets of values offered to him by his black Muslim friends and his liberal white lover. His apparent dilemma represents the position of many members of the Pakistani community in Britain, expected to adapt to or adopt social codes that do not appear to acknowledge their cultural differences or adhere to a cultural tradition that has very different expectations and ethics.

Also impinging on Shahid's life are his intimidating older brother Chili, who runs the family's travel agency business, and his sister-in-law Zulma, an assertive, rich socialite from a prominent land-owning Karachi family. The other major characters are: Chad, Riaz, and Hat, the committed Muslim students who befriend Shahid; Deedee's husband Brownlow, a history lecturer whose Marxist politics are underwritten by Sartre and Fanon; and Strapper, a drug-dealer squatting in a flat left by an Asian family who suffered long-term racial abuse. Although the major catalyst of later events is the Rushdie Affair, earlier in the book Kureishi describes Shahid moving through London after the bombing of Victoria railway station, the students assembling at a house on an estate to defend a family from racist attacks, and their later attempt to have the local Labour leader place a 'miraculous' aubergine in the foyer of the Town Hall. Like the division over Rushdie's book, all of these incidents serve to underline the racial, political, and cultural differences that typify urban Britain.

The novel draws on the traditions of the campus novel, most recently associated with Malcolm Bradbury and David Lodge, and re-inflects its codes – as Prince plays on the signification of the Beatles album. Kureishi interrogates the white assumptions of liberal education and of its fiction by interweaving complex issues of interracial attraction and Muslim fundamentalism. The book fails to find a third space between the perceived differences of black and white culture but champions an awareness of cultural roots and a respect for difference as Shahid's final choice. As such it opposes right-wing authoritarianism in any form, recommending the course of a personal and cultural fusion of ethnicities while warning against the appropriations of otherness that undermine liberal politics.

Kureishi's second novel was generally less well received than his previous one, and this has been the pattern of his fiction since. He has in some ways re-cast himself as a short story writer and perhaps has little left to say in the medium of long prose fiction. Each novel seems a little less rich and involving, but Kureishi continues to attempt to find a voice as a middle-aged writer, dealing with concerns of his own generation, rather in the manner if not the style of Martin Amis. He has also returned to scriptwriting and has found renewed critical success with some of his recent work, confronting issues of rebellion not in the young, but in the old.

References and Further Reading

Steven Connor, *The English Novel in History: 1950–1995*, London: Routledge, 1996.
Anthony Ilona, 'Hanif Kureishi's *The Buddha of Suburbia*', in *Contemporary British Fiction* edited by Richard J. Lane, Rod Mengham, and Philip Tew, Cambridge: Polity, 2003, 87–105.
Kenneth C. Kaleta, *Hanif Kuresihi: Postcolonial Storyteller*, Austin: University of Texas Press, 1998.
Hanif Kureishi, *My Beautiful Laundrette* and *The Rainbow Sign* (RS), London: Faber, 1986.
——, *The Buddha of Suburbia* (BS), London: Faber, 1993.
——, *The Black Album* (BA), London: Faber, 1995.
——, *Intimacy* (I), London: Faber, 1999.
——, *Midnight All Day* (MAD), London: Faber, 2000.
——, *Gabriel's Gift* (GG), London: Faber, 2002.
——, *Dreaming and Scheming: Reflections on Writing & Politics: Collected Non-fiction, Essays and Teachings* (DS), London: Faber, 2002.
A. Robert Lee, 'Changing the Script: Sex, Lies and Videotapes in Hanif Kureishi, David Dabydeen and Mike Phillips', in *Other Britain, Other British*, edited by A. Robert Lee, London: Pluto, 1995, 69–89.

Bart Moore-Gilbert, *Hanif Kureishi*, Manchester: Manschester University Press, 2001.
Jago Morrison, *Contemporary Fiction*, London: Routledge, 2003, 179–90.
Susheila Nasta, *Home Truths: Fictions of the South Asian Diaspora in Britain*, London: Palgrave, 2002.
Ruvani Ranasinha, *Hanif Kureishi (Writers and Their Work)*, Northcote House, 2001.
Berthold Schoene, 'Herald of Hybridity: The Emancipation of Difference in Hanif Kureishi's *The Buddha of Suburbia*', *International Journal of Cultural Studies*, 1:1, 1998, 109–28.
Nahem Yousaf, *Hanif Kureishi's 'The Buddha of Suburbia'*, London: Continuum International Publishing Group, 2002.

Web Reading

Key website: http://www.hanifkureishi.com/
http://www.emory.edu/ENGLISH/Bahri/Kureishi.html

7

Ian McEwan: The Child in Us All

7.1. Literary History

In Zadie Smith's *White Teeth*, a little joke about the literary in-crowd is made through a reference to some smart white kids in the corner of the playground called Ian, Mart and Jules. However, in spite of his reputation for the macabre, Ian McEwan (b.1948) is generally perceived as a more serious, and less postmodernist writer than the two authors with whom he is most often grouped: Martin Amis and Julian Barnes. In fact, despite the early accusations of sensationalism made against him, his approach to fiction has more in common with the reflective humanism of Kazuo Ishiguro, another graduate of the Creative Writing Masters course at the University of East Anglia.

McEwan's book-length debut, a collection of short stories he worked on during his MA, was *First Love, Last Rites* (1975). Because of the stories' preoccupation with sexualized children and violent abuse, the volume immediately won McEwan a reputation for writing 'literature of shock'. Though the stories were highly praised in many quarters, to a majority of reviewers the settings seemed sordid and bleak, the narratives lurid and morbidly compelling. *First Love, Last Rites* was followed by McEwan's second collection, *In Between the Sheets* (1978); stories which again received an outraged reaction from some sections of the press. The narratives are predominantly focussed on relationships and the book is arguably more of apiece than his first set of stories. Subjects vary from a two-timing, sexually diseased man who is castrated by the nurses he has been deceiving, to a woman writer who keeps an ape as a lover; only the final story,

160

'Psychopolis', written after a trip to the States, hints at the possibility of a broader canvas for McEwan's writing.

McEwan's first novel, *The Cement Garden* (1978), seemed to most reviewers to continue the preoccupations of the short stories. Indeed, as a short novel itself, it could be considered a treatment at greater length of familiar McEwan territory, including sibling rivalry, taboo sex, and the simmering threat of violence. With a small cast of barely more than six characters in the novel there is as strong a sense of intimacy and insularity as in the stories, but at its core the novel is about the ways in which a family of orphaned children stick together. Its narrator is the second oldest of four children, Jack, a 14-year-old whose Oedipal desires come true when his father collapses and dies of a coronary while building the cement garden of the title: 'Because of his heart attack my father was forbidden this kind of work but I made sure he took as much weight as I did' (C, 13). When their mother dies shortly afterwards, Jack and his three siblings do not report the death to the authorities but simply bury her corpse in cement in the basement. Each of the four children responds to their loss and subsequent fragile independence differently, but the dominant movement is one of regression. The story ends with Derek, the boyfriend of Jack's older sister, Julie, breaking into the mother's concrete tomb, and the police arriving at the house immediately after Jack and Julie have sex for the first time, as though installing themselves as the new parents in the family home.

The Comfort of Strangers (1981), is narrower again in its range of characters but a little broader in its setting. It is perhaps more easily considered an example of 'literature of shock' than any of McEwan's other novels. Apparently set in Venice, *The Comfort of Strangers* tells the story of a tourist couple, Colin and Mary, who become involved with a local man, Robert. When they meet Robert's wife Caroline, Colin and Mary, grow to realize that the older couple are involved in a sadomasochistic relationship. The book, whose central subject is male violence, draws parallels between the two couples, but builds towards Robert's premeditated murder of Colin. Through the arc of his simple, parabolic narrative, McEwan seems to take Blanche DuBois's famous assertion, from Tennessee Williams's 1947 play *A Streetcar Named Desire*, that she has always 'relied on the kindness of strangers', and turn it on its head to explore the way in which travellers are at the mercy of others when holidaying in alien surroundings. In several ways, McEwan's second and equally short novel appears to share the interest in isolation and incest evident in his first, largely because the central couple of *The Comfort of Strangers* are so close they could almost be brother and sister – to the extent that they sometimes find it difficult to remember they are separate individuals (CS, 17). Holidaying on the continent, Colin and Mary sleep in the afternoon, talk little, and do not even have the energy or motivation to tidy their hotel room. They revert to a child-like state, reliant on their hotel maid: 'they came to depend on her and grew lazy with their possessions. They became incapable of looking after one another' (CS, 12). Where Jack and Julie in the earlier novel are adolescents who prematurely become adults in the familial home, Colin and Mary are adults (she divorced with children) who revert to an earlier stage of life in the unfamiliar temporary home of a foreign hotel. In both *The Cement Garden* and *The Comfort of Strangers* there is an almost solipsistic feel to the lives of the main characters, a family and a couple into whose midst strangers come in search of sex and power. In each novel, too great a closeness creates its own problems for the protagonists, and they are presented as deeply vulnerable to outsiders who can expose the dangers of, and prey upon, their intimacy: 'with each step the city would recede as [Colin and Mary] locked tighter into each other's presence' (CS, 13). *The Comfort of Strangers* was shortlisted for the Booker Prize but was a controversial novel on publication because McEwan had chosen to explore sadomasochistic relationships. He has said in interview about Colin and Mary:

> I felt they had become mesmerized by Robert and Caroline in ways they could not speak about. Robert and Caroline were for me simply a sort of comic drawing of a relationship of domination, and when this decently liberal and slightly tired couple, Colin and Mary, come in contact with that relationship they find it has a sway over their unconscious life, and they begin to act out – or rather speak to each other – these incredible masochistic and sadistic fantasies while they are making love. By example, as it were, their very carefully constructed rational view – he being a mild feminist, she a rather stronger one, and their sort of balance – becomes undone, because they haven't ever addressed the matter at a deeper level of themselves; they've always seen it as a social matter. (Haffenden, 179)

McEwan's third novel is thematically linked to his first two. As in *The Cement Garden*, there is a male protagonist whose maturation is central to the narrative, but as in *The Comfort of Strangers* there is a fundamental concern with a couple in crisis. Once more, childhood is a major preoccupation, as are gender relations. However, McEwan's third novel marks a considerable change from his earlier fiction in certain other respects. Informed by the experience of writing for television and film, and after a six-year gap since his last novel, *The Child in Time* (1987) has a far broader social and political canvas than either *The Cement Garden* or *The Comfort of Strangers*. For many critics this revealed McEwan to be one of the foremost novelists of his generation though for others it exposed the fact, as they saw it, that he was at his best writing about couples and families in near-claustrophobic situations. The story of *The Child in Time* takes place over a few years in a projected future but is initially set, during the 'last decent summer' of the 1990s, in a London of beggars licensed by the government and schools offered for sale to private investors. The novel's main storyline concentrates on Stephen and Julie, a husband and wife who, upon the kidnapping of their only child, become estranged, but appear to be reconciled with the birth of a new baby at the close of the narrative. The second-string plot concerns the composition and publication of a government childcare manual. These two strands of narrative are brought together not just through events in Stephen's life but also via his concern with the idea that a generation or society can be appraised by its attitude towards the nurturing and education of children.

Like *The Comfort of Strangers*, McEwan's next work can be considered as genre fiction: as a Cold-War spy story that has at its heart the preoccupations of many espionage novels, such as deception, duplicity, ignorance, aggression, and the loss of innocence that accompanies the acquisition of knowledge and experience. *The Innocent* (1990) was McEwan's most successful book to date and, though an easier read, is more complexly plotted than his previous fiction. The prose is heavily symbolic at times, and the story aims towards becoming an allegory of how strong countries impose their wills on weaker ones, but lacks the moral and literary sophistication of much of McEwan's best work. The story is set in Berlin at the time of a stereotypical Cold-War enterprise called Operation Gold, the attempt by the British and American military to tunnel into the Soviet sector to infiltrate communication systems in 1955–56. As well as focussing on the actual Berlin Tunnel built by MI6 and the CIA, McEwan also breaks the fictional frame of the narrative by introducing the figure of George Blake, the double-agent who actually did betray Operation Gold before the tunnel was even started. *The Innocent* is most obviously concerned with the way the post-war Western world bifurcated into factions aligning themselves with the mutually suspicious superpowers, and so concentrates on the opposed political philosophies of the USSR and Euroamerica, but it is also a story about the end of the British Empire and the rise of American global cultural domination. Set in the crucial years of the mid-1950s, the time in British politics of the confusion and humiliation of the Suez Crisis (cf. Ishiguro's *The Remains of the Day*), *The Innocent* details the loss of Britain's international role and the assumption of its secondary position in the new world order alongside the other transition signalled by the division of Berlin, whose carving up is imaged in the literal dismemberment of a body in the novel's middle section.

Black Dogs (1992) purports to be a memoir or 'divagation' by Jeremy, an orphan fascinated by the families of others. Jeremy has spent his life striving to regain his childhood innocence before the death of his parents when he was eight years old. This early loss has led him to seek parental figures, those with authority but compassion, solutions but sympathy. A preface provides the reader with Jeremy's background, concentrating on his relationship with his sister and his protective love for her daughter. Yet, in several ways the principal figures in the novel are Jeremy's parents-in-law, June and Bernard Tremaine, a separated couple who met as communist sympathizers but whose experiences and temperaments have taken them in diametrically opposed philosophical directions. This concern with ideological differences continues a theme from *The Innocent*, with which *Black Dogs* shares an interest in the Berlin Wall's construction and destruction, the pulling down of which in *Black Dogs* is symbolic of the breaking down of a barrier between June and Bernard's seemingly irreconcilable perspectives. June is a spiritual being, an intuitive believer and a natural communicator, while Bernard is a logical rationalist and unswerving materialist. She searches for the 'hidden truth' of the universe, and argues that she would not take the life of another no matter what the benefit, while he believes there is no truth that science cannot ultimately reveal to humanity, and argues that he would countenance the death of hundreds of people if it were to save the lives of thousands. In the opening section of the novel after the preface, June is dying from leukaemia at a nursing home in 1987, where Jeremy visits her. While he makes notes from what June tells him, and reflects upon his conversations with Bernard, Jeremy becomes the intermediary (as adult and child) between this self-alienated couple with their warring beliefs. As he learns more of their background and the circumstances of their marriage, Jeremy increasingly becomes an image of the novelist, of the observing outsider trying to make sense of the lives and opinions of others. The narrative of the novel does not proceed chronologically but leads up to an incident in 1946, an encounter June had in France with two predatory dogs, which brought her to a belief in God. June understands the dogs to be embodiments of evil, exemplars of a pervasive, ever-present malignant force that can arise anywhere at any time. The events of the book, from the assault on Bernard at the Berlin Wall in 1989, through the history of the Majdanek concentration camp in Poland, to Jeremy's disturbing experience of the violent forces in himself, can all be considered from this perspective. Against this, Bernard would rationally argue that all examples of 'evil' are historically specific incidents of violence that could be eradicatd by improved social and political systems. Ultimately, Jeremy, and one suspects McEwan, leans more towards June's understanding of the universe than Bernard's: that the world is not entirely in human hands to control and that there are forces at work that the conscious mind will never have in its possession. A very dense book, involving numerous interconnected themes, *Black Dogs* is at heart a meditation on the nature of moral forces. The book uses the dogs of its title (who have supposedly been trained by the Gestapo not only to attack but to rape) as an emblem or manifestation of a primal evil that will periodically surface in Europe (McEwan's filmscript for *The Good Son* is also concerned with modern Western society's refusal to countenance the existence of evil). The narrative is thus concerned with the contemporary meanings of 'evil' and 'good', the latter figured as the redemptive power of love. Taking his cue from the poet W. H. Auden, McEwan forces on the reader the conviction that, whatever one takes them to be symbols of, the 'black dogs' can, and indeed will, arise again in the future, and only love can in some sense overcome the violent tragedies of history.

McEwan's next novel appeared in 1997; and while its theme is love it is concerned with how love can be obsessive and threatening as much as supportive and redeeming. *Enduring Love* is less a reflection on love's endurance than on an individual's endurance of unwanted, uncompromising love. It again has a marriage in crisis at its centre: a couple whose union is threatened by the sudden appearance of a third, deluded 'lover'. Following their meeting in a moment of emotional intensity, a five-man attempt to hold down a hot-air balloon in danger of flying away with only a child aboard, the social misfit Jed Parry fixates on the novel's narrator, Joe Rose. The reader is never quite sure until late on whether Parry is indeed stalking Joe, or, as his partner Clarissa believes, Joe is fabricating the story. Through these doubts and interpretations, *Enduring Love* develops as a novel about the different narratives, theories, and beliefs people use to interpret events in their lives. Though the plot can be accused of being overly schematic, as arguably are those of several of McEwan's books, it is in many ways a compelling and chilling study of an individual who has to endure a love as threatening and predatory as the incarnations of evil in *Black Dogs*.

Amsterdam, which won the Booker Prize in 1998, appeared only a year later. The novel is a little different from McEwan's previous work. Read as another serious exploration of themes of responsibility and rivalry, it fails to maintain the high standards of McEwan's previous work. However, read as a black comedy, the novel's 'faults' (predictability, melodrama, over-coincidence) appear to be entirely within the genre of social satire and to reveal a new strand to McEwan's writing. The plot centres on three men gathered together at the funeral of a woman to whom they have all been lovers. Following a series of bizarre plot-twists and misunderstandings, two of the men, supposedly best friends, travel to Holland to kill each other under the guise of euthanasia. The third man, husband to the dead woman, appears at the end of the novel to rise from being a foolish cuckold to stand as the orchestrator of the others' doom. The book shows McEwan's continuing skill at giving macabre twists to debates over contemporary social issues. Set in 1996, the novel attempts to explore the morality of the well-off portion of a generation brought up with 'full employment, new universities, bright paperback books, the Augustan age of rock-and-roll, [and] affordable ideals' (A, 12). It suggests that a nanny state has fostered selfish children and that the politics of sleaze and greed that characterized nearly 20 years of Conservative government were the result. Perhaps best seen as a witty diversion, *Amsterdam* reads like a potboiler, and though below McEwan's best it can be enjoyed as his first real work in the genre of satire: 'a novel, play, entertainment, etc., in which topical issues, folly, or evil are held up to scorn by means of ridicule and irony' (*Collins English Dictionary*).

McEwan's next work, *Atonement* (2001), was another foray into new fictional terrain, in that, for the first time, he set a novel mostly before his own birth. Though it ends in the present, the narrative begins in the mid-1930s and centres on a child's disastrous misinterpretation of the sexual desires of an older sister and her lover. The book received some of McEwan's best reviews, partly because it suggested he was engaging in a complex and allusive way with the canon of English literature, and particularly with a much-discussed strand: the country-house novel.

Alongside his novels and short stories, McEwan has produced a variety of other work. The first of his several film and television scripts, a half-hour confrontational dinner-party drama directed by Mike Newell, *Jack Flea's Birthday Party*, was aired in 1976. McEwan has said that he thinks of the play, written in 1974, as a part of the stories assembled for *First Love, Last Rites*. In 1979, an adaptation of one of his best short stories, 'Solid Geometry' was halted by the BBC following concerns over its subject matter (the story was eventually made into a short film starring Ewan MacGregor, in 2002), but in 1980 McEwan had his second original TV script produced when *The Imitation Game*, a story of sexual politics within English patriarchy, was directed by Richard Eyre as a BBC 'Play for Today'. McEwan's subsequent scripts have been for film: *The Ploughman's Lunch* (1983), an anti-Thatcherite story set at the time of the Falklands, again directed by Eyre, *Soursweet* (1988), a faithful adaptation of Timothy Mo's 1982 novel about a Chinese family in 1960s Britain, and *The Good Son* (1993), a dark thriller about a seemingly angelic boy whose cruel, destructive impulses are only recognized by his bereaved cousin. In 1983, McEwan's Audenesque oratorio about the threat of nuclear war, *or Shall We Die?*, was performed at London's Royal Festival Hall with a score by Michael Berkeley. McEwan has also published a novel for children called *The Daydreamer* (1995): a collection of seven interconnected stories about body-transformations, told by an adult remembering the metamorphoses of his childhood imagination.

7.2. Themes: Children and Adulteration

Throughout his fiction, McEwan has dissected relationships between children and adults, particularly the ideas and fears that the young have about 'being grown up'. To illustrate and explore this theme, I shall examine *The Cement Garden* and *Atonement*. *The Cement Garden* details the summer months of a family of newly bereaved and abandoned children coming to terms with life without their parents. In many ways, the narrative explores their simultaneous growth into adulthood and regression into childhood. McEwan's novel might indeed have been called the semen garden; it is concerned with sex and growth, with creation (nature) and procreation (animal). The narrator Jack is an adolescent who at the start of the novel successfully masturbates for the first time at the same moment as his father has a heart attack and dies. The boy jacks off on to his hand and then studies the semen drying like cement: 'As I watched, it dried to a barely visible shiny crust which cracked when I flexed my wrist. I decided not to wash it away' (C, 18). Little in this book is in fact washed away, from dirt to guilt, but almost everything is covered over: the garden, a dead body, incest.

From one perspective, *The Cement Garden* investigates the preoccupation with illusion and fantasy at the heart of an 'ordinary' family. The children re-imagine their lives through comic books, dreams, and sexual fantasies or reinvent themselves through role play, dressing up, games of doctors and nurses, and the world of science fiction with its antithetical staples of heroes and aliens. Through these various projections and daydreams, the four children suggest the desire for different fictions that they have at their respective ages: Tom (who is 5), Sue (12), Jack (14), and Julie (16). After the deaths of their parents in Part One of the book, the outside world is represented to these children in Part Two by Julie's boyfriend Derek, who is himself a young man of 23. Derek's main haunt is a snooker hall, a dark masculine world in which he is the dominant male and where he takes Jack to prove his superiority. As an only child, Derek is also envious of the orphaned children's new family unit (Jack and Julie as parents, Sue and Tom as children). His wish is to break their intimacy and independence, which he does at the end of the novel when he discovers Jack and Julie in bed together, rushes down to the basement to break open the trunk of cement in which the mother has been buried, and then fetches the police.

The Cement Garden is a book about the fears and yearnings of childhood and adolescence, and it therefore brings to mind many other novels concerned with children isolated from adults, most notably William Golding's *The Lord of the Flies*. But, whereas Golding's children run wild, fighting each other, McEwan's grow closer together, such that the reader is reminded how the adult world provides checks not on their natural aggression but on their natural sexuality. Any reference to 'nature' is problematic, but McEwan does not suggest that if adults are removed from the family, children revert to any kind of 'savage' state – instead, they adopt and adapt the role models provided by the older generation. The book's primary coverings are of the parents, but not their influence: the mother dies and is buried in cement in a trunk after the father is taken away by an ambulance, having fallen face down in the cement while suffering his fatal coronary attack: 'I did not have a thought in my head as I picked up the plank and carefully smoothed away his impression in the soft, fresh concrete' (C, 18). The absence of the parents will prove to be the determining factor in the children's subsequent life together over the long hot summer holiday as they slot themselves into the roles (sexual, parental, gendered) most suitable to them after their parents' removal. This is a somnambulistic world where the children, according to McEwan, fall asleep (Haffenden, 170), which are the words used by Jack to describe life after his mother's death: 'the house seemed to have fallen asleep' (C, 71). In this somnambulism, each of the children turns to an activity: the 'alien' Sue reads and writes in her diary (at one point McEwan considered making this diary addressed to the dead mother the book's narrative), the bullied Tom plays outside and dresses as a girl, and the beautiful Julie explores her sexual attractiveness as well as her maternal feelings. Meanwhile, it is the lethargic Jack, so attracted to but excluded from the world of men at the beginning of the novel, who finds he has nothing to do and sleeps much of the day. Yet, Jack is preoccupied with his body, particularly its new adolescent productions: acne and semen. In his semi-mature condition, Jack appears to conflate or confuse all women, such that at one point he thinks a woman on the street is his dead mother, and then changes his mind to recognize her as Julie, only to confront the person and find it is a stranger. At his mother's death, Jack seeks a replacement who will also be all women to him, as his mother was when he was a child; therefore, in Julie he seeks a mother, sister, and a lover. Until he consummates his heterosexual masculinity, completing the usurpation of his father's role, by sleeping with Julie at the novel's climax, Jack continues the act begun at the very moment of his father's death, and warned against by his mother, by masturbating each morning and afternoon (in one of his dreams Jack 'drubs' in front of his mother).

The book's title contains allusions to some central themes: the natural/unnatural taboo against incest, the modern city as concrete jungle, and culture's thin veneer over nature, illustrated by the fact that whatever is hidden away or covered over in the book refuses to stay 'buried': human remains, desire, the past. Yet, *The Cement Garden* is not just a book about nature returning no matter how hard it is pitchforked out. McEwan's novel is concerned with questioning the ways in which the lines between right and wrong, nature and culture, the social and the personal, are precariously and almost arbitrarily drawn, as well as the senses in which ordinary life is fashioned by fantasies, dreams, and role-playing. It is a narrative about social conventions, cultural norms, and the divisions between the human and the alien, the natural and the artificial. The novel's closing line is a rhetorical question: ' "There!" she said, "wasn't that a lovely sleep" ' (C, 138). It allows the reader, as much as Jack, to think of everything that has happened as a dream, and to be comforted by the adult's role as provider of safety and reassurance. Yet the waking reality of the novel is more disturbing than anything else, and Julie's suggestion that the preceding narrative has been a 'lovely sleep' not only connects with Jack's feeling that the house fell asleep when their mother died but also provides a comforting fiction that only a child would believe.

Atonement similarly deals with a child's perception of adult behaviour. It is initially set in 1935 at Tilney, a country house, and is divided into three parts, with a coda set in London in 1999. The main trio of characters, in a narrative suffused with triangles and three-way relationships, are Briony Tallis, a 13-year-old with literary pretensions, her older sister Cecilia, and Robbie Turner, the son of the Tallis family's cleaning lady. Robbie and Cecilia are down from Cambridge, where Robbie has been educated at the expense of the girls' father, a Whitehall civil servant whose rule over but absence from the young people's world of play-acting and sexual intrigue recalls that of Sir Thomas Bertram in Jane Austen's *Mansfield Park*. As with many of McEwan's previous novels, the plot hinges on a pivotal moment in the characters' lives, which opens the novel. The preoccupations of the novel are contained in Briony's observation of Robbie and Cecilia's argument by the fountain over the broken Meissen vase (echoing Henry James's novel *The Golden Bowl*), in that it mimics the presence of the third-person narrator who assumes an impossible omniscience. Confidently interpreting and fictionalizing that which she has neither experienced nor understood, Briony serves as a cautionary figure for both author and reader.

The effect of the adult world on children throughout part one is to create a disturbance which results in the children acting in ways which might or do lead to disaster. This dimension of role-playing and immature understanding is foregrounded by the lurid-yet-innocent gothic play about a romanticized adult world that Briony asks the children to rehearse at the start of the novel. Refracted through Robbie's thoughts, Part Two parallels the injustices and confusion of Part One with that of the rout of the British Expeditionary Force in France. The symbolism of the vase becomes a little clearer here. It entered the household via an uncle of the Tallises to whom it was given in the First World War by the French villagers he had saved. Its breaking by Robbie in the interwar years is now followed by his own attempt to help defend France in 1940, and he in turn is given aid and shelter by French villagers. The vase comes to signify so many broken things that people attempt to put back together: relationships, lives, the past, countries. The vase is mended in 1935 so that the cracks are barely discernible, yet, in the Second World War, it is broken again, this time irreparably. As Briony notes of the rash certainties and accusations she has been guilty of: 'the glazed surface of conviction was not without its blemishes and hairline cracks'.

While Part One disclosed that Robbie had intended to become a doctor, the novel's third part focusses on Briony's wartime experience as a nurse. It ends with the note 'B. T. London, 1999', informing the reader that the preceding narrative has in fact been Briony's account, has been a fiction within McEwan's fiction – it proves to be an imaginative rendition of the atonement Briony could have performed had Robbie and Cecilia lived. It is followed by a coda, or epilogue, narrated directly in the first person by Briony and turns on a new generation's performance of Briony's playlet, 'The Trials of Arabella', which initiated the book's preoccupation with imagined lives.

The novel's intrigues centre on perspective. Though *Atonement's* main three parts are told in the third person, the reader is forced to rely on characters' readings of events, and while dominant interpretations occur to the reader, there are few anchors to determine conclusively the meanings of scenes and actions. The entire narrative, even Robbie's war experience, proves to have been Briony's rendition of possibilities and probabilities; in fact, Robbie and Cecilia both died in 1940. The novel itself, which is the final reworked and expanded version of the story Briony sent to *Horizon* 59 years earlier, emerges as her act of reparation as she, suffering a series of minor strokes, awaits her own death. Throughout the narrative, in relation to his theme of atonement, McEwan also explores the role of society, the individual, and the novelist in a world where there appears to be no higher authority. Through its three main sections, the book thus asks a number of questions: without God, how and from whom can the individual find forgiveness for crimes against the dead, particularly unwitting crimes committed as a child; how can nations and individuals find reparation for the horror of war; and how can the novelist, as Briony becomes, find expiation in a 'fictional' world of her own creation? (AT, 371).

While its story of the relationship between two sisters seems to draw on many texts, from Austen's *Sense and Sensibility* to George Eliot's *Middlemarch*, *Atonement* is a novel in the country-house tradition for its first section. It is reminiscent of the many precedents provided by the interwar period itself, from Henry Green and Rosamond Lehmann to Elizabeth Bowen and Ivy Compton Burnett. Perhaps most of all, however, *Atonement* recalls the work of Henry James, whose *What Maisie Knew*, along with L. P. Hartley's *The Go-Between*, stands behind McEwan's story of an adult's world seen through the eyes of a child. Where the children of *The Cement Garden* had to wake up to the outside world after their 'lovely sleep', Briony has carried her childhood mistake all her life, and having atoned in the only way she feels she can, looks forward to escaping the albatross of the past – 'But now I must sleep' is *her* final line.

In McEwan's work, childhood is a sleep from which everyone must awaken to face an adult world where their former actions will have unforeseen consequences. Childhood is also a realm adults seek to control but to which they also seek to return. McEwan additionally puts under scrutiny the potentially insidious influence of adults on children through writing, whether it be childcare manuals or adventure fiction.

7.3. Key Works: *The Child in Time, Enduring Love*

In *The Child in Time*, a young married children's author living in London, Stephen Lewis, remembers how he lost his three-year old daughter in a supermarket. Kate's disappearance seems to mock any belief that an individual can confidently foresee and plan for the future, despite the fact that life requires each person to attempt to do precisely this. Yet, the attempt to police and prescribe childcare, evident for example when Tony Blair appointed the first Minister for Children in June 2003, followed by a children's commissioner for England created by the Children's Bill in March 2004, can become overly intrusive and regulatory.

The Child in Time's nine chapters all begin with an excerpt from a fictional 'Authorised Childcare Handbook' that is to be prepared by a body informed by the government-appointed think-tank on which Stephen sits: the sub-committee on Reading and Writing. Each chapter of the novel also focusses on an aspect or experience of childhood that an adult cannot escape. For example, the reader is introduced to how Stephen established himself as a children's author. Aiming to become the new James Joyce or Thomas Mann, he wrote a novel called 'Lemonade' which landed by mistake on the desk of a publisher's editor of children's fiction. It becomes a runaway success as a book for children, rather than as the great modern novel Stephen intended it to be. Once again, Stephen's hope that he can plan the future, let alone control his world, is mocked.

Central to the book's concerns with the relationship between child and parent is an uncanny and inexplicable vision Stephen has while travelling to see his estranged wife Julie in the country. It is a glimpse of his parents at the moment that his mother was deciding whether to terminate her pregnancy when she was carrying him. The mutual vision across time results, in the past, in Stephen's mother deciding to keep her baby and, in the narrative's present, in Stephen witnessing a crisis point that nearly resulted in his mother 'losing' him as he did Kate. Subsequently, the reader learns a great deal about Stephen's own childhood as he listens to a debate over how children learn, particularly in relation to language, at one of the sub-committee meetings. The connection between government policy and private practice is pointed up by the entrance of the Prime Minister, who is significantly described as 'the nation's parent'.

Equally symbolically important is a second eventful journey Stephen takes and which is marked by a life-changing incident. This strange experience signals the beginning of Stephen's maturation into a 'good parent'. He is involved in a car accident with a lorry and has to pull the driver out of his cab window in a scene redolent with birth imagery. For some critics it is also one of the moments in the book where McEwan allows Stephen not so much to empathize with, as usurp women's experience – as arguably happens when Stephen, in the vision across time, makes up his own mother's mind to bear him, and when he delivers Julie's baby at the end of the novel.

This first half of the book is set in oppressive heat but the second begins shortly before Christmas when it has rained 'every day for fifty days' (CT, 123). It is another turning point in Stephen's life, as it is in the year. Stephen is still obsessed by Kate's disappearance two and a half years earlier: he watches children on television and buys children's toys, which seem to be both presents for the missing Kate and sources of comfort for himself. Still unable fully to accept that Kate is no longer a living presence in his life, he convinces himself that he has seen her in a playground and demands that she be released to him, until the school's headteacher is able to persuade him that the girl is not in fact his daughter. As well as illustrating the stages of grieving and loss, Stephen's obsession with Kate is used by McEwan to suggest an inability to accept adult responsibility, a trait that is particularly associated with men in the novel. Accepting the responsibility of being a parent is tied with the act of letting go of childhood.

This is denied to Stephen's friend and publisher, the childless Charles Darke who has himself regressed to a childhood world of fizzy pop and tree-houses. Following a visit by the Prime Minister,

Stephen learns of Charles's death. He also finds out that the newly released 'Authorised Childcare Handbook' was not produced from any evidence provided by Stephen's sub-committee but written by Charles under the parental, possibly sexual, tutelage of the Prime Minister. The childless, regressive Charles is thus portrayed as the inadequate or immature adult, unsuited to proper childcare (care of his own inner child), just as the genderless Thatcherite Prime Minister emerges as the novel's 'bad parent'.

In *The Child in Time*'s final chapter, Stephen sets off with the exuberance of a boy on the narrative's final journey, a long-train ride. He is seeking reconciliation with Julie, which seems to be achieved with the birth of their second child soon after Stephen's arrival. The nine chapters of the book thus appear to have been equivalent or in some sense parallel to the nine months of a baby's gestation, suggesting the growth of a child or an individual, from an embryonic state to birth when fully formed. Like that of the nation's Prime Minister, the baby's sex is not revealed to the reader, exemplifying the novel's themes of uncontrollable life-factors and the social construction of gender. The complexities of life and its unpredictability are at all points in the novel represented by the theme of time, which takes each person out of an unalterable past, through a known stable moment of the present into an uncertain, contingent future. This theme is most fully explored when Stephen recounts his vision to Charles Darke's wife Thelma, a physics lecturer who details the conjectural possibilities that theoretical science could offer to explain such a curvature in time as Stephen's glimpse of his own past.

However, McEwan's overriding concern is with how society is reflected in its attitude towards childcare, and how the theories and practice of looking after children change over time. He has said of the novel's own conception:

What comes out of [Christina Hardyment's book *Dream Babies*] quite wonderfully is how any age distils itself into its childcare books. The way we look after our children or the way experts advise us to look after our children has a lot to do with how we want to be, the ideal, the dream selves we aspire to. You get late 18th century books that are very much influenced by Rousseau, then mid-Victorian harshness, then Edwardian sentimentality. The '20s and '30s in this century were dominated by the rise of the social sciences and therefore generate, too, their own harshness. The postwar era was dominated by Spock and again, libertarian, optimistic ideas of human nature. The thought that crossed my mind was – what next? I imagined, given the collapse of the libertarian consensus as a dominating force in British and American society, that the next childcare book could be authoritarian and that the state could write it.   (quoted in Slay, 'Vandalizing Time': 128)

* * *

Enduring Love (1997) starts with one of the most arresting scenes in contemporary fiction, when John Logan falls to his death from an escaped hot air balloon. This horrific event deeply affects the narrator Joe Rose, a freelance science writer, and his partner Clarissa, a Romanticist English lecturer, but it is subsequent events and not this initial incident, as was the case with the loss of Kate in *The Child in Time*, that pull the couple apart. Shortly after the balloon episode, Jed Parry contacts Joe because he believes that he and Joe forged a profound connection in the emotional intensity of the tragedy. Parry begins to show signs of an obsession, and his interest in Joe is apparently religious, though there is a suggestion of sexual desire in his proclamation of love. Only Joe is fully aware of this intense infatuation, which Clarissa thinks Joe is exaggerating and possibly even fabricating.

From this state of affairs, the book takes the reader through the narrative with three perspectives available. There is Joe's scientific, empirical appreciation of the 'facts' he thinks he is presented with: Parry is deluded and increasingly dangerous. There is Clarissa's sceptical, psycho-emotional response, which sees Joe's reaction as overblown and a sign of something else ('her father died of Alzheimer's, and it's always been a fear that she'll live with someone who goes crazy' (E, 83)). For most of the narrative, the reader is unsure which of them is correct. Also, however, there is the perspective of Jed Parry, who claims that a profound moment of religious connection has occurred. While Joe appears the victim of a homo-erotic obsession (described in an appendix as de Clérambault's syndrome), there is no means by which, until near the end of the novel the reader can know which of the characters' various views are true, though the narrative perspective is

Joe's (one chapter is imagined from Clarissa's point of view and Parry's letters are reprinted). Joe and Clarissa, who in a sense live in different professional worlds, are estranged from each other by the intervention of this unexpected, unwanted third person who occupies a radically different perspective on the important aspects and values of life. As Joe, who seeks to be objective in a world of parallax and relativity, decides: 'there isn't only one system of logic' (E, 214). Consequently, McEwan makes much of Joe's professional interest in science and rationalism, ranging from evolutionary psychology to logical positivism, while Clarissa's perspective is represented by her passion for Keats's poetry and the belief that 'truth is beauty' (from Keats's 'Ode on a Grecian Urn').

Three important scenes introduce sidelights on to these different perspectives. First, there is Joe's visit to see Mrs Logan, the widow of the man killed in the balloon accident. In a way that parallels Clarissa's mistrust of Joe, Jean Logan seems less concerned with her husband's death than with her suspicion, based on circumstantial evidence, that he was having an affair (at the end, when she is proved wrong, Jean Logan, obsessive like Jed Parry, with her own view of things is akin to Briony Tallis in that she feels unable to achieve forgiveness or atonement). Second, there is Clarissa's birthday lunch: an exploration of viewpoint and memory centred on the characters' different explanations of why a man near them in the restaurant is shot. Third, there is the chapter in which Joe procures a gun to protect himself from Parry, because he is convinced that it was he who was supposed to be shot in the restaurant. Each of these scenes shows multiple perspectives on events, with characters voicing arguments that are based on reason or emotion, intuition or logic. McEwan stresses the element of interpretation by repeatedly tempting the reader to disbelieve Joe and speculate on whether he might be mistaken or disingenuous as he arms himself and prepares to injure another human being.

McEwan's aim in the book is to present a narrator with a particular cast of mind that is often treated sceptically by novelists: a strong materialist perspective that analyses life through a combination of game theory and evolutionary science. The reader may be hostile to Joe's mindset but McEwan wishes to emphasize its virtues: logic, rationality, and empirically grounded argument. For example, when, Joe and Clarissa go to see Jean Logan, it is revealed that as a result of Joe's inquiries, John Logan was not having an affair, as his wife believed, but had given a lift to two secret lovers, the evidence of whose presence in the car Jean had misinterpreted. As Logan's fidelity is restored to his wife but she has to assume the burden of her own misplaced suspicions, Joe and Clarissa appear reconciled as they explain to the Logan children the invisible forces that hold the world together: a factual explanation that has clear symbolic resonances for human relationships.

The book concludes with two appendices. The first purports to be a case history of Jed Parry's syndrome, while the second is a letter written three years later to Joe by Parry from what would appear to be a psychiatric hospital. The novel thus has three endings, each of which focusses on a different perspective, the emotional/intuitive, the clinical/scientific, and the religious/ impassioned, reflecting the temperaments and logics of the three main characters. Concerned with an understanding of human nature existing at the intersection of biology, anthropology, and psychology, *Enduring Love*, like much of McEwan's writing, emerges as an exploration of, and exercise in, competing narratives and interpretations. Love is itself one of those forces which can be explained in different ways. Clarissa sees it in terms of Romantic ideals, Parry understands it as a gift of God, while Joe has a scientific worldview, in which human beings are like 'two atoms of hydrogen, one of oxygen, bound together by a mysterious powerful force' (E, 225): as he and Clarissa remain bound together – or perhaps as Parry has been bound to them.

References and Further Reading

Christina Byrnes, *The Work of Ian McEwan: A Psychodynamic Approach*, Nottingham: Paupers' Press, 2002.
John Haffenden, *Novelists in Interview*, London: Methuen, 1985, 168–90.
David Malcolm, *Understanding Ian McEwan*, Colombia, South Carolina Press, 2002.
Ian McEwan, *The Cement Garden* (C), London: Vintage, 1997.
——, *The Comfort of Strangers* (CS), London, Vintage, 1997.
——, *The Child in Time* (CT), London: Picador, 1988.
——, *Enduring Love* (E), London: Vintage, 1998.
——, *Amsterdam* (A), London: Vintage, 1998.
——, *Atonement* (AT), London: Jonathan Cape, 2001.

Jago Morrison, 'Narration and Unease in Ian McEwan's Later Fiction' *Critique*, 42:3, Spring 2001, 253–70

Angela Roger, 'Ian McEwan's Portrayal of Women', *Forum for Modern Language Studies*, 32:1, 1996, 11–27.

Kiernan Ryan, *Ian McEwan*, Writers and their Work, Plymouth: Northcote. 1994.

Judith Seaboyer, 'Sadism Demands a Story: Ian McEwan's *The Comfort of Strangers*', *MFS: Modern Fiction Studies*, 45:4, 1999, 957–86.

Jack Slay, *Ian McEwan*, Twayne's English Authors Series, Boston, MA: Twayne. 1996.

Web Reading

Key website: http://www.ianmcewan.ws/

Interview: http://www.randomhouse. com/boldtype/1298/mcewan/index. html

8

Salman Rushdie: A Long Geographical Perspective

Morality, judgment, character ... It all starts with memory.

(MC, 381)

8.1. Literary History

From a Muslim family background, Salman Rushdie (b.1947) is an imaginative fabulist and a secular humanist who has become a central figure in debates over the tensions between the right to freedom of speech and the religious and legislative sanctions against blasphemy. He is an author who has always embraced his cultural hybridity as a position that allows both a richer mix of experience for his writing and a better appreciation of the post-colonial condition. The borderline position occupied by Rushdie, like Omar Khayyam in *Shame*, is one that he believes makes him uniquely placed to perceive the differences between ethnocentric histories. Rushdie elsewhere argues that expatriate writers, having what he calls a 'long geographical perspective', are able to offer alternative histories to the official ones because they are situated within neither of the dominant ideologies.

Rushdie's first novel, *Grimus* (1975), is a hybrid of Asian and Norse mythology. The book is especially indebted to pre-Islamic Persian mythology, notably the twelfth-century Sufi poem *The Conference of Birds* (Rushdie's title is an anagram of 'Simurg(h)', the name of the huge, sagacious king of birds). It is the consistently experimental use of language that links Rushdie's first published novel with his second. He has said:

> Most people in India are multilingual, and if you listen to the urban speech patterns there you'll find it's quite characteristic

180

that a sentence will begin in one language, go through a second language and end in a third. It's the very playful, very natural result of juggling languages. ... When I was writing *Midnight's Children*, I was really trying to say that the way in which English is used in India has diverged significantly from standard English. That India has made its own English the way America and Ireland and the Caribbean and Australia made their own English. But even though this is the way everybody speaks in India, nobody had the confidence, when I started writing, to use it as a literary language.   ('Salon Interview')

Rushdie has elsewhere admitted that there were precedents for his experiments in Indian English, citing G. V. Desani's unjustly neglected *All About H. Hatterr* (1949) as an obvious major influence.

   Midnight's Children (1981), whose story runs from 1910 to 1976, gained its title from the speech of the first Indian Prime Minister, Jawaharlal Nehru, delivered at the stroke of midnight, 14–15 August 1947, as India seceded from the British Empire. The narrator and central character of the book is Saleem Sinai, who was born at the moment of Independence and whose life seems to mirror that of the new country – even his face is analogous to a map of the subcontinent (MC, 231). Saleem forms a group with the other 1000 children born at Independence, and their 1001 stories become a modern-day *Arabian Nights*. The children and their fates become a metaphor for the betrayed hopes of the 'tryst with destiny' Nehru spoke of in the nation's inaugural speech, with the novel culminating at the time of the dictatorial State of Emergency declared by Nehru's daughter, the new Prime Minister Indira Gandhi in the mid-1970s (cf. 'The Free Radio' in *East, West*).

   Just as *Midnight's Children* is a history of postcolonial India, Rushdie's next novel, *Shame* (1983), is a parodic fictional treatment of the history of Pakistan since Independence in 1947: 'the country in this story is not Pakistan, or not quite' (S, 29). A predominantly Islamic state in the Indian subcontinent, Pakistan was the dream of Mohammed Ali Jinnah (first governor-general of Pakistan) and his Moslem League in British India. The country was constituted as a dominion under the Indian Independence Act of 1947, becoming a republic on 23 March 1956. Its two halves, West and East Pakistan, either side of India, became respectively Pakistan and Bangladesh when the East declared its Independence in 1971. Pakistan then left the Commonwealth in protest at the recognition of Bangladesh in January 1972. From its inception Pakistan suffered from disunity, not least because of its constitution as two geographical regions, initially known up to 1956 as Pakistan and its province of East Bengal, separated by 1100 miles of Indian territory. Yet, the world represented in *Shame* is unreal, is fantastic. The narrator says: 'My story, my fictional country exist, like myself, at a slight angle to reality' (S, 29).

Shame thus focusses on a country which is and isn't Pakistan. The novel is a fable, an allegory, and a fairy tale. Rushdie's most postmodernist novel, *Shame* appears to deny that the country it aims to discuss can be represented other than mythically. Pakistan is thus said to be a 'failure of the dreaming mind' (S, 87; cf. the 'collective failure of imagination' in India, MC, 118). Much of this is linked to the idea that Pakistan is an 'invented' country, split in two at birth in 1947 and carved out of an Indian parent (mother for Rushdie) but previously ruled over by the now-departed patriarchal authority of the Raj. However Rushdie says that his 'hero' Omar Khayyam, 'who is not even the hero of his own life' (S, 24), doesn't really know whether his father was Indian or British: 'choose yourself a father and you also choose an inheritance'. Rushdie says that this also required the negation or covering up of Indian history together with its centuries of tradition and custom; so, in *Shame* the narrator explains 'every story one chooses to tell is a kind of censorship, it prevents the telling of other tales' (S, 71). Lastly, in his twining together of factions, countries, and individuals who try to separate themselves into compartments, Rushdie also tries to take apart the distinctions between East and West, for example in his allusions to the French Revolution: 'The people are not only like Robespierre. They, we, are Danton too. We are Robeston and Danpierre ... Iskander Harappa was not just Danton; Raza Hyder wasn't Robespierre pure-and-simple' (S, 241–2).

The Jaguar Smile: a Nicaraguan Journey (1987) is a cross between a travel diary and a critique of South American politics in the vein but not the style of V. S. Naipaul's non-fictional accounts of his journeys in India and Africa. It was followed by *The Satanic Verses* (1988) a novel that was banned in India and South Africa, burned on the streets of Bradford, and brought to world attention by the *fatwa* decreed by the Ayatollah Khomeini on 14 February 1989. It begins with Gibreel Farishta and Saladin Chamcha, two Indian actors, falling to earth when an Air India jumbo jet explodes 30 000 feet above the English Channel (an Air India Boeing 747 was indeed blown up in 1985, supposedly by a Sikh terrorist). Gibreel Farishta is the name in Urdu of the Angel Gabriel: the archangel regarded by Islam as delivering the *Koran* to Muhammad from God. The novel's chief intertextual concern is thus not with 'English' literature but *The Koran* and yet its setting is neither India nor Pakistan but Ellowen Deeowen, or London. In Rushdie's fourth novel, the Empire comes home to roost, and despite the greater fame of *The Satanic Verses* for the furore surrounding its critique of Islam, it is deeply critical of the West and of neo-colonial attitudes, especially the new empire within Britain (IH, 129–38).

Like those of other postcolonial writers, one of Rushdie's basic moves is to switch positions around, as when he writes of modern day migration, or colonialism-in-reverse: 'Native and settler, that old dispute, continuing now upon soggy streets, with reversed categories' (SV, 353). Again inverting colonial mimicry, Rushdie has his chief anglophile in *The Satanic Verses* observe that it is the English who are unable to live up to the standards of their national identity: 'For a man like Saladin Chamcha the debasing of Englishness by the English was a thing too painful to contemplate' (SV, 75). Chamcha's received colonial and stereotypical Englishness is something he himself has to maintain as the English do not: 'The Alps, France, the coastline of England, white cliffs rising to whitened meadowlands. Mr Saladin Chamcha jammed on an anticipatory bowler hat' (SV, 86–7).

Rushdie says of *The Satanic Verses* that it is a celebration of miscegenation and '*how newness enters the world*. It is the great possibility that mass migration gives the world, and I have tried to embrace it. *The Satanic Verses* is for change-by-fusion, change-by-conjoining. It is a love-song to our mongrel selves' (IH, 394). His work thus involves the revision of national identity in the light of postcolonial migrations and of selves constituted more by displacement and diaspora than by notions of 'home' and 'belonging'.

Rushdie's only work for children is *Haroun and the Sea of Stories* (1990). It tells of a boy whose mother leaves his father, Rashid, a great storyteller. When Haroun finds that his father's stories have dried up, the two of them embark on a magical journey to find out how to bring them back – how to get the 'storyline' reconnected. Haroun's adventures take him to the earth's invisible moon where the 'sea of stories' is being poisoned and blocked by a Cultmaster, Khattam-Shud. After encountering numerous fantastical characters and facing many trials, Haroun defeats the evil sorcerer by using 'wishwater' and the book ends happily with the 'artificial' story return of Haroun's mother. Like *Midnight's Children*, the narrative borrows from the *Arabian Nights* (many of which feature the Caliph of Bombay Haroun al-Rashid) and is an imaginative treatment of Rushdie's own position after the *fatwa* as well as a parody of Khomeini: ' "Khattam-Shud," he said slowly, "is the Arch-Enemy of all Stories, even of Language itself. He is the Prince of Silence and the Foe of Speech" ' (HSS, 39).

East, West (1994) contains three stories in each of its three sections, 'East', 'West', and 'East, West'. Its themes of home, exile, and belonging are suggested by the completion of the nineteenth-century proverb: 'East, west, Home's best', a variant on the similarly old homily 'There's no place like home', most famous from *The Wizard of Oz*. The East stories are set in modern India and concern deception and thievery. Though slight tales, they suggest that only false happiness is offered by dreams of escape from ordinary life focussed on migration, materialism, Bollywood, and religion. The middle section is more fantastical and revisionist, approaching the West in terms of its canonical literature, film mythology and imperial history. The central tale, 'At the Auction of the Ruby Slippers', hinges on the sale of the magic shoes from *The Wizard of Oz* (about which Rushdie wrote a book for the British Film Institute in 1992). The slippers promise to take the wearer home when their heels are clicked:

> 'home' has become such a scattered, damaged, various concept in our present travails. There is so much to yearn for. There are so few rainbows any more. How hard can we expect even a pair of magic shoes to work? They promised to take us *home*, but are metaphors of homeliness comprehensible to them, are abstractions permissible? Are they literalists, or will they permit us to redefine the blessed world?   (EW, 93)

The collection's final three stories have a shared theme of Indians in Britain, of the East in the West. They concern kinds of confusion and delusion, focussing on: a mystically inspired writer's paranoid schizophrenia and suicide; two Indian agents living out their mission in the days after Indira Gandhi's assassination through the coded world of *Star Trek*; and a stroke victim's traumatic attack by 'Beatle thugs' which brings back his normal speech. Diversions more than impressive stories in their own right, the nine tales of *East, West* are most helpfully considered as further explorations of hybridity, like all Rushdie's work but particularly the large novels that surround it in his oeuvre.

Rushdie's next novel was another major work, *The Moor's Last Sigh* (1995). The narrative centres not on the end of the official East–West relationship, like *Midnight's Children* and *Shame*, but on its beginnings with the spice trade:

> Cochin was the site of the first contact between India and the West, a kind of science fiction moment if you like, a meeting of two species. So the meeting and mingling of these two cultures was, you could say, my subject. And I thought I should begin at the beginning, start with the first contact in Cochin, of the activities of Vasco da Gama and his death there and burial and subsequent Eva Peron-like, post-death migration to Portugal. And it was my thought that I would start with Vasco and give him this furious dynasty. And so, really, the book grew from that germ, this image I had.   ('Salon Interview')

The moor of the title is Moraes Zogoiby, born the only son of a Portuguese Goan family in 1957. He is a child afflicted with accelerated growth, which is another of Rushdie's literalisations:

> I just thought that there is something in the air at the moment, that people think everything is speeding up, the pace of life, the rate of change, everything just seems to be going zooooom! And I thought that if there is this widespread sense of the acceleration of things, one way of crystallizing it was to make it happen to someone in a very literal way.   ('Salon Interview')

The story is narrated by the Moor from his prison on the Iberian Peninsula, where he is required to write his family history before he is killed by his captor, his mother's ex-lover Vasco Miranda. The Moor's father is a south-Indian Jew supposedly descended from the last Muslim sultan of Granada, while his mother is a famous

painter whose Christian family can trace its history back to Vasco da
Gama, the Portuguese navigator who discovered the route to India
around the Cape of Good Hope, arriving in Kerala in May 1498.
Another complex novel, its themes are familiar from Rushdie's earlier work: language, religion, miscegenation and the failure of the
postcolonial world to deliver on its promises (MLS, 51).

Spanning the period from the 1930s to the 1980s, *The Ground
Beneath Her Feet* (1999) is an exploration of popular and classical
mythology, playing ancient stories of Gods against modern ones.
Like most of Rushdie's fiction, this is a tale of migration which in
this case moves from India to England to America. The three principal characters are all linked back to Bombay: the beautiful and
gifted musician Ormus Cama, son of Parsee Anglophiles, is a surviving child of twins who is haunted by his dead brother; Rai, or
Umeed Merchant, a famous photographer in fear of his life, is
another of Rushdie's narrators born in 1947; and Vina Aspara is a
half-Indian, half-American beauty with whom both men fall in
love in Bombay in 1956. Rushdie mines rock legends, and as
usual creates a world history slightly tangential to the 'real' in
order to paint the story of Ormus and Vina's rise to pop fame.
Ormus develops fantastical 'double vision' when he recovers
from a coma after a car-crash, while Vina, on the fateful
14 February 1989, dies in an earthquake and is immortalized by
her fans. Now both stars are dead, Rai tells their story from his
place 'in a corner of their lives'. Especially indebted to the myth
of Orpheus, whose lyre adorns the book's hardback cover, *The
Ground Beneath Her Feet* is an epic love story centring on Vina and
Ormus' formation of a group called VTO, a pun on U2, the band
who released lyrics from the novel on their single, also called 'The
Ground Beneath Her Feet'. The novel thus takes Rushdie fully
into the world of 'popular culture', but both words are under
inquiry in the text.

> What's a "culture"? Look it up. 'A group of micro-organisms
> grown in a nutrient substance under controlled conditions.' A
> squirm of germs on a glass slide is all …
> In India it is often said that the music I'm talking about is pre-
> cisely one of those viruses with which the almighty West has
> infected the East, one of the great weapons of cultural imperi-
> alism, against which all right-minded persons must fight again
> and again … why raise low culture so high, and glorify what is
> base? Why defend impurity, that vice, as if it were a virtue?

Such are the noisome slithers of the enslaved micro-organisms, twisting and hissing as they protect the inviolability of their sacred homeland, the glass laboratory slide.   (GBF, 95)

The Ground Beneath Her Feet also reminds the reader once more of the importance of language's cultural mix for Rushdie, and especially of modern India's pluralistic vocabulary: 'she could prattle on in Bombay's garbage argot, *Mumbai ki Kachrapati baat-cheet*, in which a sentence could begin in one language, swoop through a second and even a third and then swing back round to the first. Our acroynymic name for it was *Hug-me*: Hindi Urdu Gujarati Marathi English' (GBF, 7).

In 1999 Rushdie also published his adapted screenplay of *Midnight's Children*, which was to be a series of five television episodes, each one introduced by Lifafa Das as though they were all parts of his fairground peep-show. The series was commissioned as a BBC project but never came to fruition because the governments, first of India and then Sri Lanka, refused permission to film. In his Introduction to the screenplay Rushdie reiterates his belief that the book was about a boy 'handcuffed to history' because of the coincidence of his birth with Indian Independence and that its roots were in Rushdie's impulse to write about his memories of growing up in Bombay/Mumbai. The failure of the film project had a major impact on Rushdie: 'the rejection of *Midnight's Children* changed something profound in my relationship with the East. Something broke and I'm not sure it can be mended' (MCS, 12). Despite Rushdie's feelings about the failure of the film project, a new stage dramatization by Simon Reade, Tim Supple and Rushdie was premiered at London's Barbican by the Royal Shakespeare Company in early 2003.

Unsurprisingly, given Rushdie's comments about the failed attempt to film *Midnight's Children, Fury* (2001) emerged as probably his least Eastern novel to date. It is the contemporary story of a fifty-five-year-old retired Cambridge historian of ideas, Professor Malik Solanka, who has suddenly left his (second) wife and son to begin a new life in New York. Solanka has created an animated doll, Little Brain (named after Winnie the Pooh), which has become a cult figure with its own TV series. He becomes involved with two women: Mila, who looks like Little Brain, and Neela Mahendra, a beautiful freedom fighter. *Fury* is a second novel suffused with popular culture and it is very much immersed in the atmosphere of New York, yet the narrative is somewhat darker in tone than

Rushdie's earlier work, not least because of the constant feeling of anger that surrounds Solanka and also hides just under his surface: 'Life is fury, he'd thought. Fury – sexual, Oedipal, political, magical, brutal – drives us to our finest heights and coarsest depths. Out of *furia* comes creation, inspiration, originality, passion, but also violence, pain, pure unafraid destruction, the giving and receiving of blows from which we never recover' (F, 30–1).

Rushdie has also edited *The Vintage Book of Indian Writing: 1947–1997* (1997 with Elizabeth West) and published with Granta two short works in response to the *Satanic Verses* affair: *Is Nothing Sacred* (1990) and *In Good Faith* (1990), which are included in the volume that is the best guide to his work and thought, a collection of essays and criticism entitled *Imaginary Homelands* (1991). A second volume of essays, *Step Across This Line: Collected Non-Fiction 1992–2002*, followed in 2003.

In 1992, Angela Carter called Rushdie Britain's most remarkable writer. His record to that year made the comment easily defensible in that, on the one hand, his output had been extremely impressive up to that date, and on the other hand, his continuing death-sentence also made him widely talked about. However, since the mid-1990s each of his works has met with further-attenuated critical praise. *The Moor's Last Sigh*, published almost a decade ago, was perhaps his last notable achievement and there is a growing suspicion among readers that, like some others of his generation, his best work may be behind him.

8.2. Themes: Identity and History

In *Midnight's Children*, Saleem has resolved to write down his story because he is 'falling apart' (MC, 109). As a metonym for India, the world's largest democracy, Saleem is fragmenting into 630 million pieces, one for each member of the population, as the country falls into Mrs Gandhi's Emergency of 1975–77. Saleem wants to prevent the 'amnesiac nation' forgetting history by telling *his* story, which is parallel to India's: 'while Indians headed blindly towards a military débacle, I, too was nearing ... a catastrophe of my own' (MC, 300). The identity of the individual and the nation are thus intertwined, such that: 'To understand just one life, you have to swallow the world' (MC, 109).

Saleem claims that in India 'Our names contain our fates' (MC, 304), and in *Midnight's Children* there is a plurality of appellations, such that identity shades into multiplicity. Saleem is 'Snotnose, Stainface, Sniffer, Baldy, Piece-of-the-moon' (MC, 118, cf. 9), while other characters change names regularly. Nadir Khan becomes Lal Quasim, Naseem Aziz becomes Reverend Mother, Mumtaz Aziz becomes Amina Sinai. Identities are also pluralized by the many cases of mistaken parentage. So, Saleem's parents should not be Ahmed and Amina but Vanita and Wee Willie Winkie, though his real father is the Englishman Methwold. Again, Parvati's baby is not Saleem's son but his alter-ego, Shiva's, whose real parents are Saleem's false ones. This element of the narrative is complemented by the many transformations in the book. 'In the Sundarbans', in which the man-dog Saleem (called 'Buddha') deserts from the army, has been said to be key to the novel because it homes in on the key theme of metamorphosis, derived from the central metaphor of the novel, of (re)birth, signaled by the novel's first lines. Rushdie has said that 'In the Sundarbans' is the descent into hell of the epic and it is the chapter that most clearly represents a flight from reality into dreams: time and space are distorted, and the soldiers are tormented, purged of their crimes, to be reborn when they find the temple of the goddess Kali. In more general terms, the story repeatedly focuses on the Indian talent for non-stop regeneration (against Indira Gandhi's sterility programme), because it is through birth that newness enters the world: 'No new place is real until it has seen a birth' (MC, 102).

In Rushdie's writing, almost everything, whether countries, individuals, or experiences, is made up of bits and pieces; such that, in *Shame* the narrator says he is 'forced to reflect the world in fragments of broken mirrors' (S, 69). In many ways this is a reaction to the totalizing systems of colonialism, where marginality has been an effective ideological weapon, one which relies on notions of a centre, a fatherland or mother country. Omar Khayyam Shakil is therefore a hero 'afflicted from his earliest days, by a sense of inversion, of a world turned upside-down. And by something worse: the fear that he was living at the edge of the world' (S, 21). Even more than *Midnight's Children*, *Shame* is a novel about postcolonial identity: a condition it debates in more terms than fragmentation, repeatedly using images of splitting, liminality, and hybridity.

Pakistan was created in 1947 on either side of India on the basis of Muslim majority populations. A number of splits mark the country's history. Separated by a thousand miles, East and West Pakistan are areas broken off from India. The idea of a divided heritage caused by exile and migration is also important. In 1947, millions of Hindus and Muslims travelled between the new Pakistan and India, many of them having to abandon homes, friends, and livelihoods. So, Pakistan in 1947 is a country split off from India and divided from itself. It is also at the same time set free from the British rule which has been in place for two centuries. A further cleavage occurs when East Pakistan becomes Bangladesh in 1971, and this is reflected in *Shame* by many of the book's characters having split pasts, parents, and personalities.

The theme in *Shame* of liminality, the feeling of being on the threshold, immediately figures Pakistan's position on the border of India. Omar Khayyam, the closest the novel gets to a central character, thinks he is 'a creature of the edge' (S, 24). Also, the notion of the Imperial centre, so common in colonial writing is replaced by a postcolonial concern for the marginalized, and *Shame* begins in the town of Q, a 'remote border town' (S, 11). Omar repeatedly calls himself 'a peripheral man' (e.g. S, 283) who is alien to both paternal and patriarchal roots, like the women of the story, who 'marched in from the peripheries' to tell their tales, such that female stories 'explain' and even 'subsume' the male ones of military history (S, 173).

Appropriate in a book about a country that has bifurcated at birth into two halves, identities in the novel as well as being split, are hybrid: are composites or amalgamations echoing the story of the creation of Pakistan (S, 87). The literary inheritance of an Indian writing in English is inescapably double, as Omar, the 'translated man', sees so clearly because he has an anonymous father and is shared by three mothers, such that he knows who neither of his parents is exactly. This hybrid postcolonial background is pitted against a colonial desire for purity – for keeping 'races' and cultures apart. Rushdie also sees himself as a product of three cultures: India, Pakistan, and Britain. This attitude extends to language of course – Rushdie is an Indian who, because of imperial history, is writing in English – and his narrator in *Shame* says he is 'a translated man. I have been *borne across*' (S, 29). Taken from east to west, Rushdie sees himself in the same light therefore as the Persian poet Omar Khayyam, a writer reconfigured by the West. The sequence of quatrains called *The Rubaiyat of Omar Khayyam* was first published and made known in the West as a translation by Edward Fitzgerald in 1859. Fitzgerald admitted that he had rearranged the order of the stanzas and translated them very freely.

This way in which literature gets rewritten, translated, borne across, also applies to history. Rushdie says in one of his essays:

History is always ambiguous. Facts are hard to establish, and capable of being given many meanings. Reality is built on our prejudices, misconceptions and ignorance as well as on our perceptiveness and knowledge. The reading of Saleem's unreliable narration might be, I believed, a useful analogy for the way in which we all, every day, attempt to 'read' the world. (IH, 25)

In its own attempt to 'read the world', *Midnight's Children* touches on the most prominent moment in early twentieth-century Indian history, the massacre at Amritsar in 1919, but then jumps to the Quit India Riots of 1942 before moving on to Independence in 1947. Post-Independence, the events that the novel focusses on are crises: the 1957 election and subsequent 'language riots' which led to the state of Bombay's partitioning, the Indo-Chinese border war in 1962 and the two Indo-Pakistan wars of 1965 and 1971 (the year East Pakistan became Bangladesh). The story ends after India's first nuclear test in 1974, with the Emergency years from 1975 to 1977. Saleem places himself at the core of this history: he triggers off the violence that leads to the partitioning of Bombay (MC, 192); he is responsible for Nehru's death (MC, 279); and war between India and Pakistan is chiefly conducted to destroy his family (MC, 338), just as Mrs Gandhi's Emergency, with its birth-control campaign (11 million sterilizations) is said to be designed to destroy the MCC. When he develops his mind-reading abilities at age nine, Saleem believes 'I was somehow creating a world' where real people 'acted at my command ... which is to say, I had entered into the illusion of the artist, and thought of the multitudinous realities of the land as the raw unshaped material of my gift' (MC, 174). He also anticipates the end of the novel when he says 'if I had not believed myself in control of the flooding multitudes, their massed identities would have annihilated mine' (MC, 175).

Rushdie's chief magic realist technique in *Midnight's Children*, as it also is in a more fantastic way in *Haroun and the Sea of Stories*, is to 'literalise the metaphor'. Rushdie says that 'reality can have metaphorical content'; therefore, the world can be used as metaphor itself. So, when Amina has a love affair she is so clouded by guilt that a fog literally develops around her.

At one point Saleem argues that 'Reality is a question of perspective; the further you get from the past, the more concrete and plausible it seems – but as you approach the present, it inevitably seems more and more incredible' (MC, 165). He likens this to being too close to a cinema screen such that the spectator cannot see the present clearly, cannot get the whole picture. Rushdie says this is,

> a metaphor for the narrative's movement through time towards the present, and the book itself, as it nears contemporary events, quite deliberately loses deep perspective, becomes more 'partial' ... I felt it would be dishonest to pretend, when writing about the day before yesterday, that it was possible to see the whole picture. I showed certain blobs and slabs of the scene.   (IH, 13)

The image is revived in *The Ground Beneath Her Feet*, when the narrator Rai is told: *'The only people who see the whole picture are the ones who step outside of the frame*. If he was right then this is the subject also. If he was wrong, then the lost are merely lost. Stepping out of the frame, they simply cease to exist' (GBF, 203). The only protection against this is narrative, in story or history. So, working in a pickle factory, Saleem will preserve the past by 'chutnification', with one jar per year of Independence: 'Thirty jars stand upon a shelf, waiting to be unleashed upon the amnesiac nation' (MC, 460). Chutnification thus emerges as Saleem's term for the processes of history and hybridity in India's rich mix of different religions, ethnicities, castes, and allegiances, each group with its own perspective.

The narrator of *Shame* says at one point that the purpose of fiction is to offer alternative histories. Appropriately therefore, the book uses alternative narrative forms to realism: shawls; fairy tales; Bilquis' oral histories; private languages invented by the three sisters; communication through an umbilical cord. Rushdie wants to offer these as different possible versions of the past of an invented country whose history lies elsewhere, in India, and whose important stories are not those of the official reports but of the migrant families uprooted by the partition following Independence.

In *Shame*, history is seen as a weave of narratives, rather like the shawls that Rani Harappa knits in the novel – a series of tableaux rather than a coherent single story. Rushdie's narrator characterizes telling a (hi)story as piecing together the past; like Aadam Aziz's future wife glimpsed in sections, history is made up of parts, creating again a 'world in fragments' (S, 69). This view is reinforced in Rushdie's essays: 'human beings do not perceive things whole; we are not gods but wounded creatures, cracked lenses, capable only of fractured perceptions. Partial beings, in all senses of that phrase' (IH, 12). Less concerned than Saleem to tie together the nation and the individual, the narrator of *Shame* sees history as a construct of power: 'History is natural selection. ... Only the mutations of the strong survive. The weak, the anonymous, the defeated leave few marks' (S, 124).

So, the alternative narratives in *Shame* are placed as a counter-balance to this 'history by natural selection', which is why Rushdie's narrator claims that the 'women seem to have taken over' (S, 173). Though he has been accused of insincerity, because his male narrator has control over the story, Rushdie here is putting forward the view that in order to tell a history that is opposed to the official one, he has to include what has been excluded. Rushdie has likened himself to women in Pakistan because he can be silenced: a 'realist' novel criticizing Pakistan would be censored and its author would run the risk of imprisonment (S, 70). Rushdie thus calls his allegorical overlay a 'palimpsest': a text which lies over another and 'obscures what lies beneath' (S, 87). In a passage that brings to mind *The Satanic Verses* affair, Rushdie's narrator tells the reading authorities (including us) that what he has written is only fiction, 'a sort of modern fairy-tale', and so 'No drastic action need be taken' (S, 70).

Yet Rushdie's narrator also addresses openly the possible objections to his position as insider/outsider writing about the events of Pakistan from England, and in English:

> *Outsider! Trespasser! You have no right to this subject! ... I know: nobody ever arrested me. ... Poacher! Pirate! We reject your author-ity. We know you, with your foreign language wrapped round you*

like a flag: speaking about us in your forked tongue, what can you tell but lies? I reply with more questions: is history to be considered the property of the participants solely? In what courts are such claims staked, what boundary commissions map out the territories? (S, 28)

In *Shame* the reader is informed that when Pakistan was created, the *Indian* history was written out of the Pakistani past. History was rewritten by immigrants, in 'Urdu and English – the imported tongues'. But Pakistan has been *'insufficiently imagined'* and to write the past back into history, it again takes an outsider: 'It is possible to see the subsequent history of Pakistan as a duel between two layers of time, the obscured world forcing its way back through what-had-been-imposed' (S, 87). Rushdie therefore sets himself up as an unofficial chronicler, someone who writes back to the past by writing overlooked or obscured elements of the past back into history.

8.3. Key Works: *Midnight's Children, Shame*

Rushdie writes in his essay 'Imaginary Homelands' that 'Bombay is a city built by foreigners upon reclaimed land; I, who had been away so long that I almost qualified for the title, was gripped by the conviction that I, too, had a city and a history to reclaim' (IH, 10). But, he says, reclamation means we 'create fictions, not actual cities or villages, but invisible ones, imaginary homelands, Indias of the mind'. *Midnight's Children*, in which Saleem's father tries to make a fortune from land reclamation, is thus 'one version of all the hundreds of millions of possible versions' (IH, 10).

Midnight's Children is a complex narrative and so a summary of the salient plot elements helps to focus in on its major ingredients. The main story begins in 1915 with Saleem's 'grandfather', the doctor Aadam Aziz, learning to love a landowner's daughter, Naseem, whose body he sees in glimpses through the perforated sheet that is used whenever he goes to treat her various ailments. After they marry, Naseem, also known as 'Reverend Mother', has five children. One of the daughters, Mumtaz, marries Ahmed Sinai when her first husband, the personal secretary of an assassinated Muslim politician, flees his hiding place in the cellar, leaving a note to say that he divorces himself from Mumtaz, with whom he never consummated the marriage. Mumtaz changes her name to Amina and gives birth to a son on the stroke of India's Independence; however at the nursing home a midwife called Mary Pereira swaps the Sinais' baby with another born at the same time. The boy who grows up as Saleem Sinai is therefore in fact the son of an Englishman, Methwold, and a poor woman called Vanita who died in childbirth. After Saleem's father receives an official letter freezing all his assets, Amina gives birth to a daughter, Jamila, a wild child who is known as 'The Brass Monkey'. Saleem, who has grown at a fantastic rate, one day discovers that he has a strange broadcasting ability when a pyjama cord gets stuck up his enormous nose. Using this new power, Saleem forms the 'Midnight Children's Conference' of the 1001 children born in the first hour of Independence.

The Sinais later separate and Amina leaves for Pakistan with the two children – where Saleem finds that his radio ability does not work. The Brass Monkey becomes famous as a vocalist by the name of 'Jamila Singer'. Ahmed and Amina are reconciled in Bombay and they trick Saleem into a nose operation that loses him his telepathic powers. When the family all emigrate to Pakistan, Amina and Ahmed are killed by a bomb in the Indo-Pakistani war of 1965. Saleem joins the Pakistani army, where he loses both his memories and his feelings, but when he is bitten by a snake in the jungle of the Sundarbans he recovers all memories except his name, which it takes an encounter with Parvati-the-Witch for him to recall.

While Saleem has fallen in love with Jamila, Parvati is in love with him and becomes secretly pregnant by Shiva to try to convince Saleem that he is not impotent. Saleem and Parvati marry and she gives birth to a new, enormously eared but unspeaking Aadam in 1975, on 25 June at the stroke of midnight, the turn of the day on which Mrs Gandhi, found guilty of electoral malpractice, declared a State of Emergency and arrested nearly 1000 of her political opponents.

Turning 31 at the end of the book, Saleem expects soon to marry his co-worker, Padma, now that Parvati is dead. However, he is plagued by thoughts of death, not least because he and all the living midnight's children have been operated upon by doctors to make it impossible for them to have more descendants. Hope for the future is only signalled by Saleem's/Shiva's son

Aadam, who suddenly speaks his first word at age three, offering some promise of new worlds about to open: 'Abracadabra'.

Midnight's Children is presented as Saleem's autobiography, narrated in a Bombay pickle factory. He is born with two attributes: the ability to create the uniting 'All-India Radio' and a colossal nose, like his 'grandfather' Aadam: 'comparable only to the trunk of the elephant-headed god Ganesh' (MC, 13; it was to Ganesh, in Hindu mythology the son of Shiva and Parvati, that the story of India, the Mahabharata, was dictated). Saleem is born at the same time as Shiva, and because the babies are switched, Saleem's real mother is in fact a street-musician's wife. Saleem the privileged Muslim should have been a poor Hindu. Much of the speculation of the novel is concerned with wondering which of these two midnight children will lead a life that mirrors that of the nation: Saleem the medium of the Midnight Children's Conference, which represents the democratic, secular, pluralist India that Gandhi envisaged, or the huge-kneed Shiva (creator and destroyer in Hindu mythology), who becomes Mrs Gandhi's war hero but never learns the truth of his parentage. The book's suggestion of hope in a new generation starting with a new Aadam, is for most critics less prominent as an ending than the fact that all India will finally trample Saleem underfoot: 'reducing me to specks of voiceless dust ... sucked into the annihilating whirlpool of the multitudes' (MC, 463).

Before he is lost, however, Saleem attempts to preserve the flavour of India's democratic foundation via the 'chutnification of history' in jars that hold not just food but also 'memories, dreams, ideas' – in recipes ready to be 'unleashed upon the amnesiac nation' (MC, 460). He is aware that the pickling process can result in sharp and unpalatable flavours but he nonetheless intends that the jars will 'possess the authentic taste of truth' (MC, 461). Saleem tells his story to the illiterate vat-stirrer, Padma, as they work together in the pickle factory. Padma's role within the text is clearly a symbolic one. As the masses of India formed into a single identity, she represents a critical incredulity towards the personal and national history Saleem unfolds in his idiosyncratic style.

Saleem's narrative method is imaged in the first chapter's perforated sheet: a metaphor for the way in which the story is revealed piecemeal to uncover an India glimpsed in fragments – 'glued together by [Saleem's] imagination'. Saleem indeed questions his own reliability, interrupts himself, and speculates on whether his story will wash with Padma, who, as a factory worker is closest to the Indian everywoman who must and yet cannot be Saleem's audience. Saleem's problem in telling his story is explained on the first page: 'there are too many stories to tell, too many, such an excess of intertwined lives events miracles places rumours, so dense a commingling of the improbable and the mundane! I have been a swallower of lives; and to know me, just the one of me, you have to swallow the lot as well. Consumed multitudes are jostling and shoving inside me' (MC, 9). The way in which he solves this problem is to assume a number of narrative styles: most prominent is the oral tradition, with its loops and circles, embodied in the boatman Tai, who is as old as memory itself and the source of all storytelling; there is also the explicit use of film techniques – close-up, zoom, long-shot – in a novel where cinema and radio are used to represent the collective life of the nation; plus there are the many slips into folk tale in the repeated 'once upon a time' clauses (e.g. MC, 9, 213).

Saleem himself, who is always also Shiva, is both India and its language, the 'teeming multitudes' and their stories. He says of the foetus growing inside his mother: 'what had been (at the very beginning) no bigger than a full stop had expanded into a comma, a word, a sentence, a paragraph, a chapter; now it was bursting into more complex developments, becoming, one might say, a book – perhaps an encyclopedia – even a whole language' (MC, 100).

* * *

While *Midnight's Children*, for all its sense of failed hopes and pessimism, can be considered a labour of love, *Shame*, as its title implies, is more like an indictment. Several critics have provided a gloss on the novel's tangential relation to Pakistan's history (e.g. see the article by Stephanie Moss in Further Reading below). Iskander Harappa is a caricature of Zulfikar Ali Bhutto (S, 70), Pakistan's only civilian ruler in several decades before being ousted in 1977 by a military coup led by General Zia-ul-Haq, who is fictionalized as Raza Hyder. Harappa's wife is Rani (meaning 'queen'): exiled and silenced she knits the fate of the future and in her truthful storytelling represents the 'soul' of the country. Their daughter is Arjumand Harappa, 'the virgin ironpants', who as Benazir Bhutto will come to govern Pakistan in the years after

Shame's publication. She regrets her sex because it denies her access to power; she argues that she needs to 'rise above her gender' and so wages a war against her body.

The three mothers Chhunni, Munnee, and Bunny Shakil can be read as India before freedom: even in their names they metonymically represent Indian, Pakistani and British influences and are looked after by 'Parsee wet nurses, Christian ayahs, and iron morality' – the last being Muslim fundamentalism (S, 13). The three sisters invent special languages, representing one country divided by different tongues. Their father's death on the novel's first page marks the end of British rule, and the girls' inheritance of his debt: so the sisters sign away their fortune and their fertile land to pay their father's bills. Their shared son is Omar Khayyam, a fragmented and translated man who will always remain on the periphery of his own life as Pakistan exists on the borders of India. He is additionally an image of the poets Rushdie saw exiled from Pakistan since the 1970s and living in England because they have offended the mullahs ruling Pakistan.

Bilquis Kemel is emblematic of Muslim Pakistan during and after the Partition. She finds protection under military rule, by marrying Raza Hyder, who covers her 'shame' with a military overcoat. Their first child, the son they have longed for, is stillborn, while their second is not a boy but a girl, and consequently another manifestation of their 'shame': 'the heroine of our story, the wrong miracle' (S, 119). This anti-heroine is Sufiya Zinobia Hyder, who embodies all of the feelings of dishonour and vengeance in the novel, though she is married to Omar Khayyam, who is shameless (S, 39). In a novel without an obvious central character, this united pair defines its cruel and destructive limits: 'Between shame and shamelessness lies the axis upon which we turn; meteorological conditions at both these poles are of the most extreme ferocious type. Shamelessness, shame: the roots of violence' (S, 115–16).

Sufiya represents the Pakistan that arose after the dust of Partition had settled. Her blood rises constantly to her cheeks – as blushes of shame but also portents of the blood that will be spilled by her on the 'Judgment Day' that ends the novel. In infancy she contracts a disease no one can cure, except the local Hakim's potion of 'Islamic fundamentalism'. Sufiya's vengeful, bloodythirsty side eventually surfaces as an untameable beast, the monstrous apotheosis of her father's aggression (he is Hyde to the Shakil's Jekyll). Rushdie says that Sufiya was born out of two stories. One of a Pakistani woman murdered by her father for sleeping with a white boy; and another of an Asian girl attacked by a group of white teenage boys. Rushdie therefore in part situates Pakistan as a woman destroyed by a patriarchial traditionalism and also by the violence of the West (S, 115 ff.).

Female oppression takes many forms in the novel, but it is brutal policing of sex and reproduction that affects most women characters. For example, Sufiya's sister Naveed 'Good News' Hyder finds herself turned into a breeding machine and finally hangs herself (S, 251). She represents only 'maternal fecundity' for her husband (a militant fundamentalist police chief) who rejects birth control and unites the country but also spawns its evils. Opposed to Good News is Atiyah Aurangzeb, the 'body' of the country fought over and lusted after by Raza and Iskander. Under her sobriquet 'Pinkie' she is the 'white tyranny that ruled over a brown nation for so long'. In the end she is worn out, old before her time.

Shame mythologizes the acts of shame committed when a divided nation was consciously brought into existence at the partitioning of the Indian subcontinent, resulting in mass migration and communal riots. It also aims to chronicle the shamelessness of barbarism that Rushdie thinks characterizes the excesses of military rule and religious persecution in Pakistan since 1947.

References and Further Reading

Lisa Appignanesi and Sara Maitland (eds), *The Rushdie File*, London: Fourth Estate, 1989.

Stephen Baker, 'Salman Rushdie' in *Contemporary British Fiction*, edited by Richard J. Lane, Rod Mengham, and Philip Tew, Cambridge: Polity, 2003, 145–57.

Damian Grant, *Salman Rushdie*, Plymouth, Northcot House, 1999.

John Haffenden, *Novelists in Interview*, London: Methuen, 1985, 231–61.

Cynthia Ho, 'Salman Rushdie', in *British Novelists Since 1960*, Second Series, edited by Merritt Moseley *The Dictionary of Literary Biography*, Volume 194, Detroit: Gale, 1998, 249–61.

Jago Morrison, *Contemporary Fiction*, London: Routledge, 2003, 133–54.

Stephanie Moss, 'The Cream of the Crop', *International Fiction Review*, 19:1, 1992, 28–30.

Susheila Nasta, *Home Truths: Fictions of the South Asian Diaspora in Britain*, London: Palgrave, 2002.

Salman Rushdie, *Midnight's Children* (MC), London: Picador, 1982.

Salman Rushdie, *Shame* (S), London: Picador, 1984.
——, *The Satanic Verses* (SV), London: Viking, 1988.
——, *Haroun and the Sea of Stories* (HSS), Harmondsworth: Puffin, 1993.
——, *Imaginary Homelands* (IH), London: Granta, 1992.
——, *East, West* (EW), London: Jonathan Cape, 1994.
——, *The Moor's Last Sigh* (MLS), London: Jonathan Cape, 1995.
——, *The Ground Beneath Her Feet* (GBF), London: Jonathan Cape, 1999.
——, *The Screenplay of Midnight's Children* (MCS), London: Vintage, 1999.
——, *Fury* (F), London: Vintage, 2002.
David Smale (ed.), *Salman Rushdie: Midnight's Children/The Satanic Verses*, Cambridge: Icon, 2001.
Richard Todd, *Consuming Fiction: The Booker Prize and Fiction in Britain Today*, London: Bloomsbury, 1996.
Twentieth-Century Literature, Special issue on Salman Rushdie, Winter 2001, 47–4.

Web Reading

http://www.trill-home.com/rushdie.html
http://www.januarymagazine.com/profiles/rushdie2002.html
'Salon Interview' (http://www.salon.com/06/features/interview2.html)

9
Zadie Smith: Searching for the Inescapable

9.1. Literary History

Zadie Smith (b.1975) was the first British literary celebrity of the twenty-first century. Her debut *White Teeth* (2000) was released to the accompaniment of a barrage of publicity and seemed to be the most assured first novel by a twenty-four-year-old Oxbridge graduate since Evelyn Waugh's *Decline and Fall* (1928). It is too early to tell, on the strength of only two novels, if Smith's precocious talent will mature but she has been more critically studied and commercially popular than any other new novelist. Of a different generation from the other authors in this study, she presents a more eclectic and exuberant image of modern British society than most writers born in the forties and fifties.

Smith grew up in northwest London, the daughter of a Jamaican mother and an English father. She graduated from Cambridge with a first in English in 1997 already armed with a lucrative contract for a debut novel. Her writing has been compared to that of several other novelists, but most regularly to the work of Salman Rushdie and Hanif Kureishi. *White Teeth* is similar in its use of repetitions, digressions and hyphenated constructions to Rushdie's style, but is closer to Kureishi's in its extensive use of social satire rather than methods that could be likened to those of magic realism. However, what is distinctive about Smith's prose is her extensive use of free indirect speech, and while *White Teeth* generally uses omniscient narration, Smith's narrator employs the vocabulary and speech-mannerisms of her characters when she wants to show events from their perspective (e.g. Archie's encouragement of the FutureMouse, W, 540). With obvious caveats, *White Teeth* can be seen as a *Midnight's Children* for postcolonial Britain. Like Rushdie centring his novel on 1947, Smith takes the year of her own birth and builds around it a national narrative as well as a personal story – especially for Irie but also for Magid/Millat, contrasting Saleem/Shiva figures born at the same moment. The narrative of *White Teeth* both starts before and develops alongside the life of Irie, the author's surrogate figure, who is born at a significant historical moment; yet Irie's birth-year is not that of a nation: it is the year of the proclaimed end of the world, inserted within a spectrum of other key dates: 1857, 1907, 1945, and 1999. 1975 is put forward as a postcolonial year zero for Britain, when the apocalyptic pronouncements of neither the fictional Jehovah's Witness Hortense Bowden nor the real-life anti-immigrationist Enoch Powell are coming true, but a new London is in the process of being born.

Prior to the publication of *White Teeth*, Smith had written fiction for *Granta* and *The New Yorker*. She had also had four stories published between 1995 and 1997 in the annual *May Anthology of Oxford and Cambridge Short Stories*, plus an inclusion in a Penguin anthology edited by Nick Hornby, *Speaking With the Angel*, a collection of monologues published in aid of The Treehouse Trust, a charity for autistic children. Between *White Teeth* and her second novel, Smith wrote three book introductions, to: *The May Anthologies 2001*, the Bloomsbury edition of Lewis Carroll's *Through the Looking Glass and What Alice Found There*, and the Institute of Contemporary Arts short-story volume *Piece of Flesh*, which she also edited (all 2001). She has also written the introductions to *The Best American Nonrequired Reading* (2003), and a collection of contemporary stories from the US: *The Burned Children of America* (2003).

Her first novel catapulted Smith to celebrity status in a way that emphasized her looks and youth over her talent as a novelist, creating a marketing phenomenon that is unrivalled in contemporary British literary fiction and whose success blurred distinctions between her and authors like Nick Hornby and Helen Fielding. Yet there is a sophisticated dissection of society and culture in Smith's fiction that is beyond the scope of most other popular contemporary writers. For example, *White Teeth* is a novel deeply concerned with national identities in a way that undermines the arguments of those who would link Britishness to ethnicity: few people in the book identify with one country or culture, and instead, through the fortunes of war, work, allegiance, heritage, identification, or travel, see either no reflection or too many reflections of themselves in the mirror of history. Magid's Englishness, the Chalfens' Catholic-Jewishness, Millat's Americanness, and even the French Dr Perret's Nazi sympathies are rebuffs to attempts at 'classification' such as Marcus's or cultural coercion such as Samad's. Supplemented by Irie's complex ancestry, these syncretic ethnicities ensure that neither history nor hybridity can be escaped. While it is in some ways less explicitly treated, this concentration on themes of identity and miscegenation in her first novel became a major theme of Smith's next book.

The Autograph Man appeared in 2002. Divided into two parts, with an epilogue and a prologue, the novel tells the story of Chinese-Jewish north Londoner Alex-Li Tandem, the professional autograph collector of the title. In the prologue, the young Alex attends a wrestling match with his father, Li-Jin, and two friends, at the Royal Albert Hall – a Hall explicitly 'ERECTED FOR THE ADVANCEMENT OF THE ARTS AND SCIENCES', but currently being used for neither, because wrestling isn't an art or a science: 'Its TV'. (A, 21) Like his teenage friends, Mark Rubinfine and Adam Jacobs, Alex 'deals in a shorthand of experience. The TV version. He is one of this generation who watch themselves' (A, 2). Like the 'International Gestures' that pepper the book, collecting autographs thus becomes the ultimate expression of a Pitman's culture and the cult of celebrity. At the wrestling match, Alex meets another boy, Joseph Klein, who turns him on to 'philography', which literally means 'a love of writing'. The four boys will grow up to be close friends, but Li-Jin, suffering from a brain tumour, collapses and dies at the end of the bout as Alex runs to get the autograph of the wrestler 'Big Daddy'. This symbolic act of fleeing the real for the artificial characterizes Alex's life until he returns to the memory of his father at the narrative's close.

Book I, set fifteen years later in Mountjoy, the fictional London suburb in which Alex lives, is subtitled: 'The Kabbalah of Alex-Li Tandem'. The chapters proceed according to Alex's version of his friend Adam's diagram of the Jewish mystical tradition:

> ten circles in strange formation. These were, according to Adam, the ten holy spheres, each containing a divine attribute, one of the *sefirot*. Or else they were the ten branches of the Tree

of Life, each showing an aspect of divine power. Or they were the ten names of God, ten ways in which he is made manifest. They were also the ten body parts of Adam, the first man. The Ten Commandments. The ten globes of light from which the world was made. Also known as the ten faces of the king. Also known as the Path of Spheres.   (A, 93)

A professional autograph man, the 27-year-old Alex is now immersed in a lucrative economy of images where everyone he knows is obsessed with celebrity value, commodified identities, and potential forgeries. Alex has the form of 'tunnel vision' called 'fandom' (A, 215) and, partly in consequence, he also has 'no love, no transportation, no ambitions, no faith, no community, no expectation of forgiveness or reward'. While there is too little love or purpose in Alex's life, 'There is so much fame in the world' (A, 202).

Alex is now writing a mammoth book that divides the world into all things Jewish and all things goyish (A, 88–91). He has a long-term girlfriend, Adam's sister Esther: 'black Harlem Jews' living in Mountjoy. But he is also fixated on the Russian-Italian-American star Kitty Alexander, an aging 1950s Hollywood actress to whom he has written weekly for thirteen years. Book One ends with the arrival of the first response he has ever received from Kitty: an autograph.

Book II has a similar structure to book I. Called 'Roebling Heights: The Zen of Alex-Li Tandem', it is modelled on the 'ten bulls' of Zen Buddhism, representing steps in the realization of Alex's 'true nature'. While Esther undergoes an operation to remove her pacemaker (Alex guiltily uses the 'phrase *routine procedure*, stolen from a long-running television show' (A, 267)), her boyfriend takes off to New York, ostensibly for an autograph fair, but actually, in one of the many quests within the novel, to track down Kitty in Brooklyn.

When they are taking a cab from the airport, Alex's travelling companion remarks that he feels he has been in New York before. Alex responds with a list of movies, to which the cab driver then adds several more, with the implication that Hollywood has made the American urban landscape instantly familiar to every cinema-goer, such that it is inevitably both pre-known and radically unknowable. 'Everyone's been here before' is Alex's final comment on the matter (A, 226). The exchange highlights the narrative's interest in vicarious living but also with the idea that almost nothing in the book is expressed directly; feelings and thoughts have to be mediated and the individual has to be aware of their mediation, such that 'It is impossible these days to follow a man or quit a job without an encyclopedia of cinematic gestures crowding you out' (A, 268). It is also a world in which value is traded in a currency of celebrity and worth is gauged by the individual's proximity to fame: Alex's autograph friends are immensely impressed when he meets Honey Smith/Richardson, a Zen Buddhist prostitute notorious for having been caught having sex with a celebrity (the contemporary obsession with the commodification of sex is discussed in Smith's Introduction to *Piece of Flesh*). Honey enlightens Alex as to what celebrity means:

> More people know you than you know people ... see, that's all it is. Ain't nothing more than that, really. It's for amputee people, fame. I mean, people who're missing something vital. That's all. I'll tell you what's messed up too. In my neighbour-hood, I'm a celebrity. Do you believe that? In certain areas of Brooklyn, I'm Elizabeth Taylor.   (A, 255)

Together, Honey and Alex track down Kitty, who is now a reclusive old lady shielded from the world by a controlling 'fan' called Max. They persuade her to return with Alex to London, where he can make Kitty rich by auctioning her autographs and letters. The auction raises even more money than expected because a television news story conveniently claims that Kitty has died, increasing her market value. Alex meanwhile is progressing sufficiently to make the gestures of altruism that will take him closer to enlightenment. Having helped Kitty, he donates his £15 000 commission to a fellow autograph man who is in hospital: Brian Duchamp. It is in this way that *The Autograph Man* moves beyond *White Teeth*, by allowing Alex to develop as a human being, to grow in wisdom in ways denied to the characters of Smith's first novel.

The book ends with Alex realising that the tenth branch, the place at the Crown of the Kabbalah, has to be taken by the hero of his life, his father: the person who most loved him and whose memory he has neglected in pursuit of signs of fame in a world of transience and artifice. The epilogue is Alex's Kaddish: a Jewish prayer recited in the daily ritual of the synagogue and by mourners at public services after the death of a close relative. With this ritual performed, Alex may be able, the book implies, to come to terms with the loss of his father and make some commitments in his own life.

Smith's second novel is a more meditative and personal one than her first. It does not aim towards broad social critique though it is a satire on a generation who Smith thinks needs repeatedly reminding 'YOU ARE NOT WATCHING TV' (A, 181). Alex is a well-drawn character, somewhere between Ishiguro's Christopher Banks in *When We Were Orphans* and Kureishi's Karim Amir in *The Buddha of Suburbia*. But, in distinction from the direct address of these characters, Alex's voice is muted by the mediating presence of the third-person narrator, who speeds knowingly from one shorthand cultural observation to another. The book is as inventive as *White Teeth* but in a very different way, presenting more believable characters but fewer socio-cultural perspectives. Its range of literary as well as contemporary cultural reference is extraordinarily wide, drawing on the writings of authors like Woolf and Kafka, included in Alex's Kabbalah, but also, for example, T. S. Eliot, whose *The Waste Land* is a touchstone for Smith's depiction of twenty-first century twenty-somethings succumbing to emotional virtual reality and in as much need of spiritual re-growth as Eliot's Londoners.

9.2. Themes: Ethnicity, Nationality, and Multiculturalism

White Teeth focuses on three families: the British and Jamaican Joneses; the Bangladeshi Muslim Iqbals; the Jewish and Catholic but atheistic Chalfens. Each of them could be considered to embody or express a different experience of multicultural Britain.

In the words of one chapter title, the Chalfens are taken to be 'more English than the English'. This is because of their liberal middle-class values, and also their empiricism, which is traditionally a core characteristic of Englishness. However, they are also third-generation Poles, originally Chalfenovskys: not more English than the English, but as English as anyone else. Smith rings this theme of hybridity and cross-fertilization through numerous parallels, drawn from horticulture, eugenics, and meteorology. One of the dominant extended metaphors belongs to Joyce Chalfen's 1976 book entitled *The New Flower Power*:

Where once gardeners swore by the reliability of the self-pollinating plant in which pollen is transferred from the stamen to the stigma of the same flower (autogamy), now we are more adventurous, positively singing the praises of cross-pollination where pollen is transferred from one flower to another on the same plant (geitonogamy), or to a flower of another plant of the same species (xenogamy) … Yes, self-pollination is the simpler and more certain of the two fertilization processes, especially for many species that colonize by copiously repeating the same parental strain. But a species cloning such uniform offspring runs the risk of having its entire population wiped out by a single evolutionary event. In the garden, as in the social and political arena, change should be the only constant. Our parents and our parents' petunias have learnt this lesson the hard way. The March of History is unsentimental, tramping over a generation and its annuals with ruthless determination.   (W, 309)

As the title of Joyce's book suggests, being English for the Chalfens is rooted in a set of 1960s images, such that they emerge as 'an ageing hippy couple both dressed in pseudo-Indian garb' (W, 131). Joyce expresses the idea that miscegenation is valuable in itself, and her marriage to Marcus is an expression of their shared belief in 'good genes' rather than 'pure blood'.

The second central family of the book, the Iqbals, have come to England from Bangladesh. Samad arrives in 1973. Like Archie he marries a woman who is much younger than himself: Alsana. Initially, they live in the East End of London but the racism they experience causes them to move to Willesden where Samad knows Archie lives. The Iqbals' second-generation children spend their teenage years apart, the one in London, the other in Chittagong. Each finds his identity is located elsewhere: Millat, living in London, wishes to be an American gangsta-rapper (W, 218) or Hollywood Mafia tough before he becomes in the words of his father a 'fully paid-up green bow-tie wearing fundamentalist terrorist'; while Magid, sent to Bangladesh, becomes 'a pukka Englishman, white suited, silly wig lawyer' (W, 407). It is Magid who insists on a bacon sandwich at the Iraqi Abdul-Mickey's café where the most sacred rule is 'no pork'. Through these unexpected twists in cultural identifications, Magid and Millat's story parodies traditional attempts (opposed to Marcus's modern scientific attempt) at social control, and all their father's endeavours to mould their lives fail.

By contrast to the Chalfens' easy adoption of Englishness, the person in the novel who most considers herself to be 'a stranger in a strange land' (W, 266) is Irie Jones, whose mother is 'from Lambeth (via Jamaica)' (W, 27) and whose father, Archie, is a white war veteran from Brighton. In the novel's terminology, Irie sees no reflection of herself in the 'mirror of Englishness'. This largely explains her attraction to the Chalfens: 'she *wanted* to merge with the Chalfens, to be of one flesh; separated from the chaotic, random flesh of her own family and transgenically fused with another. A unique animal. A new breed' (W, 342).

Also in contrast to the masculine culture of the Iqbals, Irie later turns to her matrilinear heritage, to her grandmother and to Jamaica for a sense of her 'roots' (W, 400) – though she concludes that the idea of belonging is itself a 'lie' and there has to come a time when 'roots won't matter any more' (W, 527). Irie's mother Clara arrives in the UK in 1972 with her own mother, Hortense, several years after her father Darcus. The Bowden family is identified in a female tradition going back through Hortense to her mother Ambrosia, who gave birth to Hortense in the 1907 Kingston, Jamaica earthquake. Hortense's father was the colonial Captain Charlie 'Whitey' Durham; and, in keeping with the history of the family's genealogical chart (W, 338), Irie doesn't know for sure who is the other parent of her own child, Millat or Magid; such that the girl will be 'fatherless ... a puppet clipped of paternal strings' (W, 541). This signals the unpredictability of the future, like the escape of Marcus's mouse at the end of the narrative, but it also continues the mixing of Irie's colonial history, in which fathers have been British (Whitey Durham), Jamaican (Darcus), English (Archie), and now British Bandgladeshi (Magid/Millat).

To underscore the polarized views on multiethnic Britain, Smith introduces the second part of the book with a quotation of the most infamous pronouncement on race relations since Enoch Powell's 'Rivers of Blood' speech in 1968. This is a comment from 1990 by the Conservative politician Norman Tebbit, who mounted an attack on those who in his view had refused to 'assimilate': 'The cricket test – which side do they cheer for? ... are you still looking back to where you came from or where you are?' (W, 123). Samad's response to this expresses the other end of the range of opinion: 'People call it assimilation when it is nothing but corruption' (W, 190). Corruption then becomes Samad's word for cultural diversification, while for Archie how things change seems to be a matter of chance, on which it is virtually pointless to try to assert one's will. Consequently, fundamental beliefs, like Samad's in 'purity', appear to be repeatedly put out-of-joint by the twists of the narrative (such as the sexual advances of Poppy Burt-Jones). 'To the pure all things are pure' is Samad's creed, but no one is pure in the novel: ethically or ethnically. Typical of a book that parodies both ends of opinion from an undefined middle point, Samad's perspective and Tebbit's are equally satirized by the novel.

Samad's attempts at social engineering are no more endorsed by the book, and no more successful, than Marcus Chalfen's genetic engineering of the FutureMouse (whose real life counterpart is the 1988 patented OncoMouse™) that disappears out of the door to Archie's delight on the closing page of the novel. Life in *White Teeth* is itself characterized by contingency, coincidence, and the drive to freedom; and its mutations and permutations celebrate the hybrid and mongrelized rather than the pure and well bred. Consequently, it is Samad's wife Alsana who actually expresses the dominant view of the novel: 'You go back and back and back and it's still easier to find the right Hoover bag than to find one pure person, one pure faith, on the globe. Do you think anybody is English? Really English? It's a fairy-tale' (W, 236). *White Teeth* itself could be considered a fairy-tale in that its view of race-relations, though far from Utopian, seems more closely to resemble hopes for Britain's future – satirized as 'Happy Multicultural Land' (W, 465) – than observations about its past. In Smith's view, that future is not to be engineered like Marcus's mouse, predestined to die after seven years and predetermined to live according to its artificial genetic programming, but enriched by cultural commingling, accident, and chance.

The book thus works politically far more at the level of representation than any kind of confrontation. But it is harsh to expect *White Teeth* to do more than it has. The novel disseminates a multiethnic view of London, where currently over 40 per cent of children are born to at least one black parent (*Guardian*, 11 December 2000). *White Teeth*, as Caryl Phillips concluded in his review of the novel, ably dramatizes the fact that 'The "mongrel" nation that is Britain is still struggling to find a way to stare into the mirror and accept the ebb and flow of history that has produced this fortuitously diverse condition' (Phillips, 286). Smith's horti-multicultural view of Britain is best summarized within the novel by this key passage:

This has been the century of strangers, brown, yellow and white. This has been the century of the great immigrant experiment. It is only this late in the day that you can walk into a playground and find Isaac Leung by the fish pond, Danny Rahman in the football cage, Quang O'Rourke bouncing a basketball, and Irie Jones humming a tune. Children with first and last names on a direct collision course. Names that secrete within them mass exodus, cramped boats and planes, cold arrivals, medical checks. It is only this late in the day, and possibly only in Willesden, that you can find best friends Sita and Sharon, constantly mistaken for each other because Sita is white (her mother liked the name) and Sharon is Pakistani (her mother thought it best – less trouble). Yet, despite all the mixing up, despite the fact that we have finally slipped into each other's lives with reasonable comfort (like a man returning to his lover's bed after a midnight walk), despite all this, it is still hard to admit that there is no one more English than the Indian, no one more Indian than the English. There are still young white men who are *angry* about that; who will roll out at closing time into the poorly lit streets with a kitchen knife wrapped in a tight fist.   (W, 326–7)

Smith's narrative paints a generally optimistic view of multicultural Britain; one that largely directs its gaze away from issues of social difference between ethnic groups. It celebrates diversity by implication while mocking those who try to celebrate it explicitly.

White Teeth thus seems to satirize the excesses of both liberalism and illiberalism. The former is lampooned when Mrs Owens, the headmistress at Manor School, says: 'the school already recognises a great variety of religious and secular events: amongst them, Christmas, Ramadan, Chinese New Year, Diwali, Yom Kippur, Hanukkah, the birthday of Haile Selassie, and the death of Martin Luther King. The Harvest Festival is part of the school's ongoing commitment to religious diversity, Mr Iqbal' (W, 129). While Samad points out that he believes that there aren't any pagans in the school, Mrs Owens's argument simply appears to be that all faiths *must* be represented in the school calendar, and this is supported by a majority of parents, to Samad's annoyance: 'I am certain the Manor School Witches and Goblins will be delighted' (W, 131).

In contrast to this catch-all approach to religious inclusion, many characters in the book are associated with hardcore beliefs, ranging from Hortense Bowden's vision of the world's end to Joshua Chalfen's decision (because he falls in love) to become a frontline animal rights activist, (in)conveniently making his father his number one enemy. Magid becomes a follower of the scientific convictions of Marcus, and so also becomes the friend of his father's enemy, while Millat joins the Keepers of the Eternal and Victorious Islamic Nation, even though he cannot 'purge [himself] of the taint of the West' (W, 444). Most conscious decisions thus seem undercut by personal considerations or undermined by the vagaries of others.

The book repeatedly contrasts individuals' attempts to control their identity and their future with life's unpredictability. For example, Samad tries to determine the future for Magid and Millat, but the twins simply turn out a grotesque reverse parody of his imaginings, while Irie becomes pregnant but cannot know which of Magid or Millat is the father (just as when someone needs to be arrested for shooting Archie, the police witnesses cannot tell the twins apart, confusing evidence and identity). Similarly, Archie tries to avoid making his own decisions by tossing coins, yet it is oddly the act of tossing the coin, rather than its outcome, that gets him shot: twice.

The importance of this repetition is to illustrate that Smith feels history is as inescapable as the here and now. As indicated by the two dates that introduce each part of the novel, Smith is working with the links between past and present. She also eschews linear plot development, preferring to move fluidly between characters and times while allowing the narrative to drift into the future. The culmination of the book's implied viewpoint is embodied in its critique of the idea of the copyrighted FutureMouse. Marcus Chalfen wishes to deliver a future free from human weaknesses and vagaries, but his careful planning has missed Millat's fundamentalism, Joshua's activism, and Archie's past encounter with the French geneticist working for the Nazis, 'Dr Sick'. Nothing is in fact in Chalfen's control and the FutureMouse escapes from captivity and out of the door. Nature and chance supplant attempts to dictate life despite individuals' and groups' attempts at religious, social, and genetic engineering.

9.3. Key Works: *White Teeth*

False as her own white teeth.

(W, 355)

White Teeth oscillates between personal acculturation and ethno-cultural diversity, the two forces together creating a new British social landscape. The latter influence is present in Millat's hybrid 'Raggastani', a 'strange mix of Jamaican patois, Bengali, Gujarati and English' (W, 231), whereas Magid feels the former pressure and responds to his sense of difference by trying to flatten it out, by calling himself 'Mark Smith' at the school chess club (W, 154), just as all the sons in Abdul-Mickey's family add an English name to their patronymic one (186). A corollary to this is Irie's desire to take command of her appearance and her identity by changing her hair: 'straight long black sleek flickable tossable shakeable touchable finger-through-able wind-blowable hair' (W, 273). The extensions she is given to make her feel more European, and less African, are of course Asian.

Itself an endorsement of uncontrolled cultural mix and random, passionate stirrings of the gene pool, *White Teeth* presents a series of images of modern London's heterogeneity. Smith's title of course plays with the idea that everyone is the same under the skin, but the novel charts the variety of molars, canines, incisors, root canals, false teeth, dental work, and damage that constitute the history behind different smiles. The commonsensical idea of the uniformity of teeth, which could also be divided into a host of shades from pearly to black, is itself a fiction within the novel.

One of the few explicit mentions of 'white teeth' occurs when Magid, Millat and Irie go to see Mr Hamilton to take him Harvest Festival gifts. He tells them: 'One sometimes forgets the significance of one's teeth. We're not like the lower animals – teeth replaced regularly and all that – we're of the mammals, you see. And mammals only get two chances. ... But like all things, the business has two sides. Clean white teeth are not always wise, now are they?' (W, 171). He goes on to explain that when serving in the army in the Congo he knew where to shoot by seeing the flash of the Africans' white teeth (in a comparable way, the adulterous Samad spots his sons' white teeth biting into symbolic apples at the end of the chapter (W, 182)). Hamilton goes on to say that 'Fibs will rot your teeth' (W, 173) 'and when your teeth rot … there's no return. … But while you're still young, the important matter is the third molars. They are more commonly referred to as the wisdom teeth, I believe. You really must deal with the third molars before anything else' (W, 173). Thus, teeth become an image of care and wisdom, neglect and rot: they must be looked after, brushed three times a day, and protected. Clara of course loses her teeth, but is given another set – her 'false' teeth – as she gets another life, with Archie. Their daughter, Irie decides towards the end of the novel that she is going to become a dentist – arguably a metafictional reference to the fact that her closest real-life equivalent, Zadie Smith, is writing a book called *White Teeth*.

Through these and other references, the reader develops an understanding that teeth are being used as a symbol of history, memory, and a shared colonial past. Of the books four parts, the first three all have a chapter on 'root canals' – those of Archie and Samad; of Mangal Pande; of Hortense Bowden. Teeth are to this extent used as a metaphor for a sense of identity: they have roots, they grow, they decay, and are in one sense the same and in another sense different for everyone. Even Archie's second chance in life is seen in terms of his transition from baby teeth to adult teeth: his 'Teething Trouble', in the words of one chapter title.

This is later followed by chapters entitled 'Molars' and 'Canines'. Molars are explained to the younger generation, Magid, Millat, and Irie, but the canines, the ripping teeth, are associated with the Chalfens who are older Europeans associated with the rapacity of English colonialism on Joyce's side (the *Daily Mail* letter-writing Connors), and the Frankensteinian manipulations of genetic science on Marcus's side. When Millat and Irie arrive, the friendless, culturally inbred Chalfens are bored and looking for something new to get their teeth into, because 'there was no one left to admire Chalfenism itself. Its gorgeous logic, its compassion, its intellect. They were like wide-eyed passengers of *The Mayflower* with no rock in sight. Pilgrims and prophets with no strange land' (W, 315).

By alluding to the first European settlers in the New World, Smith links a primal colonial encounter to the situation she is describing in Willesden at the end of the millennium. A recurring phrase throughout the book is: 'Past tense, future perfect'. This is Smith's shorthand for the multicultural social vision, in which 'history' is a source of conflict, but it is only through the efforts of her 'new world' pilgrims, living together in the same community, that there will be a multiethnic future of peace, love, and understanding. Like the hopes expressed through the birth of Helen Schlegel's baby at the end of Forster's *Howards End* (Smith has claimed to be Forster's 'ideal reader'), Irie's daughter at the close of Smith's novel embodies *White Teeth*'s most optimistic vision of the future. The narrator informs the reader that she will be brought up by Irie and by Joshua Chalfen, but the baby's natural father is either Magid or Millat. Thus, in Irie's daughter all the families of the book are brought together, mixing British, Caribbean, Bagladeshi, and Jewish heritage. But the novel also has a sceptical attitude towards any pronouncements of a happy ending and merely gestures towards the future at its close.

The perception of a tense past is also evident in Irie's life, as when she, perhaps naively, thinks of other families:

> What a *joy* their lives must be. They open a door and all they've got behind it is a bathroom or a lounge. Just neutral spaces. And not this endless maze of present rooms and past rooms and the things said in them years ago and everybody's old historical shit all over the place. They're not constantly making the same old mistakes. ... As far as they're concerned it's the *past*. (W, 514–15)

Though Irie is talking about her own family, her words echo those the narrator has used when describing the scene in which Magid and Millat are reunited 'in a blank room': 'they cover the room with history ... they take what was blank and smear it with the stinking shit of the past like excitable, excremental children. They cover this neutral room in themselves. Every gripe ... Every contested belief' (W, 464). History, this suggests, is escapable, but this is something that the individual perceives unevenly, either seeing its truth for themselves but not for others, or believing they alone are immune to its universality.

As is suggested by the book's epigraph from *The Tempest*, 'What's past is prologue' (in the hardback edition this is attributed to the inscription on Robert I. Aitken's 1930s statue 'The Future' in the Washington museum), neither personal nor political history is ever left behind, but at the same time life does not remain static. This is illustrated by O'Connell's bar, which Archie likes for its supposed unchanging familiarity: 'Everything was remembered, nothing was lost. History was never revised or rein-terpreted, adapted or whitewashed' (W, 192). Yet, O'Connell's does change. Pork is introduced when Magid returns from Bangladesh; and women are allowed into the café for the first time at the close of the book on 31 December 1999 (W, 541).

The theoretical belief that history cannot be escaped is contrasted with the physical facts of change through one of the paradoxes of Zeno. According to Zeno's story of Achilles and the tortoise, Achilles would never be able to overcome the tortoise's headstart because whenever he makes up the distance between them, the tortoise will always have moved on (the logic of this is illustrated by Tom Stoppard in his 1972 play *Jumpers*). Smith uses this to illustrate the impossibility of escaping history, whether personal or collective:

> The harder Achilles tries to catch the tortoise, the more elo-quently the tortoise expresses its advantage. Likewise, the brothers will race towards the future only to find they more and more eloquently express their past, that place where they have *just been*. Because this is the other thing about immigrants ('fugees, émigrés, travellers): they cannot escape their history any more than you yourself can lose your shadow.   (W, 466)

Zeno's philosophical arguments against material plurality can also be paradoxically taken as examples of xenophobia (*Xeno(s)* meaning stranger in Greek – as in Joyce's mention of xenogamy, W, 309), because they propose the impossibility of movement, in theory, despite the evidence of lived experience.

That the past cannot be escaped, and that the future hangs on it, is the fundamental message of Dr Perret's (the French 'Nazi sterilizer' Dr Sick) return at the end of the novel. He reappears to haunt Archie, and to forge a link for the reader between Marcus and wartime geneticists, over fifty years after Archie supposedly killed him (the quotation from Forster's *Where Angels Fear to Tread* that precedes Archie's part of the novel is significant here (W, 1)). If this seems a strange coincidence then it is at least in keeping with the novel's emphasis, through Archie, on chance.

The novel thus comes full circle to end with Archie as it began, though Smith chooses to add a postmodern faux-proleptic ending, supposedly informed by demographics. Archie's ending also reasserts the importance of 1945: the key date whose legacy he cannot escape. Samad's important point in time is 1857, the year of the 'Indian Mutiny' in which he believes his ancestor played a key part. Because Irie fixes on the importance of her ancestral history from the time of the Jamaican earthquake, her identity is rooted in 1907, the one date of which she can be sure in her family's past. However, Archie's defining year is 1945, because of his fateful encounter with Dr Sick and his moment of pivotal bonding with Samad, but also because Archie appears to have no other history – he knows nothing of his heritage but remembers and understands how he shares in the key event of recent British 'triumph' (and the last British Imperial one): the victory at war to which his generation returns for its sense of identity but which means little to those growing up in the twenty-first century, all of whose histories must now be acknowledged to have been characterized by myriad pasts, by diaspora, migration, and cross-fertilization.

References and Further Reading

Dominic Head, *The Cambridge Introduction to Modern British Fiction, 1950–2000*, Cambridge: Cambridge University Press, 2002.
——. 'Zadie Smith's *White Teeth*' in *Contemporary British Fiction*, edited by Richard J. Lane, Rod Mengham, and Philip Tew, Cambridge: Polity, 2003, 106–19.
Laura Moss, 'The politics of everyday hybridity: Zadie Smith's *White Teeth*', *Wasafiri*, 39, Summer 2003, 11–17.
Caryl Phillips, *A New World Order: Selected Essays*, London: Vintage, 2002.
Zadie Smith, *White Teeth* (W), Harmondsworth: Penguin, 2001.
——, *The Autograph Man* (A), London: Hamish Hamilton, 2002.
Claire Squires. *Zadie Smith's White Teeth: A Reader's Guide*, London: Continuum, 2002.

Web Reading

Interview: http://www.randomhouse.com/boldtype/0700/smith/
http://www.geocities.com/SoHo/Nook/1082/zadiesmithpage.html
http://www.penguin.co.uk/static/packages/uk/articles/smith/

10

Graham Swift: Past Present

10.1. Literary History

To date Graham Swift (b.1949) has published seven novels and one collection of short stories. His work is remarkably consistent in its concentration on ordinary language and its emphasis on ordinary lives. Swift's novels almost invariably allow the central characters to tell their own story, but use disturbed chronology, reminiscence, and flashback to juxtapose individuals and situations across time, casting the borrowed light of the past on family relationships in the present. His first book, *The Sweet Shop Owner* (1980), is his only novel narrated in the third person, though the extensive use of free indirect speech and strong focalization through the main character's eyes make it read at times like a first-person narration. As much concerned as his later work with revealing the extraordinary in seemingly unexceptional lives, Swift's first novel tells the story of the last day in the life of the eponymous Willy Chapman: a widower whose only child, Dorry, is estranged from him. Typical of Swift's fictional method, the book unfolds a plain story in the present while the protagonist mines his memories of the past. Willy, who has (and has been) offered money instead of intimacy all his life, has decided to commit suicide so that his daughter can have her full inheritance. As Willy edges towards his willed death, the possibility of a reconciliation with Dorry remains for a short time, but from his reflections it is clear that while Willy has craved love he has been unable to express it. Focussed around the unbreakable relationship between past and present, the conflicts and misunderstandings between generations, and the connections between private and public history, the themes prominent in *The Sweet Shop Owner* are also characteristic of Swift's later work.

Shuttlecock (1981) is another novel that explores the genealogy of a dysfunctional family, though in Swift's oeuvre there is perhaps no other kind. Set in 1977, it is narrated by Prentis, a man in his thirties who works for the London police, filing and documenting 'dead cases': ones that have never been fully investigated, usually because suicide or death has intervened. The book develops as an inquiry into the obligations of those with power and privileged knowledge to safeguard both truth and the happiness of others. It concerns itself with corrupt power – Prentis's torturing of his pet hamster as a child grows into a cruelty towards his wife and children as an adult – and also the possible abuses of power exercised benignly. The latter is what Quinn, Prentis's boss, thinks he is doing in withholding files: 'power mishandled ... plain and simple corruption. ... But what about the opposite of that? What if you just as surely pervert your power and overstep the bounds of your responsibility under the notion that you are doing good? Is that wrong too?' (S, 177) The connection from the private world to the public is made through Prentis's father, a wartime spy tortured under interrogation by Gestapo police. He emerged from this ordeal a hero, and his book of war memories, entitled *Shuttlecock: the Story of a Secret Agent*, was a minor success. In his late fifties, however, Prentis's father broke down and became hospitalized and incapable of communication. The novel's climax then confronts Prentis with the opportunity to read and/or preserve the files that supposedly expose his father as a fraud who betrayed his country and his family: an impostor who gave information under torture and an adulterer who slept with his best friend's wife. Prentis elects not to read the files and burns them with Quinn, coming to the conclusion that for most people, their 'contentment somehow depends on their ignorance' (S, 212). Yet this is a comment he makes on his family while he takes over Quinn's job, so becoming the powerful custodian of others' secrets as well as his own.

Swift's short-story collection *Learning to Swim and Other Stories* (1982) brought together ten previously published stories, and one new one, 'The Tunnel', which has some similarities to *Shuttlecock*. Both the novel and the story use the image of burrowing to represent escape and to provide a metaphor for digging deeply into the past or the self. *Shuttlecock* begins with a burrowing creature, Prentis's pet hamster, and concludes with Prentis's family escaping to the seaside, where he and his wife make love on the beach, 'burrowing in the sand' (S, 219); one chapter in the novel also concludes with Prentis's father describing his escape from the Gestapo culminating in him digging a hideaway in the undergrowth: 'no better than some burrowing animal' (S, 108). 'The Tunnel' is another story of a private, insular world in which a couple have started to torment each other. The narrator and his girlfriend, Clancy, are school leavers who have holed up together and created a life that begins idyllically but sours as practical matters press in on them and their initial sexual and emotional intensity loses its power. Their journey inwards and then their escape are metaphorically represented by the ex-pupils that the narrator watches digging a tunnel in the disused grounds of a closed school. The narrator says that, though the boys are just playing: 'it seemed that their escape was real ... I did not want to imagine them failing' (LS, 28). Immediately the boys' tunneling succeeds, the narrator and Clancy find freedom through an inheritance and celebrate by deciding to 'get a train to somewhere in the country, and talk' (LS, 30).

The stories in *Learning to Swim* contain a broader European canvas than most of Swift's fiction by including in their narratives Greek, Hungarian, Turkish, and Polish characters or settings. But the themes and subjects are similar to his novels: the war, couples in crisis, death and the importance of family. Two of the most resonant and effective stories are 'Seraglio' and 'Learning to Swim'. In both stories couples use children to goad each other. In 'Learning to Swim', a husband and wife on the beach in Cornwall separately weigh up their relationship: how they came to be married and the many occasions on which they have thought of leaving each other. All that seems to keep them together is their son Paul. It becomes clear that the parents use the child in a tug of war: Mr Singleton teaches his son to swim because this was the sport he excelled at before he married, and for Mrs. Singleton her son's distress at learning is 'a guarantee against Mr. Singleton's influence' (LS, 142). While the six-year-old Paul is terrified of water, Mr Singleton thinks that if his son can learn to swim, he can finally leave his wife. The narrative ends with the parents arguing about whether Paul should come out of the sea, as the boy kicks 'half in pride, half in panic, away from his father, away from the shore [where his mother stands], away, in this strange new element that seemed all his own' (LS, 146). A story apparently concerned with two adults seeking escape from each other concludes with their son starting to find his independence. In 'Seraglio', set in Istanbul, a liminal city joining Western Asia and South-East Europe, the narrator and his wife are a couple who take increasingly exotic holidays to make up for the fact that they can't have children, following a miscarriage. Seven years after this misfortune, the couple are figured as two continents (LS, 6), physically next to each other but temperamentally opposed, paradoxically joined and separated by so little distance and so much mistrust and history. Everything that happens to either of them is the opportunity for more guilt and recrimination; no sympathy passes between them as they distrust each other's motives and expect the metaphorical 'daggers' that are the story's chief image of suspicion and pain. Unable to propel their relationship forwards they move through a cycle of blame. The couple go away on holiday but are incapable of escape, only finding their frustrated lives mirrored in the history and geography of Turkey: 'The Bazaar itself is a labyrinth with a history. ... People have entered, they say, and not emerged' (LS, 1).

Waterland was first published in 1983 and reissued in a revised edition in 1992. Generally regarded as Swift's masterpiece, it is a rich and complex but immensely readable novel that explores the ways in which seeming opposites seep into each other: story and history, the past and the present, the personal and the political, and especially the waterways and the land. It is narrated by a history teacher in London, Tom Crick, whose sixth form classes have broadened out from the French Revolution to include Crick's own family history, that of his wife Mary, and that of the Fenland country in which he grew up. Though its multilayered narrative is more intricate than anything else Swift has attempted, *Waterland*'s themes overlap with those of his other novels: generational conflict, incest, loss, adoption, secrecy, betrayal, war, genealogy, and regeneration.

After publishing a book a year for four years, Swift took five years to produce his next novel. *Out of this World* (1988) uses two parallel narratives to tell the story of a father and daughter's ten-year separation and their possible reconciliation. Harry Beech is in his sixties, a well-known aerial photographer and ex-photojournalist whose Greek wife and powerful father have both died, while his only child, Sophie, lives in New York with her husband and twin sons. The two have not spoken since the funeral of Robert's father, a successful arms manufacturer and Great War veteran, rewarded by the state with the Victoria Cross but killed by the IRA. Sophie's narrative largely takes the form of her monologue to her therapist, Dr Klein. Harry's loss of Sophie as well as his wife surfaces in a new relationship with a woman forty years his junior, while Sophie's love–hate relationship with her father leads her to indulge in indiscriminate adulterous couplings which she recounts to Klein. *Out of this World* is a novel closely concerned with the relationship between the real and the illusory: as Sophie remarks to her therapist, 'But what's the point of life, and what's the point of goddam movies, if now and then you can't discover that the way you thought it isn't, the way you thought it only ever is in movies, really is the way it is?' (OTW, 145) The novel is absorbed with the truths and illusions of family relationships as well as of photographs and memories. In a world based on imitation and deception there is little foundation for secure knowledge: 'how terrible … not to know, at the end of it, what is true or false' (OTW, 72). Which is why Harry bears public witness through his photography and Sophie bears personal witness through her therapy: 'Do we see the truth or do we tell it?' she ruminates (OTW, 76).

Swift's next novel *Ever After* (1992) also deliberates on the possibility or desirability of knowing the past. The narrative complexity of *Out of this World* is increased in *Ever After*, which like *Waterland* provides a family history across several generations. The story works in two time frames. In the twentieth century, a widower whose father committed suicide, Bill Unwin is a second-rate academic with a death wish. In the nineteenth century there is Unwin's great-great-grandfather Matthew Pearce (almost a cross between Matthew Arnold and Charles Darwin), whose notebooks Bill has discovered. These documents describe how Pearce, echoing the experience of his own father, who gradually renounced his faith after the death of his wife, lost both his religious belief and his marriage as a result of two factors: his son's death and his growing appreciation of the arguments of Darwin and Lyell (EA, 95). Through Pearce's story, Unwin looks for traces of his own identity, believing that in the absence of God, human meaning must exist in genealogy and ancestry. As a child, Bill felt that the 'sunshine was made up of countless particles of irreducible, indestructible, eternal gold' (EA, 24). Now, surrounded by death, Unwin seeks in vain for anything permanent, something like the belief in an omnipotent God that his ancestors would have subscribed to before the mid-nineteeth century. Apart from the notebooks, all that Bill has of this past is a clock made by Matthew's father and handed down through the generations as a reminder of the unstoppable passing of time and the truth of not permanence but change. The clock has an engraved brass plate with the motto: *Amor Vincit Omnia* (EA, 46). What the notebooks suggest has been taken away from the family is compensated for by the clock, and Bill's narrative ends with a long love letter to his own dead wife, which echoes Matthew's last letter to his wife Elizabeth. Only through the bonds of love and family can Bill or Matthew find solace and meaning. Bill concludes from Matthew's replacement of faith with human truths: 'You see, it is the personal thing that matters. The personal thing. It is knowing who Matthew Pearce *was*. And why he should matter so much to me. And why things mattered so much to him when (what difference did it make? what difference does it make?) he might have gone on living happily ever after' (EA, 49). While truth is paramount, there is still the chance of happiness, in the personal, in love and memory.

Like *Out of This World*, *Last Orders* (1996) is composed of a series of interleaved first-person narratives that includes one by a character who is dead in the present of the story. Through the course of 75 interior monologues, *Last Orders* pieces together the car journey of four bereaved men – three friends and the adopted son of the dead man – as they take the ashes of Jack Dodds to be scattered in the sea at Margate. The four men are Ray Johnson, an insurance clerk, Vic Tucker, an undertaker, Lenny Tate, a grocery stall owner, and Vince Dodds, a second-hand car dealer who significantly chose not to become a butcher like his 'dad'. Included in the segments are short narratives by three other characters: Amy, Jack's wife, Mandy, Vince's wife, and Jack himself. Through their individual thoughts and recollections, the seven characters describe the ways in which their lives have become intertwined, revealing the grudges, rivalries, and secrets that have arisen between them as well as the ties that have bound them together. The book slowly assembles the personal histories and shared pasts of the characters as the quartet's Chaucerian journey winds from Bermondsey via the Old Kent Road, New Cross, Blackheath, Dartford and Gravesend, on to Rochester, Chatham, Canterbury and finally Margate. Several of the place names contribute to the accumulated images of death and burial: *Grave*send, Canter*bury*, where Thomas à Becket was murdered by four knights, and Chatham, where at Vic's request they visit the naval memorial. Like Swift's earlier books, *Last Orders* tunnels into the past to uncover complex histories behind the events of the present. However, unlike the increasingly sophisticated self-reflexive narratives of Swift's preceding four novels, respectively told by a police librarian, a teacher, a photographer, and an academic, *Last Orders* returns to the language of Willy Chapman. From one angle, the story of *Last Orders* begins with a man and woman, Jack and Amy, joining together in 'the Garden of England' (LO, 106), and accretes around this origin the multiple narratives that slowly document their fall from happiness. But there is a feeling of pathos and of release by the end of the book when Amy decides she is free to begin her life anew while Jack joins all those whose death unites them after the hostilities and grievances of life. As the undertaker Vic realises: 'In life there are differences, you make distinctions. ... But the dead are the dead, I've watched them, they're equal. ... It's what makes all men equal for ever and always' (LO, 143).

In 2003, Swift published a seventh novel *The Light of Day*, about an imprisoned woman, Sarah Nash, visited every other week by divorced and disgraced ex-policeman George Webb, the private detective she hired to follow her husband on the last day of his affair. The story is told by George and is set on the second anniversary of Sarah's fatal stabbing of her husband. The book has several themes, such as freedom and incarceration, guilt and innocence, betrayal and justice, but central to Swift's narrative is the phrase 'To love is to serve, what else is it for?' (LD, 156) Love is evident throughout the novel – between father and daughter, husband and wife, man and woman, woman and woman – but the element of service provides its context: to serve a prison sentence for murdering an unfaithful husband, to serve a meal as an act of hospitality and acceptance, to serve as a police officer or a private detective. In the novel's present of November 1997, 'Saint George' (LD, 156) also serves by visiting Sarah, the woman he has fallen in love with and might have prevented from murdering her husband when he returned from the airport having dropped off his lover, Kristin Lazic, a Croatian refugee. To underline its epigraph, 'All's fair in love and war', the book has two key historical touchstones: the Croatian civil war and the story of Napoleon III, the disgraced Emperor who fled with his wife Eugénie to die in England. *The Light of Day* is told in a simple, limpid prose that attempts to follow the Wordsworthian injunction to compose literature in a common social language; in this it is broadly of a piece with Swift's approach in his previous books, just as it is consonant with them in focussing on fathers and daughters, death and trauma, love and betrayal, family and history.

In *Ever After*, it is said that 'A great deal of literature is only (only!) the obvious transformed into the sublime' (EA, 70), and this is the most complimentary way to view Swift's work. Two of his novels have received great praise, but there have also been accusations of misogyny and repetition levelled at him. His novels, perhaps in a way similar to Ishiguro's or Winterson's, tend to range over a comparatively circumscribed range of subjects, but repay close attention as a great deal of artifice is concealed in the plain, seemingly almost artless style.

9.2. Themes: Family and History

> *A zone ... of verges and double garages and wrought iron and speed bumps and private nursery schools ... where – with all they've got – they can still (you'd be surprised) do the strangest things. ... This home-and-garden land, this never-never land where nothing much is ever meant to happen.*
>
> (LD, 19)

Married couples nearly always have their secrets and their separations in Swift's novels: these come in several forms, from incestuous connections to silent witnesses.

First, there are betrayals and infidelities in nearly all of the novels, including *The Light of Day* where, in addition to recounting Sarah's revenge on her husband's adultery, George tells the reader how his 'private' detection work began long ago when he tracked his own father to uncover the affair that his mother was ignorant of until she sat at her husband's death bed. To take another example, in *Out of This World*, Anna, Harry Beech's wife, was unfaithful to him with one of his closest friends – a fact that has been kept a closely guarded secret in the family. Also, Sophie feels betrayed by Harry's absences from home when she was growing up, and is herself unfaithful to her husband, Joe, while he goes behind her back to write to Harry. Adding to this pervasive atmosphere of infidelity, Harry's father feels betrayed by his son's refusal to take over Beech munitions. Second, there are incestuous acts and feelings In *Waterland*, Dick is thought to be the child of his mother and *her* father. In *Last Orders*, Vince sleeps with each of his foster parents' semi-adopted daughters, Sally and Mandy (who declares explicitly that it was 'like *committing incest*' (LO, 157)). Third, in Swift's novels it is always clear that being a member of a family entails responsibilities and obligations, the routine acts that acknowledge the past and fall somewhere between duty and love. In *Shuttlecock*, Prentis remarks about going to see his silent father that 'there is something terribly perfunctory, terribly pointless and mechanical about these twice-weekly visits. Sometimes I think it is not a man who walks or sits beside me, but some effigy I push and trundle about on a wheeled trolley' (S, 43). Prentis's father is like Amy's daughter June in *Last Orders* and Crick's wife Mary in *Waterland*: someone whose incapacity contains the novel's central enigma, suggesting how only the past can start to explain the present. The inability of these characters to communicate tortures the visitors who want to understand them and to be loved by them.

While husbands and wives, sons and daughters, are bound together by ties of blood or history, there are as many rifts between them as they are links. In *Last Orders* Jack and Amy are still together but have been in deep disagreement all their married life; Ray's wife Carol has left him because of his inadequate ambitions and his support for their daughter, who Carol has renounced. Couples are frequently foster parents or simulating parenthood in Swift's novels. For example, there is Vince's observation of Amy and Jack in *Last Orders*: 'they've been playing at being Sally's parents but now they've got me again' (LO, 64). The irony here is that Vince is about to be told that he is adopted, that Jack and Amy are in fact also 'playing' at being his parents. Meanwhile, in the same novel, Lenny thinks that Mandy, Vince's future wife, was also taken in by Jack as a surrogate daughter, 'thinking of June for once. Thinking of Amy' (LO, 68); as Vince tells Mandy: 'you're *supposed to be the sister I aint got*' (LO, 103). In *Waterland* Tom Crick takes Price under his wing to provide himself with a kind of son while his barren wife Mary steals a baby to compensate for her sense of loss. Couples are often childless, as in *Waterland* and *Ever After*, or at odds with their children, as in *Shuttlecock* and *Last Orders*, where one of Vince's deepest desires is for his father to be forced to come to him for money one day.

Through these repeated examples, Swift creates a pervasive feeling of the artificiality of families alongside repeated images of individuals attracted to constructed ties that are sought to compensate for the disappointments of blood relations. Families appear to be composed of fragments in search of a whole. In *Out of This World*, a narrative about personal loss and emotional investment in falsity, the primary image of fragmentation and artificiality is Harry's father's prosthetic arm. Harry says after his father's heart attack: 'I remember that his metal arm lay, detached, beside him on the bedside table. ... And I remember feeling a stab of pity for that bereft arm that I did not feel for my father' (OTW, 70). He later remembers: 'I always wondered which way round it was: was he trying to make his arm like the rest of himself, or the rest of himself like his arm?' (OTW, 199) Noticing that the 'earlier ones are shapely ... [while] the later ones look like nothing human, but actually simulate the function of an arm', Harry concludes that his father's array of false limbs are 'like an index of the twentieth century' (OTW, 200) because the world itself has moved from aesthetics to prosthetics.

While sons, like Bill Unwin in *Ever After*, often profess to hate one or other of their parents, there are as many alienated daughters in Swift's work, expecially in *The Sweet Shop Owner* and *Last Orders*. In *Last Orders*, Mandy comes to London after running away from home; Ray's daughter Susie has emigrated to Australia against her mother's deepest wishes; Lenny's daughter Sally has never forgiven him for insisting on her abortion and she now has no family living with her but 'paying' visitors instead (LO, 276), while Vince's daughter Kath has started 'pulling in punters of her own' (LO, 49). All of these disappointments and estrangements between daughters and parents are metaphorically represented by June, who has been incapable of speaking to her devoted mother and who has never been acknowledged by her father.

In some ways similarly, the narrator decides in Swift's short story 'The Son': 'what a shameful thing for a man to live thirty-five years not knowing that his parents are not his parents at all' (LS, 54). Mistaken paternity is common in Swift's work; in *Waterland*, where genealogies are shrouded in mystery and rumour, it is never known who the father of Mary's aborted child was and Dick's true parentage is a secret. In *Out of This World*, Anna dies pregnant but Harry later learns that the child would not have been his, while in *Ever After* Bill Unwin is told that his real father was killed in the Second World War, just as Vince Dodds in *Last Orders* is informed that his real parents were killed in an air raid. Vince's childhood alienation from Jack (who at this stage of his life he has no reason to believe is not his father) is illustrated by his decision, as a boy in the back of the Dodds and Son van, to reject a daily job handling meat for a world of mechanics that will define him:

> I'd hate him and hate the meat smell until they were one and the same ... and I'd think, I aint going to be a butcher never. ... I'd feel the metal throbbing underneath, I'd hear the grind and grip of the transmission, the thrum of the shafts taking the power to the wheels, and I'd think, This is how a motor works, I'm lying on the workings of this van. I aint me, I'm part of this van.   (LO, 63)

In Swift's novels ancestry and also 'parental' influence is to a degree destiny. No matter how much children try to rebel against their real or foster parents, connections and repetitions keep appearing. In *Last Orders*, Vince is sure he hates Jack, but he repeats his experience of army life in the Middle East to emulate or imitate him. At one point in his childhood he asks Amy for a photograph of Jack – one of him laughing in the desert during the war: 'He doesn't look like a soldier, he doesn't even look like a grown up. He looks like a kid on the beach' (LO, 137). For Vince to find affection for the man who has been his father he has to identify with him, see him as the kid on Margate beach that he often feels he is himself.

Shuttlecock brings to light similarities between the males of successive generations. At first, Prentis appears different from his father, as a weak and cowardly man who is cruel but breaks under pressure (his two sons worship the Bionic Man on television but have little respect for their own father). Only at the close when Prentis learns a different story of his own father, and takes over from Quinn as the gatekeeper of personal files and national secrets, is he able to love his own family, particularly his eldest son Martin, who had taken to spying on him as he spied on Quinn, and Martin's grandfather spied for his country. The novel couches these activities in terms of the abuse of privilege, born out of the corruption brought about by power: 'this creature which I loved was also at my mercy' (S, 6). Prentis is speaking here of Sammy, his pet hamster, who 'tries to squirm free but I catch him by the collar' (S, 10). Sammy is like many of the humans in the story, captive and tormented in the service of knowledge and control: 'animals are really kept in zoos so we can understand them scientifically' (S, 153). This is the pursuit of knowledge and power that is inseparable from the desire for freedom and control. Prentis speculates that: 'We are all looking for a space where we can be free, where we cannot be reached, where we are masters' (S, 36). This applies to his own father, about whom Quinn says: 'If he did betray, he only did what any ordinary natural human being would have done – he saved his own skin' (S, 190). Only those outside of nature, such as the Bionic Man, are able to escape both captivity and the demands and desires of a cruel, frail animality ('The thing that most embodies the evil of war, is ... its wilful disregard for nature' (S, 108)). Everyone else can be tormented by confrontation with 'the face of someone who knows what you don't' (S, 90), like Prentis's own father: 'sometimes I get the impression that this silence of his is only a pretence, an elaborate, obstinate pretence' (S, 48). The reader has to decide the extent to which Swift is exploring Prentis's particular fears, such as when he decides Quinn 'is playing games with [him]' (S, 22), and the extent to which Prentis is just like the reader: 'everybody is trying to search out everybody else's story, everybody else's secret, and the assumption is that this secret will always be a weakness' (S, 25). The principal metaphor here is nakedness as exposure and vulnerability: Prentis's wife Marian bathing is 'defenceless', reminding him of the naked children in the bath when they were small and 'at my mercy' (S, 149). 'Everyone is trying to strip everyone else bare, and everyone, at the same time, is trying not to be stripped bare himself' (S, 25); because, as Prentis's father writes of his captivity in the war, nothing is 'more appalling than this nakedness' (S, 147).

Connections and patterns across Swift's writings suggest wider meanings that concern matters of home and history. A sense of belonging exists separately from the houses and families in the novels. Mandy says to Vince in *Last Orders*:

> To run away from home and find another home in less than a day, though the new home wasn't a real home, any more than the one I left. The new home was all the opposite of what it seemed: a son whose home it wasn't but it was, a daughter whose home it was but it wasn't because she had to be kept in

a Home, a mum and dad who weren't really a mum and dad, except to me (LO, 157)

This can be considered irony and confusion, but is also history repeating itself – as in the madnesses that come back with each generation in *Waterland*: these are matters of heredity that cut across the homes that people live in. The force that often creates these complexities is the same one that redeems them in the narratives: love. A good example is the triangle of Jack, Amy and Ray in *Last Orders*. Ray's fondest memory is of Amy's words: ' "Oh Ray, you're a lovely man." To have lived and heard a woman say that to you' (LO, 284); while Amy's parallel memory is of some of the first words that Jack spoke to her: ' "You're beautiful." It's not what you expect from a butcher's boy. It turns you over to hear a man say that, fills you up. To be alive, to have lived to hear a man say that' (LO, 240).

Throughout Swift's work, his protagonists are connected in one way or another with wider social and political events, and with a public history that is connected to their family history. 'History. Now I've always been fascinated by history' (SSO, 179) says Willy Chapman in *The Sweet Shop Owner*. Willy lives a marginalized life, but like Swift's other main characters he is both touched by world events and the subject of his own history, with its individual meanings and events. When he goes towards his death he asks his daughter, in her absence on her twenty-fifth birthday, about the money she wants: 'what will you buy with it, Dorry? History?' (SSO, 221) History can neither be bought nor chosen, but its presence is always impinging on the characters' lives whether they are aware of it or not. For this reason, the narrative of the present in *Waterland* is pointedly set in Greenwich, at Longitude 0, the point from where all time and space is judged.

'History fitted them into patterns' (SSO, 44–5) Willy says of his school friends and this is what Swift shows history to be doing in his narratives. So, like *Waterland*'s more obvious use of multiple key political, military, and social events, from the French Revolution to the First World War, *Out of This World* contains a wide array of historical reference points: it is initially set in April 1982, at the time of the Falklands conflict; it additionally encompasses both World Wars, an IRA car bombing, the moon landing, the 1974 military coup in Greece, the Nuremberg trials and the

Vietnam War. But in each of his novels Swift tries to explore history in a different way. One example is how in *Out of This World* history itself is different in the second half of the twentieth century: 'The first rule of photography: that you must catch things unawares. The camera doesn't manufacture. But that night was the first time perhaps that I thought: No, times have changed since then. The camera first, then the event. The whole world is waiting just to get turned into film. And not just the world but the goddam moon as well' (OTW, 13). Harry's view is partly a comment on himself, because his estrangement from Sophie stems from his photographing his own father's death – an action Harry might justify as bearing witness: 'Half my pictures, of course, they buried. You aren't supposed to see, let alone put on visual record, *those* things. ... what I'd say is that someone has to look. Someone has to be in it and step back too. Someone has to be a witness' (OTW, 49). To Harry it is this act of bearing witness that is more important than believing in the documentary evidence of photography. 'Seeing is believing and certain things must be seen to have been done. Without the camera the world might start to disbelieve' (OTW, 107). Indeed, Harry's knowledge of the possibilities of film manipulation has made him sceptical of visual images. Of the moon landing he muses 'How do we know they're really there? It could all be a happening in some studio mock-up. It could all be a trick to con the Russians. To know, you'd have to go yourself' (OTW, 170).

In *Waterland*, Tom Crick is interested in the complexity of the past's answer to 'the Question Why'. 'Why', for Crick, is a different kind of question from 'when', 'what', 'how' and 'who', all of which have comparatively simple answers. When asked 'Why History?', Crick replies: 'Your demand for explanation provides an explanation. Isn't this seeking of reasons itself inevitably a historical process, since it must always work backwards from what came after to what came before? And so long as we have this itch for explanations, must we not always carry round with us this cumbersome but precious bag of clues called History?' (W, 106). Crick therefore asserts that life is in fact only one tenth 'the HERE&NOW' (p. 62: only animals live entirely in the HERE& NOW) and nine-tenths the past, just as humans are seemingly solid but are actually three-quarters water.

Swift's most celebrated novel is above all concerned with how 'history' and 'story' cannot be kept apart. History purports to be dryland (see W, 86), as opposed to the fluidity of stories, but they cannot be fully separated – it is only possible to keep sifting, to keep asking 'why' as we dredge up the past. History is really 'mud': the mud of Flanders, the mud in which the eel procreates. *Waterland* is also concerned with all kinds of history coming to an end, with the closure of Crick's history department, the threat of nuclear war, Mary's inability to have children and so continue the history of the family. Yet, history moves forward in two ways, symbolized by the pub called 'The Pike and the Eel', showing history as revolution (in the French revolution there were 'heads on pikes' on Bastille Day) and as evolution (the natural history of the eel). The book also goes to great lengths to avoid telling a linear story; its last page is set many years back in the past, and its circularity is suggested by its final word, 'cycle', which is as much about continuity as the novel's first word: 'And'. Similarly, the 52 chapters are there to suggest the yearly cycle, but also to represent Tom and Mary's position within this cycle: they are both 52-years old. The chapters of *Waterland* are also evenly divided between those that begin 'About' and those that don't – half for history and half for story.

Waterland thus takes a very catholic view of what history is, suggesting that it is as broad as the capacious art of 'storytelling'. The novel includes the theory of history as *hubris* (W, 72), or as religion, as magic or as natural selection. Its two families represent different genealogies: the Cricks are storytellers whereas the Atkinsons rely more on industry and science: 'While the Atkinsons made history, the Cricks spun yarns' (W, 17), but the two seeming opposites come together as a family. History is histrionics, is 'an accredited "sub-science"', is an inquest and a yarn, is natural and artificial, is cause and effect, is accident and repetition: "First it was a story ... then it becomes real, then it becomes here and now. Then it becomes a story again"' (W, 328). This belief is illustrated again and again in the narrative, as with the way in which Sarah Atkinson's story not only haunts the future but is repeated in Mary's life.

Overall, in Swift's fiction, families and history are marked by repetition. The novels detail the attempts of individuals to break free from the past and to construct a better future, but in seeking to do so they merely become ignorant of the forces impinging on their own lives as well as on the lives of their parents and those who tried to love them.

10.3. Key Works: *Waterland, Last Orders*

Like a lesson in cause and effect within personal histories,
Waterland unearths the consequential past of history teacher Tom
Crick and his infertile wife Mary, who has been driven to snatch a
baby from a South London Safeway store. As with all of Swift's
narratives, the novel reveals seemingly unremarkable lives as
always unusual and unexpected events as almost predictable. It is
an elemental book, concerned with water and earth but also the
East Wind and the power of fire. These are basic forces that drive
nature and influence history, where people are acted upon but also
strive to act as agents. While the Atkinsons see the wisdom of
'investing in land reclamation' (W, 15), the Cricks 'did not forget,
in their muddy labours, their swampy origins; that, however
much you resist them, the waters will return; that the land sinks;
silt collects; that something in nature wants to go back' (W, 17).

To match the diversity of its approach to themes, *Waterland* utilizes a number of different narrative forms and genres. Its concern
with the relationship between story and history is illustrated by its
presentation in the hybrid form of an autobiography: as Tom
Crick's hi/story of the self within wider social pressures. In terms
of the fictional forms of story, it begins with 'Fairy-tale words' in its
first sentence and it contains fairy-tale characters – witch, beauty,
simpleton – wrapped in the romance narrative of the quest. The
quest tale is also the antecedent of the detective story, which surfaces in many ways in the novel, from the mystery of Freddie
Parr's murder to the question of Dick Crick's paternity. The factual
aspect to the inquiry into a death is an inquest, to which oral history and historiography are likened in the novel. However, what
drives all the genres, such as fairy stories, detective stories, and histories, is curiosity: searching for answers to questions. The prime
example of this interest in origins and puzzles is the eel, the enig-
matic central symbol of natural and sexual curiosity: ' "*Historia*" or
"Inquiry" (as in Natural History: the inquiry into Nature)' (W, 107).

Alongside its interest in history, *Waterland* also makes use of
geography, particularly its fenland setting, to amplify the book's
themes. The world of the Atkinsons and the Cricks is one in
which humans struggle to separate the water from the land, and
its concern with land reclamation is echoed in small ways
throughout the book, from Tom and Mary's attempt to 'reclaim
our marriage', to their child-substitute of a golden retriever. The

fens represent the flux and change of history, but they also emblematize the way in which people have adapted to the land from the ocean, have changed from water creatures to amphibians to land-based animals, yet their origins remain in the sea, to which they return: a theme especially linked to the eel-like Dick, who returns to the water at the end, as does Mary's aborted baby.

Waterland's interest in national history is present in its other hybrid images. For example, phlegm is considered an English humour, and is linked in the novel with the Cricks. It is 'an ambiguous substance. Neither liquid nor solid: a viscous semi-fluid. Benign (lubricating, cleansing, mollifying, protective) yet disagreeable (a universal mark of disgust: to spit)' (W, 344). The phlegm, 'or watery disposition', of the Cricks is counterposed to the beer of the Atkinsons, because phlegm 'is to be remedied by infusions of strengthening liquors ...: the administration of alcohol'. But beer is similarly a hybrid, which is also a mixture of elements: of water and hops and grain.

The book's form, its mazy twists and narrative turns come directly from its subject, of history as river, as cycle, as revolution. Crick sees that this history is always a circular flow, 'progress' is always one step forward and one step back. He says that 'It goes in two directions at once. It goes backwards as it goes forwards. It loops. It takes detours. Do not fall into the illusion that history is a well-disciplined and unflagging column marching unswervingly into the future' (W, 135).

Yet, the fears for history in *Waterland* are that it will end because of a lack of curiosity. Price's belief that history is coming to a nuclear end is mirrored by his opinion that the past is of no interest, paralleling the school headmaster's decision to close the history department because he's never been interested in the subject (W, 21), and Mary's lack of curiosity about stories is seen as her descent into madness, while 'everything's coming to an end' (W, 296). Only through curiosity, by wanting to 'use the key' that occurs as a metaphor throughout the book, will the past be unlocked or will history continue to open to the future.

* * *

The themes of *Waterland* are continued in *Last Orders* where the importance of history and heredity is again figured as both force and farce: 'I reckon every generation makes a fool of itself for the next one' (LO, 44). Swift's Booker-prize winning novel has been compared in its structure and narration to Faulkner's *As I Lay Dying*, in its use of Margate and closing-time as an image of mortality to Eliot's *The Waste Land*, and in its story-soaked journey to Chaucer's *The Canterbury Tales*. But alongside its debts to literary ancestors, the novel also brings in the importance of popular songs, with their evocations of love affairs and especially journeys or dreams of escape: 'I Get Around', 'No Particular Place to Go', 'Running Scared', 'She's Leaving Home', and 'Blue Bayou'. Travelling becomes a major theme of *Last Orders*. It functions both to bring people together and to draw them apart, as the journey to Margate does for the four men. Vince, for whom the motor business represents getting away from his parents, just as leaving his dealership represents escape from her father for his daughter Kath, muses on the importance of cars as symbols of freedom: 'Aint it amazing there's this thing that exists so everyone can jump in and travel where they please?' (LO, 71) Ray tries to rekindle some excitement in his marriage by buying a van: 'It's a dormobile. A camper-van, deluxe model. A travelling home for two' (LO, 60). Instead his wife Carol sees this as 'the last straw' and leaves him, but Ray temporarily fulfils his dream by seducing Amy in the van on one of their trips to the races. This is the same van in which Vince sleeps with Mandy, telling her: 'The world was changing all right ... But I said I'll tell you what the big change is ... It's mobility. Being mobile. ... Time was when the only way you got to travel was in the Army. ... But watch 'em all on the move now, watch 'em all going places' (LO, 105). The significance of the Middle East and Egypt, the part of the world in which all the men except Vic serve in the army, is also to do with the romance of travelling and escape: Ray sings the song 'Gypsy in my Soul' (LO, 169); Mandy likens herself and Vince in the camper van to 'a pair of gypsies' (LO, 157); and the catalyst for Jack and Amy's story is Amy's lust for a gypsy she sees hop-picking, transferring it on to her future husband (LO, 238).

The novel's title works on several levels. Its immediate reference is to final orders at the bar, intimating the pub world of the Coach and Horses, with its suggestion of past journeys and rest stops, and its brass-lettered 1884 clock reminding them of the pub's hundredth anniversary as they celebrate Vince's fortieth birthday. 'Last Orders' of course also refers to Jack's dying wishes and to the Order of the Burial of the Dead, but it can additionally remind the reader of the war service the four friends saw, three of them in the army and one in the navy. Several of the book's principal themes derive from this: duty, loyalty and mutual support. For the surviving men, these are forces and obligations that bring them together on their journey for Jack; and they travel together despite other forces: jealousy, guilt, and resentment. They are also important responsibilities for Amy, the competing calls on whose time and affection have resulted in her deciding to decline to go on the journey to Margate, ostensibly because it is her day to see June, the daughter she and Jack conceived on their first time together, before they were married (June has lived her life in a 'home' and has never spoken – never called Amy 'mummy'). Yet Amy's refusal to acquiesce to Jack's last wish is also because Margate has multiple meanings in the story, several of them painful to her. It is where Jack, not Amy, wished to move, thus abandoning June (LO, 14); it is where the couple went on their belated honeymoon in the summer of 1939 (LO, 29); and it is also where they quarrelled over June – where Amy first chose to side with their daughter when Jack rejected her (LO, 253–5). Margate ultimately represents an alternative reality of past and future hopes, as well the inevitability of death: 'It's what Margate's famous for, it's what people come here for, *Dreamland*' (LO, 273). (Except for Vic, whose serenity and contentment is an index of the others' frustrated desires, all the men have dreams of alternative lives they'd have wished for themselves: Jack wanted to be a doctor, Lenny a successful boxer, and Ray a jockey.) Amy also does not wish to participate in the 'Boys' outing' for further reasons, not least because of her relationship with two of the other men. She has had a brief affair with Ray, who has been in love with her since Jack showed him her photograph when they met in Egypt (LO, 89), and she knows also that Lenny has always fancied her (LO, 209) while being deeply resentful of the Dodds family since Jack and Amy used to take his daughter Sally on Sunday outings that he and his wife could not.

A final element of the story to mention here is that of luck and chance, which play their part in personal lives and in death – Jack supposedly 'picks' Ray as his friend in the war because he's a small target, and 'lucky' to be so (LO, 87). Ray, who thinks luck is less important than confidence, is then christened 'lucky' Johnson, a view of him that is reinforced when he develops a knack for choosing the right horses. On several occasions he places bets for the other characters and wins for them, bringing about changes in their lives from the chances of the racetrack. The book presents life as in general a kind of race and lottery as much as a matter of choices. Beside Jack's death bed, Amy thinks: 'and he says, like it's his last word on everything, on why he's lying there and why I'm sitting there holding his hand, and why it had to be him, why I was saddled with him and not a thousand others, luck of a summer night, "All a gamble, aint it?" ' (LO, 268)

References and Further Reading

Tamás Bényei 'The Novels of Graham Swift' in *Contemporary British Fiction*, edited by Richard J. Lane, Rod Mengham, and Philip Tew, Cambridge: Polity, 2003, 40–55.

Pamela Cooper, *Graham Swift's 'Last Orders'*, London: Continuum, 2002.

Damon Marcel Decoste, 'Questions and Apocalypse: The Endlessness of Historia in Graham Swift's *Waterland*', *Contemporary Literature*, 43:2, Summer 2002, 377–99.

David Leon Higdon, ' "Unconfessed Confessions": the Narrators of Graham Swift and Julian Barnes', in *The British and Irish Novel Since 1960*, edited by James Acheson, London: Macmillan, 1991, 171–91.

Frederick M. Holmes, *The Historical Imagination: Postmodernism and the Treatment of the Past in Contemporary British Fiction*, English Literary Studies, Victoria: University of Victoria, 1997.

Alison Lee, *Realism and Power*, London: Routledge, 1990.

Richard Pedot, 'Dead Lines in Graham Swift's *Last Orders*', *Critique*, 43:1, Fall 2002, 60–72.

Adrian Poole, 'Graham Swift and the Mourning After', in *An Introduction to Contemporary Fiction*, edited by Rod Mengham, Cambridge: Polity, 1999, 150–67.

Lars Ole Sauerberg, *Intercultural Voices in Contemporary British Literature*, London: Palgrave, 2001.

Graham Swift, *The Sweet Shop Owner* (SSO), London: Penguin, 1983.

——, *Shuttlecock* (S), London: Picador, 1997.

——, *Learning to Swim and Other Stories* (LS), London: Picador, 1985.

——, *Waterland* (W), Revised Edition, London: Picador, 1992.

——, *Out of This World* (OTW), London: Penguin, 1988.

——, *Ever After* (EA), London: Picador, 1992.

——, *Last Orders* (LO), London: Picador, 1996.

——, *The Light of Day* (LD), London: Hamish Hamilton, 2003.

Richard Todd, *Consuming Fiction: The Booker Prize and Fiction in Britain Today*, London: Bloomsbury, 1996.

Peter Widdowson, *Graham Swift*, Plymouth: Northcote House, 2004.

Web Reading

http://www.scholars.nus.edu.sg/landow/post/uk/gswift/gsov.html

11

Irvine Welsh: Sex and Drugs and Violence

11.1. Literary History

Though starting as a novelist Irvine Welsh (b.1958), has also become a writer for theatre, film, and television. Welsh's debut novel appeared over a decade after Scottish fiction was given a shot in the arm by the publication of Alasdair Gray's *Lanark* (1981), and some years after the first appearance of fiction by James Kelman, whose *How late it was, how late* became the first Scottish novel to win the Booker Prize in 1994. Welsh is now one of the established names of the Scottish new wave, alongside such writers as Janice Galloway, Iain Banks, Alan Warner, and A. L. Kennedy.

Welsh began his first novel when he was a student at Heriot-Watt University, studying for an MBA. He began it as a reflection of and response to his experience of Edinburgh, and the lives of his old friends in the city, after several years spent in London. The novel had a long gestation period and sections of *Trainspotting* (1993) appeared in magazines as early as 1991. Though it failed to win awards, despite nominations for the Booker and the Whitbread prizes, Welsh's book soon became a bestseller and received very strong reviews for its blend of stark realism with a strain of black humour that varies from the uncomfortably unusual to the sharply familiar. The novel's lack of conventional structure was for most critics offset by its pace, with incidents and anecdotes creating a distinctive rhythm to the narrative. The style of the novel seemed to imitate its subject matter in that the voices and stories come thick and fast like the characters and conversations in one of the book's pubs, creating the sense of an

interconnected group of friends, family, and acquaintances that
the reader comes to know through a long series of adventures and
micronarratives. The ironic title itself comes from the fact that no
trains now stop at Leith Central Station, suggesting that no one
comes and no one goes. Welsh implies that Leith's inhabitants
live in a forgotten town that Edinburgh's more prosperous inhabitants overlook and that the Festival tourists hardly realize exists;
he also implicitly contrasts the anodyne metroland hobby of
trainspotting with the escape into drugs that is the alternative
pastime for his characters in Thatcher's eighties Britain.

Trainspotting ends with its main character, Mark Renton,
leaving Britain for Amsterdam, which provides the setting for
'Eurotrash' in Welsh's next book, *The Acid House* (1994). (While
Euan's experience in 'Eurotrash' reads like a segment of Renton's
experiences between *Trainspotting* and *Porno*, several of the narratives have unnamed narrators and could be outtakes from the
first novel.) This second work was also greeted with critical
acclaim. It is a collection of 21 short stories and one novella that
moves from the speeded up realism of *Trainspotting* into fantasy,
not least because Welsh believes that through the proliferation of
media and the pervasiveness of visual culture modern readers
require multiple and competing narratives to reflect their experience of reality – a fabulous strand that appeared rarely in
Trainspotting except in delusions and hallucinations, or in the dis-
parity between the 'myth' and 'reality' of Begbie. In the title story
of *The Acid House*, a baby and a man on acid exchange minds in a
satire on political correctness and child-rearing; in the inverted
world of 'Where the Debris Meets the Sea' celebrity figures like
Madonna sexually fantasize about lads from Leith; and in 'The
Granton Star Cause' a man on an intense streak of bad luck is
confronted by a drunk and cynical God who condemns him to a
life as a fly, soon after which he is swatted to death by his mother,
but not before he has watched his parents indulge in S&M.
Weaving disparate worlds, the book also brings classes together
more than in Welsh's first novel: in 'Lisa's Mum Meets the Queen
Mum', or when middle-class homeowners are confronted by
working class burglars in 'A Smart Cunt' and academics take
their lifelong intellectual feud into a locals' pub to see what the
'ordinary person' thinks in 'The Two Philosophers'.

Marabou Stork Nightmares (1995) is set in the mind of a comatose
hospitalized computer programmer and football fan, Roy Strang,

who has tried to commit suicide out of guilt over his supposedly
simulated part in a gang rape. The narrative oscillates between
his past life, his present incarceration and a quest for the Marabou
Stork across a fictionalized African 'Jamboland': Roy was sexually abused by a racist uncle in Johannesburg and as a Hibernian
supporter hates Hearts fans as 'Jambos'. The Marabou Stork itself
seems to stand as a symbol for all the pain and violence of Roy's
life. Welsh uses different typography and fonts to represent Roy's
shifts between the three layers of his mental activity: sensory perception, memory, and fantasy, all of which vie for control of his
consciousness. When his rape victim, Kirstie, appears at the hospital to take revenge, the reader learns that Roy not only anally
raped her extremely violently, but planned the attack on her too.

   Ecstasy: Three Tales of Chemical Romance (1996) took the full force
of a backlash against Welsh, with many critics perceiving him to
have succumbed to sensationalism and sentimentality, to have
published too much too quickly and to have produced a novel
that was a pale imitation of his former books. 'Lorraine Goes to
Livingston: A Rave and Regency Romance' concerns a pulp
romance writer and stroke victim, Rebecca Navarro, whose discovery that her husband Perky squanders her money and collects
pornography leads her to introduce overt bestiality into her novels, while she also seeks revenge on a game-show host who
indulges his penchant for necrophilia in the hospital morgue, the
use of which he secures by repaying National Health Service trust
debts. Rebecca's collaborator is Lorraine, the Scottish nurse she
originally aimed to cast as a consort of Lady Caroline Lamb in
one of her historical novels but with whom she comes to enjoy
ecstasy and jungle music as well as her real-life revenge plots. In
'Fortune's Always Hiding: A Corporate Drug Romance', set in
Bavaria, a victim of (what might be) Thalidomide teams up with
a Baader-Meinhof terrorist to wreak revenge on a drug company
with a chainsaw. 'The Undefeated: An Acid House Romance'
returns to Edinburgh, where the alternating narrators, Heather
and Lloyd, are brought together by the highs of house music; but
eventually she persuades him to give up his drug cocktails for the
sake of their relationship. The stories' difference from Welsh's
earlier work is their interest in love in the mid-1990s: courtship on
a chemical high; but the finale of the book suggests that ecstasy
provides temporary, indiscriminate affection and joy while love is
the only reliable long-term drug.

Welsh has declared that *Ecstasy* was published too soon and reads like a pastiche of his earlier books. His next novel, *Filth* (1998), was another commercial bestseller and hailed as a return to form by some critics but considered Welsh's nadir by others. It received better reviews as a piece for theatre, a monologue by the actor Tam Dean Burn adapted by Harry Gibson. The principal narrator is Detective Sergeant Bruce Robertson, of the Lothians and Borders constabulary, an Edinburgh police officer who indulges in almost all prejudices and most vices. It therefore comes as little surprise that he himself turns out to be the murderer of a black journalist he has been pursuing throughout the story. Robertson's wife has left him and he drowns his sorrows in whisky and other women, such as the wife of his brother and of his best friend, while immersing himself in an underworld of drug pushers and gangsters. Though Robertson's narration is represented as dialect, a tapeworm in his gut (a parasite within the parasite) literally overwrites the story of its host in standard English, confronting him with his actions but also recasting him as a victimized and neglected child whose first love died and who now takes out his anger and frustration on the world. As his daughter Stacey unexpectedly appears at the door, Robertson finally hangs himself – before his worm of conscience can consume him, though the parasite has the last word as it slips free from his dangling corpse.

Glue (2001) is a long multilayered story about the lives of four friends from Edinburgh's housing schemes. It follows their adventures from their school days to middle age. The four are Carl Ewart, who becomes a DJ, Billy Birrell, who becomes a barowner, Andrew Galloway, who becomes a heroin addict and, the most vivid character in the book, 'Juice' Terry Lawson, who uses everybody else in the name of a good time. Though it contains cameos for characters from his first novel, the book marks Welsh's attempt to break into a new style and work on a larger canvas. However, *Glue* is in many ways an overfamiliar Welsh mix of unreflectingly narrated stories of sex, drugs, and violence forging for his protagonists an uneasy camaraderie over the decades from the 1970s to the millennium. The music business adds glamour to the narrative in the unlikely final section as an American pop star slums it in Leith with Welsh's cronies only to discover that they have 'life' while she just has a constricting fame that prevents her from enjoying ordinary pleasures. The view is predominantly male until this final section and at times Welsh seems to wish to make Terry Lawson into the endearing rogue he resurfaces as in *Porno*, where a more believable female voice also comes through.

Welsh began a sequel to *Trainspotting* before his first novel was even published but it took nearly ten years for one to appear. *Porno* (2002) features many of the principal characters from Welsh's debut, plus other familiar figures such as Lexo from *Marabou Stork Nightmares* and 'Juice' Terry from *Glue*. Sick Boy is working in a London strip club, but soon moves to take over his aunt's pub in Leith, the Port Sunshine. Mark Renton is running a club, Luxury, in Amsterdam. Begbie is about to be released from jail after committing murder (perceived as manslaughter because he has injuries, which were actually self-inflicted afterwards) in his rage at Renton's elopement with the money at the end of *Trainspotting*. Spud remains unchanged except he now lives with Alison, and they have a son, but he intends to change people's perceptions of him by writing a history of Leith since its unwilling incorporation into Edinburgh in 1920. The main new character is Nikki Fuller-Smith, an undergraduate media and film student and part-time masseuse who becomes a pornstar in the movie that is at first being developed by Terry Lawson, and then by Sick Boy. The novel moves towards a similar conclusion to Welsh's first novel, with Renton escaping from Leith once more, and letting down Spud, fleecing Sick Boy, and narrowly avoiding Begbie's wrath.

Welsh's commercial success has been praised and condemned for spawning a decade of 'lad lit.', in which the likes of Nick Hornby, John King and Tony Parsons have explored the landscapes of contemporary masculinity and generated huge sales by appealing to a readership that had found little reflection of itself in fiction before 1990. *Trainspotting* marked a literary shift because it created a new bestseller that was distinctly Scottish as well as distinctly working-class; it dealt with a subject and with an underclass that both society and fiction had largely chosen to ignore – in a dialect and a demotic language it had also largely chosen to ignore – which is why Alan Sinfield compares its significance with that of another working-class novel that appeared 35 years earlier: Alan Sillitoe's *Saturday Night and Sunday Morning*. *Trainspotting* was read in clubs and appealed to the chemical generation; it encouraged music shops to sell fiction, alerted the middle-class to another side of Edinburgh, which has the highest HIV infection rate in Britain, and reaffirmed the potential of literature to provoke moral outrage. The story also had as great if not greater success in its adaptations as film and play.

11.2. Themes: Scotland, England and Empire

Welsh is often thought of as being directly and unforgivingly critical of Scottish nationalism and of Scottish identity, as in this representative passage from his first novel: 'Some say that the Irish are the trash aye Europe. That's shite. It's the Scots. The Irish had the bottle tae win thir country back, or at least maist ay it' (T, 190). Certainly, many of the characters' feelings of failure in *Trainspotting* are projected onto Scotland. The most famous example is Renton's speech:

> Fuckin failures in a country ay failures. It's nae good blamin it oan the English fir colonising us. Ah don't hate the English. They're just wankers. We are colonised by wankers. We can't even pick a decent, vibrant, healthy culture to be colonised by. No. We're ruled by effete arseholes. What does that make us? The lowest of the fuckin low, the scum of the earth. The most wretched, servile, miserable, pathetic trash that was ever shat intae creation. (T, 78)

Those characters in the novels who valorize Scottishness are usually undermined. In *Porno*, when a professor asserts that it is 'impossible to escape the contention that migratory Scots enriched every society they came into contact with' he is met with this unspoken response from the English Nikki: 'I won't mention their role in slavery, racism or the formation of the Ku Klux Klan' (P, 53). Again, as Spud remarks in *Trainspotting* when considering the attacks on his black friend Dode: 'Ah sortay jist laugh whin some cats say that racism's an English thing' (T, 126). Many of the definitions of Scotland with which Welsh has little sympathy are in fact characterized in this way, by the creation of a dialectic with Englishness. In 'Eurotrash' Richard accuses Euan of being British and Euan is 'almost tempted to go into a spiel about how I was Scottish, not British, and that the Scots were the last oppressed colony of the British Empire. I don't really believe it though; the Scots oppress themselves by their obsession with the English' (AH, 17).

In line with this, Nikki remarks in *Porno* that ' "Rule Britannia" was written by a Scotsman. It was a plea for an inclusion you can never have' (P, 220). But Welsh actually appears to aim at undercutting all national identities as a meaningful or helpful banner under which to unite the characters in his fiction, as Renton decides on a trip to London:

> The pub sign is a new one, but its message is old. The Britannia. Rule Britannia. Ah've never felt British, because ah'm not. It's ugly and artificial. Ah've never really felt Scottish either, though. Scotland the brave, ma arse; Scotland the shitein cunt. We'd throttle the life oot ay each other fir the privilege ay rimmin some English aristocrat's piles. Ah've never felt a fuckin thing aboot countries. ... They should abolish the fuckin lot ay them.   (T, 228)

Renton reinforces the impression of a failed British national identity in *Porno*: 'Someway along the line the British went from being the cunts who had it sussed out to being the biggest wankers in Europe' (P, 125). Renton of course flees Britain for Amsterdam at the end of *Trainspotting* and for San Francisco at the end of *Porno*. The impression is that these other cities have a cultural life that is vastly different from Britain's: San Fransisco and Amsterdam represent places of possible freedom away from the binary of a colonizing England and a colonized Scotland.

Britain's enervating cultural life is defined by two things, the first of which is the heritage industry. At the start of *Trainspotting*, Renton berates 'fat, rich festival cunts too fuckin lazy tae walk a hundred fuckin yards fae one poxy church hall tae another fir thir fuckin show' (T, 4). Later he adds to this complaint in a way that aligns 'heritage' with Welsh's second, greater target: 'Ah remember walkin along Princes street wi Spud, we both hate walkin along that hideous street, deadened by tourists and shoppers, the twin curses ay modern capitalism. Ah looked up at the castle and thought, it's just another building tae us. It registers in oor heids just like the British Home Stores or Virgin Records' (T, 228).

What Welsh therefore suggests has ruined both Scotland and England is a homogenizing consumerism allied to a general embrace of middle-class values, with its commodification of the city and Edinburgh's past. Spud tells Begbie: 'it's aw changing, man. Yuv goat the Scottish Office at one end and the new Parliament at the other. Embourgeoisement, man, that's what the intellectual cats call it. Ten years' time, there'll be nae gadges like me n you left doon here ... very soon, Franco, auld Leith will be gone' (P, 261). Spud is in fact himself in several respects an example of the creeping homogenization brought about by globalized consumerism, at the same time as he is excluded from the affluence it promises. He is notable for his embrace of TV culture, and his speech is peppered with Americanisms while his conception of other cultures is based on soaps (e.g. Spud thinks Australia must be 'really crap' because of what he sees as the dull suburbia of *Neighbours* and *Home and Away* (T, 292)). Similarly, Sick Boy's self-image is fashioned by popular culture, most particularly Connery's Scottish macho version of James Bond. Overall, the characters' rejection of heritage and consumerism is largely predicated upon their exclusion from its benefits, and while they opt instead for the manufactured nihilism of Iggy Pop and punk, there is evidence of a clear underlying desire for affluence and designer individualism that is economically rather than ideologically alien.

The theme of national identity crosses over into other fundamental allegiances explored by Welsh, from football teams to religion. Racism (central, for example, to *Filth* and to 'Stoke Newington Blues' in *The Acid House*) and Protestant–Catholic antagonism appear on several occasions throughout the fiction: for example, in *Trainspotting* when Spud and Dode get into a fight in 'Na Na and Other Nazis', or when Renton attends the funeral of his brother Billy, blown up on patrol in Ireland, in 'Bang to Rites'. Like the more famous animosity in Glasgow between Rangers and Celtic supporters, the antagonism in Edinburgh between Hibs and Hearts fans is not just between rival football teams, but between 'Fenian' and 'Orange' factions. Welsh's interest is in the thin line between the animus behind this local feud and the dynamics of wider group behaviour in which difference is always configured negatively. In *Trainspotting* Stevie remarks about the hatred between Hearts and Hibs: 'He was a London boy now, what did all this shite have to do with his life at the moment' (T, 49), but the narrative soon explains when his assailants turn to berating an Asian woman ('Fuck off back tae yir ain country' (T, 50)), displacing their enmity on to any 'other' who crosses their path.

Most directly however, echoing one of his characters railing against the Festival scene, Welsh himself has in interviews attacked Edinburgh's image, which he characterizes as 'shortbread Disneyland' or 'Brigadoon'. *Porno* also has digs at post-devolution Scottish nationalism: for example, one violent attack in the novel pointedly takes place outside the Scottish Parliament building, while on another occasion Spud feels an outsider – like he's 'breakin in' – when he goes to the Central Library's Edinburgh Rooms to write the history of his own town. Only the upwardly mobile Sick Boy is celebratory about twenty-first century prosperity, because he thinks he can have a slice of the 'new Leith': 'Royal Yacht Britannia, the Scottish Office, renovated docks, wine bars, restaurants, yuppie pads. This is the future, and it's only two blocks away The next year, the year after maybe, just one block away. Then bingo!' (P, 47)

11.3. Key Works: *Trainspotting* and *Porno*

Trainspotting appears to be set in the mid- to late-1980s and the early 1990s though the novel itself provides few temporal markers or direct references to dates. Based almost entirely in Edinburgh, in the north of the city, from Muirhouse to Leith, Welsh's narrative seems to proceed chronologically though its shape is less founded on a linear progression than based on repetitions and parallels. The book is divided into 43 chapters in seven sections. The section titles appear to mark an oscillation: between going on and off drugs, between going away and coming back, between moving on and returning: 'Kicking', 'Relapsing', 'Kicking Again', 'Blowing It', 'Exile', 'Home', and 'Exit'. The last, which is also by far the shortest section, is a final 'quitting' whose longevity will only be addressed in *Trainspotting*'s sequel, *Porno*.

Some of the chapters are narrated in standard English by the third-person narrator (e.g. 'Victory on New Year's Day', 'Grieving and Mourning in Port Sunshine', and 'There's A Light That Never Goes Out'). The language of the remaining chapters varies with the narrators, each of who speaks a mix of blended English, idiolect and dialect, from Dave Mitchell's minimal variations on English dictionary spellings ('Bad Blood', 'Traditional Sunday

Breakfast') to the major variations of characters like Spud, which led to the inclusion of a glossary in the US edition (it is also notable that in *Porno* only Begbie and Spud remain native Leith speakers). The importance of this is that it draws the reader's attention to the significance of narrative voice, or rather voices; Welsh takes care to identify each narrator with particular patterns of speech and expression in their use of dialect. Thus, though it is not always clear to the reader from the content or context at the outset as to who is narrating each chapter, the language is an immediate clue. Also, though one of the most important aspects of *Trainspotting* is its use of multiple narrators, thus creating a sense of community in the novel (a common approach in working-class fiction from John Sommerfield's *May Day* in the 1930s to Pat Barker's *Blow your House Down* in the 1980s), Welsh does not attempt to homogenize the characters but to accentuate their differences by his use of distinct voices (even the speech of minor characters is represented phonetically, 'That's joost wot oi was tro-ing to tell the bastid, he sais in a Brummie accent' (T, 238)).

The novel has a very large cast but the central characters are those who go to London in the final chapter: (Mark) Renton, Spud (Danny Murphy), Sick Boy (Simon Williams), Second Prize (Rab McLaughlin), and (Frank) Begbie. Of these, the closest to a protagonist is Renton, a 25-year-old with spiky hair dyed to lose the 'McLeish image' (from orange-haired football manager Alec McLeish (T, 136)), a Catholic mother, a Protestant father from Glasgow, an older brother in the army and a younger handicapped one, now dead. If the book has a trajectory, it is described by Renton's attempts to escape the influences of his upbringing (of which his drug abuse is a symptom), something he appears only to achieve at the book's close. On the one hand, snatches of his history reveal that Renton has spent his schooling trying unsuccessfully to escape the psychopathic Begbie's corrosive influence (T, 83); on the other hand, his family represent for him the internecine warfare of Catholics and Protestants that leads to many fights in the novel and results in the death of Renton's brother Billy in Crossmaglen, near the border between Ireland and Northern Ireland. Welsh's narrative opens with Renton trying to watch the end of a video as Sick Boy selfishly insists that they go for a hit; it ends with Renton deciding that, 'free from them all, for good, he could be whatever he wanted to be. He'd stand or fall alone' (T, 344). Seen from Renton's point of view the book thus culminates in a rejection of home, family, religion, and friends that echoes Stephen Dedalus's self exile at the end of Joyce's *A Portrait of the Artist as a Young Man*; but where Stephen Dedalus has been searching for, and has discovered, his true vocation, Renton is clearly escaping from various kinds of dependency (even 'Begbie is like Junk, a habit' (T, 83)) and tight bonds of kith if not kin. He is also escaping from various kinds of threat: the police, Sick Boy's narcissistic selfishness, Begbie's violence, the risk of becoming HIV-positive, like Tommy, Wee Goagsie and Dave Mitchell, and the forces of death that have taken others, such as his older brother (killed in the army), his uncle Andy (heart-attack), Matty (toxoplasmosis) and Danny Ross (self-injected with whisky). He is also haunted by the death of his younger, handicapped brother and the cot-death of Wee Dawn.

Written towards the tail end of over fifteen years of Conservative rule, the book also portrays a world of unemployment and social deprivation in which social and personal relations have deteriorated alongside economic decline: few of the characters have jobs, the men are almost exclusively homophobic and misogynistic, and there are very few happy or stable relationships. *Trainspotting* portrays a society in which masculinity has been stripped of its dignity to such an extent that the only outlets for male pride are violence and sexual promiscuity. While babies are disowned or neglected by their fathers in the home, frustration and resentment result in random and unprovoked violence on the streets (the most striking example of this is Begbie's attack on a man in Duke Street for the sole reason that he has just caught sight of his father, 'an auld wino' (T, 309)). The attitudes of the women towards relationships with men are generally cynical: 'Nina had not been with anyone yet, had not done it. Almost everyone she knew said it was crap. Boys were too stupid, too morose and dull, or too excitable' (T, 36). In fact, this seems to be a view held by many of the male characters, but few include themselves in the criticism. Sick Boy declares early on:

> Ah shake off Rents, he can go and kill himself with drugs. Some fucking friends I have. Spud, Second Prize, Begbie, Matty, Tommy: these punters spell L-I-M-I-T-E-D. An extremely limited company. Well, ah'm fed up to ma back teeth wi losers, no-hopers, draftpaks, shemies, junkies and the likes.

I am a dynamic young man, upwardly mobile and thrusting, thrusting, thrusting... (T, 30).

Amid all the voices, Renton, who starts and finishes the novel, becomes the character with whom the reader is encouraged to empathize and who in turn is capable of showing some empathy (e.g. T, 279). He values education and reflection, reads books (to Begbie's disgust), discusses youth cultural reference points (e.g. T, 136–7), has temporarily attended University, and is by far the most cerebral of the main characters – a fact that leads to him avoiding the custodial sentence that Spud receives when they appear in court (T, 166–7). It is also only Renton who articulates his condition and expresses a view of society and psychology that offers a rationalization of his circumstances. Reflecting on his conversations with a counsellor he observes that: 'Tom refuses tae accept ma view that society cannae be changed tae make it significantly better, or that ah cannae change tae accommodate it' (T, 186). In a passage that sheds light on his 'Exit' at the end of the novel, he declares: 'Society invents a spurious convoluted logic tae absorb and change people whae's behaviour is outside its mainstream. Suppose that ah ken aw the pros and cons, know that ah'm gaunnae huv a short life, am ay sound mind etcetera, etcetera, but still want tae use smack? They won't let ye dae it, because it's seen as a sign ay thir ain failure' (T, 187). This is sum-marized as the exhortation to 'Choose life', which the film of the novel makes the decision of the story's conclusion but which the book avoids endorsing by having Renton, somewhat vaguely and perhaps naively, choose to 'escape' to Amsterdam so that he can 'be what he wanted to be' (T, 344). This connects with and is the culmination of a decision he makes when he goes cold turkey in the middle section of the book: 'Ah huv tae get oot ay Leith, oot ay Scotland. For good. Right away, no jist doon tae London fir six months' (T, 201). Renton is however full of frustration and hate: for Begbie, for his brother Billy (illustrated by his having sex with his pregnant sister-in-law Sharon immediately after his brother's funeral), and even for cats and dogs (T, 230). It is to escape his despair that Renton is most frequently seen shooting up: 'cook up a shot and git a hit, in the cause ay oblivion' (T, 222). For Renton and others, the oblivion of heroin is part of Iggy Pop's 'psychic defence' (T, 75) against globalization and homogenized mass consumer society, though the 'defence' emerges as a self-destructive one that is poorly modelled on the excesses of rock stars whose endorsement of drugs is as commodified as the lifestyle products on sale along Princes Street ('heroin' was itself coined in German as a trademark, most likely drawing its name from the word 'hero' and from the drug's aggrandizing effect on the personality).

As drugs have also replaced courtship as a means of temporary relief and escape, it is less surprising that expressions of love in *Trainspotting* are for the most part limited to romancing suppliers ('Sick Boy serenades Johnny Swan: 'Swanney, how ah love ya' (T, 11)), whereas relationships are rarely presented in terms of affection. Renton's sexual relations are limited to Hazel (their sex life is a 'disaster', and we discover Hazel was abused by her father (T, 76)), Dianne, who is underage (T, 150), and Kelly, who has had an abortion that Renton seems to think is none of his business (T, 11). Similarly, Begbie ignores his children and Sick Boy is indifferent to his daughter Dawn (that he is her father is confirmed in *Porno*, 386).

The 1996 Danny Boyle film, in which Welsh appeared as the dealer Danny Forrester, has noticeable differences from the novel. Most clear is the attempt to provide a centre to the narrative by using Renton as a voice-over narrator, connecting the scenes and explaining the characters to the viewer. Also of importance is the end of the film, which has Renton explicitly declaring that he is choosing the viewer's lifestyle, assumed to be one of mortgages and three-piece suites, over his previous rejection of 'life', the most direct assertion of which opens the movie. To lighten Renton's 'guilt' he also leaves some money behind for Spud, to reduce the number of friends he has betrayed to Begbie, whom he hates, and Sick Boy, who he thinks would have done the same to him. More than the novel therefore, the film assumes a moral position for its audience and aims to situate Renton within it, asserting that his theft is to facilitate his transformation into a 'good' person rather than to fuel his new life in Amsterdam. The film thus ends optimistically, whereas the novel suggests that Renton may not escape so easily, as the final, seventh section is only one stage in the oscillation between kicking and relapsing: 'Ma problem is, whenever ah sense the possibility, or realize the actuality ay attaining something that ah thought ah wanted, be it girlfriend, flat, job, education, money and so on, it jist seems so dull n sterile, that ah cannae value it any mair. Junk's different though. Ye cannae turn yir back oan it sae easily. It willnae let ye' (T, 90).

* * *

The sequel to *Trainspotting* brings its four main characters back together after years of separation: Renton in Amsterdam, Sick Boy in London, Begbie in prison, and only Spud still in Leith. The novel has comparatively little to do with drugs – only Spud is seemingly burdened with a disabling junk habit. The focus moves towards another underground industry and addiction, which is approached far more lightly than heroin was in *Trainspotting*. Indeed the shift between *Trainspotting* and *Porno* is in many ways most strongly marked by a change of tone, because in the sequel Welsh treats his subject with more humour than realism or pathos.

The book's three-part structure is straightforward and its narration moves between five voices, each identified by a different style of chapter heading: Sick Boy's are always a numbered 'Scam' beginning at 18 732; Begbie's chapter titles are in capitals as though he is shouting; Renton's are part-numbered 'Whores of Amsterdam' from one to twelve; Spud's are in regular title case; and Nikki's chapter headings are formed from snippets of her narration encased in ellipses. Welsh accentuates the characteristics of each of the four main characters from *Trainspotting*, making Renton thoughtful, Sick Boy irredeemably selfish, Spud kind but perennially unsuccessful, and Begbie humourless and violently aggressive. Renton's betrayal of the others hangs over the narrative, but it emerges that, as in the film version of *Trainspotting*, Renton has compensated Spud: by sending him money earned from the nightclub Renton runs in Amsterdam. He also wishes to recompense Second Prize, who is a very minor character in *Porno*, but Begbie and Sick Boy end the sequel worse off than they did in *Trainspotting*: the former is hospitalized, having been run over while racing across a street to attack Renton; the latter is robbed by Renton as well as by his 'dream girlfriend' Nikki. *Porno* thus serves to underline and even endorse Renton's decision in the first novel by having history repeat itself. Welsh sets up a third instalment ('Can you imagine us ten years on?' Renton asks Sick Boy towards the end of the narrative (P, 434)) by ending *Porno* with Sick Boy and Begbie having twice as much motivation as they had at the end of *Trainspotting* to seek revenge on Renton, who this time has escaped to the United States.

Though she is Welsh's most convincing female figure in *Porno*, Dianne from *Trainspotting* lacks a narrative voice, whereas Nikki Fuller-Smith emerges as both a stereotype and Welsh's most sustained woman character. Her portrayal balances her sense of female sexual freedom and a belief in liberation from male possession with her negative body-image and her realization that whatever degree of self-determination she exercises, the porn industry will ultimately exploit her, as does her director, producer, and boyfriend, Sick Boy. In this light, the 'erotic adult entertainment' business, for all the sense of homemade self-amusement involved in Juice Terry's initial visual-karaoke camcorder experiments, appears just as exploitative as the drug industry at the first moment that a commercial element is introduced, as inevitably happens when Sick Boy sees the potential to sell a product and work a scam. He explains to Nikki:

> porn is mainstream now. Virgin sells porn movies. Greg Dark directs Britney Spears videos. Grot mags and men's mags and women's mags are the same. Even repressed, censored British TV teases us with the hint of it. Young people as consumers don't make the distinction now between porn or adult entertainment and mainstream entertainment. In the same way they don't between alcohol and drugs.   (P, 347)

Porno is thus about the wider cultural climate as much as it is about sex, and indeed, as Dianne says, 'I don't think porn per se is the real issue. I think it's how we consume' (P, 266). A central observation Welsh is making concerns the contemporary cultural desire to perform on film or television, such that he sees 'reality' TV shows like *Big Brother* on a par with karaoke and DIY porn. The fascination with appearing on camera that used to stop people outside Dixons, staring at their own image on a television screen in the shop window, has fuelled an industry of home-movie production in which those who cannot professionally act, sing, or otherwise entertain, hold the attention of the viewer through sex. While Spud's ideal job would be to act 'as an agent for aw they blonde burds thit they huv oan the telly' (P, 72), Nikki declares that if she appeared on television or on a magazine cover: 'I would feel great because at least I would have been there. At least I would have achieved something. That's what it's all about. I want to be up there. I want to act, sing and dance. Me. I want them to see that I lived. Nikki Fuller-Smith fucking well lived' (P, 69).

But most of all the book is about capitalism's exploitation of even the most intimate and private aspects of people's lives: 'That's the thing with sex work, it always comes down to the most basic of formulas. If you really want to see how capitalism operates, never mind Adam Smith's pin factory, this is the place to study' (P, 88). Riddled with addictions, Spud is consequently the most vulnerable character in the book, immune to the forces of capitalism that aim to turn him into the defeated individual that everyone in the novel thinks he is: 'Cigarettes, alcohol, heroin, cocaine, speed, poverty, and media mind-fucking: capitalism's weapons of destruction are more subtle and effective than Nazism's and he's powerless against them' (P, 384). *Porno's* motto, repeated several times, is first flagged by Sick Boy and then turned against him: 'Look at humiliation television, look at the papers and the mags, look at the class system, the jealousy, the bitterness that oozes out of our culture: in Britain we want to see people get fucked' (P, 179). In saying this, Sick Boy of course pronounces his own future, as the novel confirms and conforms to this belief by assuming the reader will most want to see Sick Boy get 'shafted' at the story's end.

Porno is itself a much slicker narrative than *Trainspotting*. The sequel's structure, plot and ending are all carefully arranged in a way that shows the changes that have developed in Welsh's writing over a decade. While the rough edges have been lost there has been an increase in sentimentality and contrivance and his characters generally lack the force they had in his first novel. But, in bringing the characters of *Trainspotting* back in *Porno*, Welsh has also increased their degree of reflection, such that many of the novel's points about capitalism, sexuality, drug dependency, and the cult of celebrity are told to the reader rather than illustrated dramatically. This is perhaps a consequence of age, as Renton and Sick Boy are now better able to rationalize their position, but it results in more didactic narrative voices. For example,

That's our tragedy: nobody, except destructive exploiters like Sick Boy, or bland opportunists like Carolyn, has any real passion. Everybody else is so beaten down by the crap and mediocrity around them. If the word in the eighties was 'me', and in the nineties 'it', in the millennium it's 'ish'. Everything has to be vague and qualified. Substance used to be important, then style was everything. Now it's all just faking it.   (P, 374)

The characters pitted against exploitation and simulation are Renton and Dianne, a couple who turn down the chance to have sex with others because they love each other (P, 421); yet it is of course also they who con the scammer Sick Boy at the end of the novel.

While Welsh has been accused of misogyny and sensationalism, his response to this charge has been to claim that he refuses to sanitize his characters' views in the name of political correctness and that he faithfully represents the world in which he grew up. Several of the narratives, critics have argued, also represent and often endorse a (radical) feminist perspective, ranging from Lauren's arguments in *Porno* to Kirstie's revenge on her rapists in *Marabou Stork Nightmares*, culminating in the attack on Roy in which she slices off his genitals and stuffs them into his mouth before killing him. Arguably, however, Welsh appears to see sexual inequalities less in terms of feminism's battle with patriarchy than in terms of 'girl power' losing out to exploitation and capitalism, as Dianne argues in *Porno*: 'All those girls I've spoken to, they've got all the power, all that tits, arse and fanny power, and they sell it too cheaply. They practically give it away for nothing. That's the fucking tragedy, girl' (P, 312). Welsh's gay characters also appear to be victimized throughout his distinctly masculinist stories, but Welsh's protagonists such as Renton are not 'straightforwardly straight', and there is narratorial compassion in the portrayal of Denise in 'A Smart Cunt', as well as understanding for the sex-change Chrissie in 'Eurotrash'. While keeping the characters accurate to his experience, Welsh aims to undercut stereotypical hypermasculine Scottish culture in the same way that Sick Boy undermines Begbie's aggressive sexual confidence in *Porno* by sending him gay porn.

At the end of *Porno* it is Sick Boy who argues that pornography is not just logical but necessary in a consumer-driven society:

Because we're consumers. Because those are things we like, things we intrinsically feel or have been conned into believing will give us value, release, satisfaction. We value them so we need to at least have the illusion of their availability. For tits and arse read coke, crisps, speedboats, cars, houses, computers, designer labels, replica shirts. That's why advertising and pornography are similar; they sell the illusion of availability and the non-consequence of consumption. (P, 450)

To put this another way, in the terms of *Trainspotting*, the compulsion to 'Choose Life' ten years on has sucked in the very characters that Welsh was presenting as outside the middle-classes' frames of reference or understanding: consumerism has resulted in the embourgeoisement of Leith.

References and Further Reading

Cairns Craig, *The Modern Scottish Novel: Narrative and the National Imagination*, Edinburgh: Edinburgh University Press, 1999.
Ian Haywood, *Working-Class Fiction: From Chartism to Trainspotting*, Plymouth: Nothcote House, 1997.
Christie L. March, *Re-Writing Scotland*, Manchester: Manchester University Press, 2002.
Drew Milne, 'The Fiction of James Kelman and Irvine Welsh', in *Contemporary British Fiction*, edited by Richard J. Lane, Rod Mengham, and Philip Tew, Cambridge: Polity, 2003, 158–73.
R. Morace, *Irvine Welsh's Trainspotting*, New York: Continuum, 2001.
Alan Sinfield, *Literature, Politics and Culture in Postwar Britain*, Second Edition, London: Athlone Press, 1997.
G. Wallace and R. Stevenson (eds) *The Scottish Novel Since the Seventies*, Edinburgh: Edinburgh University Press, 1993.
Irvine Welsh, *Trainspotting* (T), London: Vintage, 1995.
——, *The Acid House* (AH), London: Vintage, 1995.
——, *Porno* (P), London: Jonathan Cape, 2002.
C. Whyte, 'Masculinities in Contemporary Scottish Fiction', in *Forum for Modern Languages*, 34:2, 1998, 274–85.
M. Williams, 'The Dialect of Authenticity: The Case of Irvine Welsh's *Trainspotting*' in *English Literature and Other Languages*, edited by M. Buning and T. Hoenselaars, Amsterdam: Rodopi, 1999, 221–30.

Web Reading

Key Website: http://www.irvinewelsh.net/
http://www.irvinewelsh.com/index.php
'Salon Interview': http://dir.salon.com/people/conv/2001/07/09/welsh/index.html

12

Jeanette Winterson: Boundaries and Desire

On the day I was born I became the visible corner of a folded map.
(PB, 155)

12.1. Literary History

In addition to eight novels, Jeanette Winterson (b.1959) has written short stories, film scripts, essays and even a guide to well-being. In interview, Winterson has said that she is interested in strong emotions like love and desire because they recreate the world and are: 'a chance element which unsettles all the rules, which forces people back onto their own resources, and away from their habits. ... Always in my books, I like to throw that rogue element into a stable situation and then see what happens' ('Salon Interview', 28 April 1997). Adopted by members of a Pentecostal church, she was raised as a working-class evangelist in Lancashire: an upbringing which provided the material for her first and still best-known novel. Though the basic details of *Oranges Are Not the Only Fruit* (1985) correspond to the facts of Winterson's early life, she has said that the novel is no more autobiographical than her other fiction. Instead, she has referred to the book as 'a fiction masquerading as a memoir' (AO, 53). It is a novel that interweaves a realist Bildungsroman with episodic fairy tales, most of which feature Winnet Stonejar, an alter ego for the novel's protagonist, Jeanette. Winterson has said that she aimed in the book 'to create an imaginative reality sufficiently at odds with our daily reality to startle us out of it' (AO, 188).

In the same year as *Oranges*, Winterson published a short comic novel that she now considers peripheral to her main work: *Boating for Beginners* (1985), an alternative version of Genesis, with God as the concoction of a capitalist Noah. This was followed by *The Passion* (1987), a book in which Winterson created an imaginative 'mirror' to the actual world of the Thatcher boom years, set in the Napoleonic Europe of the early nineteenth century: 'My own cities were invented; cities of language, cities of connection, words as gang-ways and bridges to the cities of the interior where the coin was not money, where it was emotion' (note to 1996 Vintage edition). The mirror here then is not a looking glass but a reflector of possibilities: 'I see a little boy watching his reflection in a copper pot he's polished. His father comes in and laughs and offers him his shaving mirror instead. But in the shaving mirror the boy can see only one face. In the pot he can see all the distortions of his face. He sees many possible faces and so he sees what he might become' (P, 26). A novel in four parts, *The Passion* has two narrators. The first is Henri, a peasant from Boulogne who becomes a cook and a special attendant on Napoleon, and finds it 'Odd to be so governed by an appetite' when he discovers the Emperor has such an enormous passion for chicken (P, 3). Henri is by contrast from 'a lukewarm people': 'Not much touches us, but we long to be touched' (P, 7). The second narrator is Villanelle, the daughter of a Venetian boatman born in 'the city of mazes' (P, 49) that Napoleon captured in 1797. Villanelle is the first woman in the city to be born with the fabled webbed feet of the gondoliers.

The Passion has several recurring themes, one of which is gambling, which is 'not a vice, it is an expression of our humanness' (P, 73): 'It's the playing that's irresistible. Dicing from one year to the next with the things you love, what you risk reveals what you value' (P, 43). Cross-dressed, Villanelle goes to work in the Venice Casino where she smells the allure of risk and urgency 'somewhere between fear and sex: Passion I suppose' (P, 55). At the Casino, Villanelle meets a woman she knows as 'the Queen of spades': the symbol of Venice. The two women begin an affair and Villanelle enters a new world: 'without warning you find the solid floor is a trapdoor and you are now in another place whose geography is uncertain ... for us, who travel along the blood vessels, who come to the cities of the interior by chance, there is no preparation. ... Somewhere between God and the Devil passion is and the way there is sudden and the way back is worse' (P, 68). Villanelle makes the bet that can be made 'only once' and gambles her heart on the Queen of spades (cf. Pushkin's short story of the same name).

Despairing of winning the Queen from her husband, Villanelle marries a man who two years later, after he wins a wager with her freedom as the stake, sells her into the army. Henri and Villanelle thus meet on Napoleon's ill-fated zero-winter march to Moscow. Henri's passion for Napoleon (P, 108) is transferred to Villanelle and they return to Venice to rescue Villanelle's 'stolen' heart from the Queen of spades but are arrested after Henri kills Villanelle's husband. In the final part of the book, after he has been declared insane, Henri is imprisoned for life, like Napoleon, in San Servolo on 'The Rock'. Villanelle visits Henri over many years as he grows more insular and mentally disordered. Despite the fact that she bears their daughter, Henri refuses to see Villanelle because 'she hurts me too much'; instead he sits alone and nurses his love for her and his hate for Napoleon: 'What am I interested in? Passion. Obsession' (P, 153). Though he could walk free, Henri feeds the seagulls from his prison window and mulls over his life: 'Love, they say, enslaves and passion is a demon and many have been lost for love. I know this is true, but I know too that without love we grope the tunnels of our lives and never see the sun. When I fell in love it was as though I looked into a mirror for the first time and saw myself' (P, 154).

The Passion contains similar fantastical elements to *Oranges* but they are more directly woven into the main narrative: Patrick's preternatural long-distance vision; Villanelle's webbed feet and her heart in a jar; the perpetually frozen miraculous icicle with a gold thread through it (Henri says that the thought of not seeing Villanelle each day 'froze my heart more cleanly than any zero winter' (P, 122)). Both novels use allegorical images to intensify the presentation of emotion and identity in the main storylines.

Winterson experimented with fantasy and history more extensively in her next novel, *Sexing the Cherry* (1989). The narration is once more split between two characters, Jordan, an explorer, and his adoptive gargantuan mother, Dog Woman. The time now is the seventeenth century and the events that form a backdrop to the narrative are the Puritan Revolution and the English Civil War, the Great Fire of London and the Plague; but the narrative also reaches forward in its last section to the present and makes reference to events such as the Falklands war. In its plotting the book challenges conventional notions of time, querying history with physics and reality with fantasy. This is flagged in the novel's epigraphs, which note that according to physics matter is empty space and points of light (cf. SC, 144), and that the language of the Hopi Indians has no past, present or future tense (cf. SC, 134–5). Through such references as well as through the counter-intuitive turns of the story Winterson indicates how ideas and beliefs about history and reality are social constructs, which can be changed and can be re-imagined. *Sexing the Cherry* builds on the theme of blurred or disguised genders developed in the figure of Villanelle in *The Passion* by dressing Jordan as a woman to further his quest for the dancer he loves. He muses: 'I have met a number of people, who, anxious to be free of the burdens of their gender, have dressed themselves men as women and women as men. ... In my petticoats I was a traveller in a foreign country' (SC, 31). Jordan's journeys begin as spatial explorations but become interior investigations of the self. At one point, Jordan wonders whether he could apply to himself the art of grafting which he has learned in relation to the cherry: 'Grafting is the means whereby a plant, perhaps tender or uncertain, is fused into a hardier member of its strain, and so the two take advantage of each other and produce a third kind' (SC, 78). The sex of the cherry remains the same but a new strain is created.

A concern to challenge further the social constructions of gendered identity underpins *Written On the Body* (1992), in which the narrator's sex is unknown. The book is in essence the story of the at-times obsessive love that the narrator, a translator of Russian literature, has for Louise, who is married to a doctor called Elgin. When Louise develops cancer, a kind of appropriation of the body that threatens to overtake the narrator's desire, it is only Elgin who can treat her. The narrator's response to this putative double-loss, of Louise to cancer and to Elgin, is to explore Louise's body in and through writing: to anatomize love and to celebrate its beauties in order to counter the view questioned in the novel's opening line: 'Why is the measure of love loss?' (WB, 9)

Art & Lies: A Piece for Three Voices and a Bawd (1994) returns to Winterson's more experimental mode but is constructed around three figures, as are all her recent novels (these triads are likened to a trefoil knot in *Written On the Body* (WB, 87)). Its narrators are Sappho, a version of the ancient Greek poet, Handel, a doctor and ex-priest, and Picasso, a female painter. Each of them has been traumatized by abuse – respectively, mutilated poetry, castration, rape – and, as they travel on a high-speed train in the year 2000, each discloses deep feelings of alienation in the modern world. Only Art provides solace for the characters, all of whom are out of step with social conventions and contemporary mores.

Gut Symmetries (1997) employs some elements similar to those found in Winterson's earlier work but it is more indebted to scientific theories than any of her previous novels. Like *Written on the Body* it is concerned with the forces that operate upon and within three lovers – but this time it is a love triangle with all the corners connected, all the love lines joined – and like *Oranges*, the novel describes the religious upbringing of its main characters. The protagonists are the 24-year-old Alluvia (Alice), and the middle-aged married couple Giovanni (Jove, a lapsed Catholic) and Sarah (Stella, half-German, half-Jewish, GS, 92). The book begins on the QE2 when Alice starts an affair with Jove and ends with Alice fleeing the same ship months later to rescue her new love Stella, who is lost at sea alone with her husband. Winterson uses numerous devices and metaphors to develop the novel's imagery, from the Tarot cards that provide the chapter titles to the astrological signs that seem to mark each character's fate and personality as much as their names (Jeanette also plays Alice in Wonderland to her mother's Queen, in *Oranges*, e.g. ONF, 125, and the narrator in *Written On the Body* says 'I shall call myself Alice', WB, 10). The overriding imagery of the book is signalled by the title: 'Grand Unified Theories that sought to unite the strong, weak, and electromagnetic quanta in a sympathetic symmetry. ... GUTs had their heart in the right place; they wanted to recognize the true relationship between the three forces' (GS, 97).

The PowerBook (2000) has familiar Winterson ingredients: fairy stories, a case of adoption, a love triangle, displays of passion and discussions of sexual freedom. But it adds a new element to her manipulations of literary form by employing cyberspace to explore gender roles and identities. Winterson parallels the freedom to explore subjectivity with the anonymity of email: 'Take off your clothes. Take off your body. Hang them up behind the door. Tonight we can go deeper than disguise' (PB, 4). The novel retains the same lesbian relationship throughout but transports the lovers from one place to another in the book's central conceit of free movement through virtual reality. Like Winterson's other novels *The PowerBook* is about the risks that the individual takes in entering into an intense relationship, one that will transform both people: 'In fierceness, in heat, in longing, in risk, I find something of love's nature. In my desire for you, I burn at the right temperature to walk through love's fire. So when you ask me why I cannot love you more calmly, I answer that to love you calmly is not to love you at all' (PB, 189).

Winterson has also written and published the script for the TV adaptation of *Oranges Are Not the Only Fruit* (1990), a filmplay for BBC television called *Great Moments In Aviation* (1994), and a collection of short stories from across her career, *The World and Other Places* (1998), which contain characters and stories, such as 'The Poetics of Sex' and 'The Three Friends', which will be familiar to readers of the novels. She has written a regular column for *The Guardian*, contributes to other newspapers, and has made forays into writing for the stage and TV documentaries, most notably her exploration of the background to and impact of Virginia Woolf's *Orlando*, for the BBC in 2002 (cf. *The PowerBook*, 237–8). Her collection of essays entitled *Art Objects* was issued in 1995 and a book for children, *The King of Capri*, was published in 2003.

Winterson is an uneven but consistently interesting writer. She is best known for her early works up to *Written On the Body*, but this is perhaps because of the order of their publication as much as anything else. There is a constancy of theme and focus, despite enormous variety of style and setting, that makes each book appear a variation on familiar preoccupations, teasing away at them in fresh ways using new ideas. However, a claim might be made for her recent work expressing a new maturity as she explores love's triangularity using art, science or technology. *Gut Symmetries*, in particular, is a complex and richly layered narrative that warrants greater attention than it has so far received, and it is to be hoped that Winterson's 2004 novel *Lighthousekeeping* proves to be considered among her best.

12.2. Themes: Love, Life, the Universe and Storytelling

In *The PowerBook* the narrator Ali writes of Rembrandt: 'No artist had so conspicuously made himself both the subject and the object of his work' (PB, 214). However, this is something that could be said of Winterson; not that her writing is extraordinarily autobiographical but that it is intimately concerned with the emotions and feelings of the individual self, which are revealed and scrutinized, displayed and studied. Ali admires Rembrandt because he was 'shifting his own boundaries' and Ali is a novelist like Winterson whose books are, she says, about 'Boundaries. Desire' (PB, 36).

A passage in *Gut Symmetries* seems to bring together Winterson's preoccupations: 'To live differently, to love differently, to think differently, or to try to. Is the danger of beauty so great that it is better to live without it (The Standard Model)? Or to fall into her arms fire to fire? There is no discovery without risk and what you risk reveals what you value. Inside the horror of Nagasaki and Hiroshima lies the beauty of Einstein's E = MC^2' (GS, 103). To recognize and embrace the gamble of loving, is to risk having your world blown apart in order to experience something beautiful, pointed up here by the direct echo of a phrase from *The Passion* (the novel is also referred to in *The PowerBook*, PB, 26).

To love differently emerges as a goal achieved by telling stories differently, of re-imagining and re-mapping life. Throughout her fiction, Winterson returns to this theme and provides different metaphors for that re-imagining:

> Break the narrative. Refuse all the stories that have been told so far ... and try to tell the story differently – in a different style, with different weights. ... In quantum reality there are millions of possible worlds, unactualised, potential, perhaps bearing in on us, but only reachable by wormholes we can never find. If we do find one, we don't come back. ... I can't take my body through space and time, but I can send my mind, and use the stories, written and unwritten, to tumble me out in a place not yet existing – my future. The stories are maps. Maps of journeys that have been made and might have been made. (PB, 53)

This passage in *The PowerBook* occurs when the narrator has been told 'I think someone has cut out your heart' (PB, 52), which is another recurring trope of Winterson's fiction. In *The Passion* this carving out has happened 'literally' to Villanelle when her heart is kept in a jar in the house of the Queen of spades. In all the stories, whether the images are derived from folk tales or quantum theory, Winterson keeps to this idea of love as a precious possession, which can be locked away or lost. Love is always a secret treasure buried in the heart, even in the least fantastical stories throughout Winterson's novels, such that in *Written On the Body* the narrator declares about Louise: 'A treasure had fallen into our hands and the treasure was each other' (WB, 99). In *The PowerBook* it is even suggested that this buried treasure of love is perhaps all that actually exists (PB, 187). The endless search for this treasure is what drives the narratives, whose journeys take place in forests, cities, continents, and cyberspace:

> My search for you, your search for me, is a search after something that cannot be found. Only the impossible is worth the effort. What we seek is love itself, revealed now and again in human form, but pushing us beyond our humanity into animal instinct and god-like success.   (PB, 78)

What this last phrase means is perhaps best explained by a passage in *The Passion* when Henri thinks to himself that philosophers speak of passion but 'there is no passion in them', yet a woman 'can turn a man through passion into something holy' (P, 26–7). For Winterson the heart is there to be broken apart in this impossible search: 'The truth is that love smashes into your life like an ice floe, and even if your heart is built like the *Titanic* you go down' (PB, 51).

But love is not ethereal, it is embodied in the loved one, and it is not general, it is particular. This is revealed when Gail, the new lover of the narrator of *Written On the Body* asks for a bedtime story and the following paragraph simply states: 'Louise, dipterous girl born in flames, 35. 34 22 36. 10 years married. 5 months with me. Doctorate in Art History. First class mind. 1 miscarriage (or 2?) 0 children. 2 arms, 2 legs, too many white T-cells. 97 months to live' (WB, 144). The narrator is unable to fabricate a story that is not about Louise and the love the narrator feels for her, even after scientifically investigating her body: the body on which the narrator's desire is written and in which the narrator's love is sealed.

Gut Symmetries adds a universal dimension to the idea of the written body: 'Paracelsus was a student of Correspondences: "As above, so below." The zodiac in the sky is imprinted in the body. "The galaxa goes through the body" ' (GS, 2). This novel envisages human life as a ship of fools, sailing through a sea of stars, searching for love and meaning. Winterson's perennial concern with the rogue ingredient that upsets the familiar recipe of people's lives is brought in through 'the sub-atomic joke of unstable matter', because below the level of the atom matter only has a *tendency* to exist. Similarly the book uses physics to undermine objectivity: 'Any measurement must take into account the position of the observer. There is no such thing as measurement absolute, there is only measurement relative. Relative to what is an important part of the question. ... I cannot help you to take a measurement until we both know where we stand' (GS, 9–11). The book uses the theories of Einstein, Planck, and Oppenheimer (GS, 82) to explain and explore unanswerable questions that we are compelled to ask about human relationships as well as humans' relationships with the universe. Much of Winterson's writing aims at taking apart binaries, such as those outlined by Jeanette's mother on the first page of *Oranges*, and replacing them with symmetries.

> There is physical reality, the table, the chair, the cars on the street – what appears to be the solid, knowable world, subject to proof, all around us. But there is also the reality of the psyche, imaginative reality, emotional reality, the things which are not subject to proof and never can be. We understand the world as oppositions: black/white, good/evil, male/female, mind/matter. What can be touched and what cannot be. But what's invisible to us is also so crucial for our own well-being or health. Life is full of things which are unexplained, full of incidents which happen from nowhere. And those are forces, literally, to be reckoned with. Now, whether you want to call it God or the mystery of the cosmos doesn't matter to me. ('Salon Interview', 28 April 1997)

Winterson develops parallels in order to question the limits of objective thinking: Jove and Stella are presumed dead at sea; Jove even convinces himself that Stella is dead beside him – yet they both live. Alice's father has died and yet in quantum terms death and life do not exist, there are only states of potentiality, just as in relativity there are only observations – relative to Alice at her moment in space and time her father is dead but this is not universally true. The only universal for Winterson is love: 'Love bears all things, believes all things, hopes all things, endures all things. Love never ends' (GS, 164). Alice tries to explain this at one point, in terms that would well apply to many of Winterson's other narrators, from Jeanette on: 'There are children who grow up as I did, with the love clamped down in them, who cannot afterwards love at all. There are others who make fools of themselves, loving widely, indiscreetly, forgetting it is themselves they are trying to love back to a better place' (GS, 126). In *The Passion*, Henri is one of these, and it drives him beyond the brink of sanity. He speculates that romance is: 'not a contract between equal parties but an explosion of dreams and desires that can find no outlet in everyday life' (P, 13). To represent desire and passion Winterson therefore turns to stories and to other 'worlds'.

In one of her short stories, 'Turn of the World', Winterson writes: 'some stories go further than others. Some take the traveller as far as the line of mountains bordering a vast forest. At this place, lonely and silent, the story falters. The traveller turns to look back at the distance and while he or she is busy with other thoughts, the stories disappear into the forest from where they came' (WOP, 160). This seems to intimate how the forest of fairy tales, so prominent in Winterson's books from *Oranges* to *The PowerBook*, is the primal home of all stories, which spin off or spiral in their own generic directions but remain variations on a few themes. 'I keep telling this story – different people, different places, different times – but always you, always me, always this story, because a story is a tightrope between two worlds' (PB, 119).

In contrast to her faith in love, what Winterson does not believe in is the truth of history, whether public or personal. The refrain of *Art and Lies* is 'There's no such thing as autobiography, there's only art and lies.' In *The PowerBook*, Ali writes: 'I was typing on my laptop, trying to move this story on, trying to avoid endings, trying to collide the real and the imaginary worlds, trying to be sure which is which. The more I write the more I discover that the partition between real and invented is as thin as a wall in a cheap hotel' (PB, 93). Which is to say that it is an invented partition not a real one. Consequently, in *Gut Symmetries*, the reader is made to feel sceptical of Jove, a lecturer on time, when he asserts that quantum physics is only real at a level that does not affect human lives. Nothing is mystical he declares and there are only things that cannot be explained yet: 'I don't mind my wife telling me stories. I worry when she can no longer distinguish between the fanciful and the actual' (GS, 193). For Winterson's narrators however, the human world is not so scientific, and there are few facts and rules: 'life is not a formula and love is not a recipe. The same ingredients cook up differently every time' (PB, 184).

In *The Passion*, Henri tells a story about the Empress Joséphine and adds: 'It may or may not be true. It doesn't matter. Hearing about it comforts me' (P, 158). Stories perform the function of reassurance and of hope. The great storyteller of *The Passion* is Patrick, a de-frocked Irish priest with one eagle eye that can see for miles: 'He was always seeing things and it didn't matter how or what, it only mattered that he saw and that he told us stories. Stories were all we had' (P, 107). It is Patrick who provides Henri with the recurring phrase of the book and indeed of Winterson's fiction overall: 'Trust me, I'm telling you stories' (P, 40).

Stories are thus a way to re-envision the world and appropriate it for oneself. When Jeanette goes to school she decides 'the daily world was a world of Strange Notions, without form. And therefore void. I comforted myself as best I could by always rearranging their version of the facts' (ONF, 47). So, when she learns that Tetrahedron is a mathematical shape Jeanette counters by constructing her own story: 'But Tetrahedron is an emperor' whose sworn enemy is 'the foul Isosceles' (ONF, 47). Stories are also a matter of relativity and 'Everyone who tells a story tells it differently, just to remind us that everyone sees it differently' (ONF, 91). Considering the other side of the story, so to speak, what applies to the relativity of the writer also applies to the reader: 'if I were not telling this story to you but to someone else, would it be the same story? ... It is just as likely that as I invent what I want to say, you will invent what you want to hear' (GS, 24–5). As Jeanette concludes in *Oranges*: 'Of course that is not the whole story, but that is the way with stories; we make them what we will' (ONF, 91).

Stories are ultimately about relativity, about the observer's position in space and time: 'I can't go back into the past and change it, but I have noticed that the future changes the past. What I call the past is my memory of it and my memory is conditioned by who I am now. Who I will be. The only way for me to handle what is happening is to move myself forward into someone who has handled it. As yet that person does not exist' (GS, 45). It is the power of stories to reinvent the world that creates new possibilities, that exposes the objective as relative and history as at best partial. Stories are lies, but because they do not claim to be otherwise they are to be trusted far more than the truth-claims of history or the certainties of science.

12.3. Key Works: *Oranges Are Not the Only Fruit, Written on the Body*

> *All things fall and are built again*
> *And those that build them again are gay.*
> (W. B. Yeats, 'Lapis Lazuli' quoted ONF, 30)

Winterson says of *Oranges* that 'It exposes the sanctity of family life as something of a sham; it illustrates by example that what the church calls love is actually psychosis and it dares to suggest that what makes life difficult for homosexuals is not their perversity but other people's' (ONF, xiii). Like many of Winterson's novels it is a hybrid of a realist narrative and fantasy, but in *Oranges* the first-person life-story and fairy tales are laid alongside each other for the reader to *make* connections. In addition to this, the stories of the eight books from the beginning of the Bible are used implicitly to mirror Jeanette's early life, from her origins in Genesis, through her 'going out' to school in Exodus, to her decision to leave her old life behind in Ruth. Against the Old Testament logic of her mother, there is however a New Testament counter-narrative running from Jeanette's 'miraculous' birth to the story's conclusion on Christmas Day. The novel also contains a direct address to the reader in its short middle chapter, Deuteronomy, the last book of Mosaic law: a chapter Winterson says is central to *Oranges* in both senses. It marks a turning point in the novel because Jeanette has just begun her sexual relationship with Melanie and discovered the enormous difference between her own feelings of love and the 'psychosis' offered by her mother and the Church. Deuteronomy precedes three more chapters, all named after those that follow the Pentateuch in the Bible and whose combined titles illustrate the Church's treatment of Jeanette: 'Joshua Judges Ruth.'

The realist narrative is set in a Northern mill town in the early 1960s and the 1970s. It recounts the key events of Jeanette's adoption and her life from the age of seven to 21. She grows up in an evangelical, matriarchal society under the guidance of a patriarchal god and his pastors. The chapters follow Jeanette from her infancy through her time at the 'breeding ground' of school, her holidays in Morecambe, her love for Melanie and then Katy, to her leaving the Church and her home before winning a place at university. The driving force of the narrative is the principal theme of conversion and transformation: religious, sexual, nominal, and fictional.

Jeanette's mother is the dominant force in Jeanette's life, but she is more complex than her fundamentalist views make her first appear. She likes to tell her daughter 'her own conversion story' now and then; how she found God at the hands of Pastor Spratt, which was, according to Jeanette, 'very romantic': 'He was very impressive. My mother said he looked like Errol Flynn, but holy. A lot of women found the Lord that week' (ONF, 8). Immediately, there is a suggestion that something coyly sexual, or at least 'Mills and Boon' (ONF, 8), lies behind the ecstatic religious rebirth. After her conversion, Jeanette's mother, in order to save the souls of the drinkers, goes to pubs and clubs singing 'Have you any room for Jesus?' We are told that the men 'cried into the tankards' and, because she was 'plump and pretty', called her the 'Jesus Belle' (ONF, 35); but this is all told to Jeanette from her mother's point of view and the reader is left to speculate on why the men were crying into their tankards and on the similarity between 'Jesus Belle' and 'Jezebel'. Jeanette's mother says she had her 'offers' and 'they weren't all Godly' (ONF, 35). On the next page, she talks to Jeanette about her old flames but in her photograph album there is also an anomalous picture of 'a pretty woman' (ONF, 36). Jeanette's enquiry about the woman is brushed off with the remark that it is 'just Eddy's sister' and the next time they look at the album the photograph is gone. This incident and the woman are not discussed again but the reason Jeanette's mother kept this photograph among pictures of her ex-boyfriends and the reason she removed it again suggest a stronger emotional life than is explicitly revealed in most of the book. The nature of Jeanette's mother's sexuality is never resolved, but, certainly, she adopts Jeanette not because she couldn't have her own child, 'more that she didn't want to do it' (ONF, 3).

Adoptive mother and daughter have parallel stories of ignorant sexual adventure based on self-misunderstanding bred from what they have been told about love. When they sleep together, Jeanette asks Melanie whether she thinks it is 'Unnatural Passion', but Melanie thinks it cannot be, because, 'According to Pastor Finch, that's awful.' All Jeanette feels is 'something crawling in my belly' (ONF, 86). This anecdote succeeds a passage in which Jeanette's mother tells her about her romance with Pierre in Paris. Jeanette's mother sleeps with Pierre because she feels 'fizzy in the belly' (ONF, 85) and takes this sensation to be love, when in fact she has a stomach ulcer. Her advice to Jeanette is to take care because 'what you think is the heart might well be another organ' (ONF, 85). Yet, what Jeanette takes to be a strange new feeling in her stomach is actually to do with her heart. Jeanette's mother says she felt nothing for Pierre after the ulcer was removed and there is little suggestion that she has had strong feelings for anyone else, except perhaps Eddy's sister – the incident with her photograph is echoed by Melanie telling Jeanette to throw away any of their love letters: 'As though letters and photos made it more real' (ONF, 166). While the novel arguably presents Jeanette's mother as asexual throughout most of its narrative, it becomes clear that she pours her sexual energy, however it might otherwise have been channelled, into the Church. One of the last comments Jeanette makes about her mother, suggesting Jezebel more than a Jesus Belle, is 'If there's such a thing as spiritual adultery, my mother was a whore' (ONF, 132).

The theme of conversion and discovery, developed in terms of religion, sexuality, and betrayal in the realist narrative, is rendered in more literal ways in the quests and transformation stories of the fairy tales, in which Jeanette's mother is metamorphosed into, for example, a sorcerer or a queen. Jeanette herself is transformed into several guises but is finally transposed into Winnet Stonejar, who embarks on several quests, which focus on a brown pebble, a raven's heart, a chalk circle and other images of love and truth. The fairy tales follow Jeanette's life; so, the first story tells of an old hunchback woman who adopts a princess to take over her three duties, milking the goats, educating the people, and composing songs for the village festival. It is immediately followed by Jeanette's mother deciding to realize her dream: to find a child and train it to be three things: a missionary child, a servant of God, and a blessing (ONF, 10).

The intersection of the fairy tale and realist worlds occurs because, at the library one day Jeanette finds a book of fairy tales (ONF, 70), which provide her with another imaginative landscape of princesses and beasts, wolves and beauties: allegorical figures that function as a Greek chorus commenting on Jeanette's life by analogy. For Jeanette, who grew up in a house with only six books, a love of Bible stories is expanded into a love of all imaginative, parabolic narratives. The authority of religious accounts is likened to the power of fairy tales, both of which deliver moral fables that can indoctrinate children in ethical codes and gender roles – except that fairy tales can be more easily re-imagined, as we see in the work of Carter and A. S. Byatt as well as Winterson.

Fairy stories, like religious teachings, deal in imagery and metaphor. One symbol that suffuses both genres is that of the demon. To Pastor Spratt demons are spirits tempting individuals towards evil, and there is an 'epidemic of demons even now spreading through the north west' (ONF, 83). Providing a bridge between the fairy tales and her life, Jeanette discovers she has her own demon at the end of a long day in which the Church elders have prayed over her, urging her to repent her 'sins'. The demon tells her that in fact everyone has a demon, but not everyone knows how to use it. Demons are like passion, 'just different, and difficult' Jeanette is told: 'the demon you get depends on the colour of your aura, yours is orange which is why you've got me' (ONF, 106). In Jeanette's 'madness' it is the demon who keeps her in one piece, but the sex of the demon is Jeanette's 'problem': her choice. The demon thus seems to represent self-possession and self-knowledge: it offers Jeanette the opportunity to be herself and not be split between her nature and her socialization.

Here emerges the importance of *Oranges* as Jeanette's narrative: that she gets to tell her own story (through art not autobiography). This is not a pretence to authority or authenticity but a belief in the ordering of one's own story: 'that is the way with stories; we make them what we will' (ONF, 91). The discussion of this takes place in the central Deuteronomy chapter, where the narrator says: 'the past, because it is past, is only malleable where once it was flexible. Once it could change its mind, now it can only undergo change. The lens can be tinted, tilted, smashed. What matters is that order is seen to prevail. ... There is an order and a balance to be found in stories' (ONF, 93). But where stories only claim to make sense and order for the individual, history pretends to make sense of the past from an objective standpoint: 'It's an all-purpose rainy day pursuit, this reducing of stories called history' (ONF, 91). *Oranges* prefers to assert that 'We are all historians in our small way' (ONF, 92), and it is better to turn to these personal and multiple stories to construct our own viewpoint than to trust to others' history: 'I can put these accounts together and I will not have a seamless wonder but a sandwich laced with mustard of my own' (ONF, 93).

Lastly, it is not just stories, but their different genres, that are important. *Oranges* uses realism, fantasy, folk tale, poetry, rhymes, and quest romance to weave a multiplicity of parallel narratives. It is therefore important that, when Jeanette recounts her version of the past to Melanie the last time they meet, Melanie laughs and decides that whereas 'the way [Jeanette] saw it would make a good story, her vision was just the history, the nothing-at-all facts' (ONF, 166). From the perspective offered in *Oranges* this is ironically true: Melanie's matter-of-fact account is *just* history whereas Jeanette's way of seeing the past makes a *good* story.

* * *

'The most prosaic of us betray a belief in the inward life every time we talk about "my body" rather than "I". We feel it as absolutely part but not at all part of who we are. Language always betrays us, tells the truth when we want to lie, and dissolves into formlessness when we would most like to be precise' (SC, 90).

At one point, the ungendered voice recounting a series of love affairs in *Written On the Body* stops telling the story to address the reader: 'I can tell by now that you are wondering whether I can be trusted as a narrator' (WB, 24). The reader can take this as a sign of unreliability but it seems more to act as a reminder that the narrator is 'telling stories': the fact that the narration has an emotional veracity is more important than its simple accuracy or consistency. We know from *Oranges* that Winterson is not interested in constructing an objective history but provides instead a 'cat's cradle' of entangled narrative threads: 'string full of knots' (ONF, 91 and 166). This metaphor is developed in *Written On the Body* to include the narrator's relationship to Louise: 'The interesting thing about a knot is its formal complexity. ... For the religious, King Solomon's knot is said to embody the essence of all knowledge. For carpet makers and cloth weavers all over the world, the challenge of the knot lies in the rules of its surprises. ... Louise and I were held by a single loop of love' (WB, 88).

Like Winterson's other novels, *Written On the Body* is a novel of disguises. The narrator assumes many personas in the novel: masculine and feminine stereotypes abound, suggesting they are adopted roles, selected self-images rather than a matter of the narrator's sex. Self-comparisons are made with Lewis Carroll's Alice, with Lauren Bacall, with Sir Launcelot, with Lothario: a final comparison that follows from the narrator's list of love affairs: Inge, Catherine, Bathsheba, Judith, Estelle, Frank, Carlo, Gail, and most importantly Jacqueline then Louise. Love and sex are for the narrator not a matter of reproduction but of passion, the desire to be loved, and the transformation of love into art (WB, 108): when Renoir died 'they found nothing between his balls but an old brush' (WB, 22) and when Henry Miller died 'they found nothing between his legs but a ball-point pen' (WB, 60). Desire is not a matter of gender but of larger forces that draw people together, whether those forces are deemed magical, emotional or scientific: 'astrology, chemistry, mutual need, biological drive' (WB, 96). Above all, both desire and who is desired are encoded in the flesh: 'Written on the body is a secret code only visible in certain lights; the accumulations of a lifetime gather there. In places the palimpsest is so heavily worked that the letters feel like braille. ... I didn't know that Louise would have reading hands. She has translated me into her own book' (WB, 89).

In *Written On the Body* the narrator becomes 'obsessed with anatomy' (WB, 111) in order to know Louise fully, to know what is happening to her body. The book's anatomy of love works beyond the level of gender: 'there are many ways to fit molecules together but only a few juxtapositions that bring them close enough to bond ... Molecules and the human beings they are a part of exist in a universe of possibility' (WB, 62) Love exists at a cellular level, like cancer:

> On a molecular level success may mean discovering what synthetic structure, what chemical, will form a union with, say, the protein shape on a tumour cell. If you make this high-risk jigsaw work you may have found a cure for carcinoma ... Docking here inside Louise may heal a damaged heart, on the other hand it may be an expensively ruinous experiment.   (WB, 62)

At the end of the book, Louise is now divorced and has 'gone away', perhaps to die alone. The narrative ends, as do all of Winterson's texts, ambiguously. A friend tells the narrator that with Louise the narrator had a 'perfect romance' because it ended in tragedy not failure. But this viewpoint rings false and the narrator questions whether this can be considered a 'happy ending'. Once again, 'what you risk reveals what you value' (WB, 81) and the narrator ends by risking everything in trying to win Louise through 'Operatic heroics' (WB, 187). Yet the narrator has little choice: 'Shall I submit myself sundial-wise beneath Louise's direct gaze? It's a risk; human beings go mad without a little shade, but how to break the habit of a lifetime else?' (WB, 80) The habit of a lifetime is not broken and the novel's final lines occur when the narrator sees or imagines Louise's appearance in the doorway: 'This is where the story starts ... Beyond the door, where the river is, where the roads are, we shall be. ... let loose in open fields' (WB, 190).

Another repeated theme of Winterson's novels appears in the novel's close: 'What then kills love? Only this: neglect' (WB, 186). Arguably, this answers the question at the beginning of the text: 'Why is the measure of love loss?' (WB, 9). The measure of love is not loss but the degree to which it is neglected. A view that sutures together *Oranges* and *Written On the Body* in their shared refrain: 'Time is a great deadener' (ONF, 91, WB, 189). In time, all that will remain of love is art, is stories: 'It's as if Louise never existed, like a character in a book. Did I invent her?' (WB, 189)

References and Further Reading

Helene Bengston et al., *Sponsored by Demons: the Art of Jeanette Winterson*, London: Scolars Press, 1999.

Helena Grice and Tim Woods (eds), *'I'm Telling You Stories': Jeanette Winterson and the Politics of Reading*, Amsterdam: Rodopi, 1998.

Dominic Head, *The Cambridge Introduction to Modern British Fiction, 1950–2000*, Cambridge: Cambridge University Press, 2002.

Frederick M. Holmes, *The Historical Imagination: Postmodernism and the Treatment of the Past in Contemporary British Fiction*, English Literary Studies, Victoria: University of Victoria, 1997.

Andrea L. Harrias, *Other Sexes: Rewriting Difference from Woolf to Winterson*, New York: State University of New York Press, 2000.

Kim Middleton Meyer, 'Jeanette Winterson's Evolving Subject', in *Contemporary British Fiction* edited by Richard J. Lane, Rod Mengham, and Philip Tew, Cambridge: Polity, 2003, 210–25.

Jago Morrison, *Contemporary Fiction*, London: Routledge, 2003, 95–114.

Lynne Pearce, *Reading Dialogics*, London: Arnold, 1994, 173–85.

Margaret Reynolds and Jonathan Noakes, 'Interview with Jeanette Winterson', in *Jeanette Winterson: the Essential Guide*, London: Vintage, 2003.

Jan Rosemergy, 'Navigating the Interior Journey: The Fiction of Jeanette Winterson', in *British Women Writing Fiction*, edited by Abby H. P. Werlock, Tuscaloosa: University of Alabama Press, 2000, 248–69.

Jeanette Winterson, *Oranges Are Not the Only Fruit* (ONF), London: Vintage, 1991.

——, *The Passion* (P), London: Vintage, 1996.

——, *Sexing the Cherry* (SC), London: Vintage, 1990.

——, *Written On the Body* (WB), London: Cape, 1992.

——, *Art & Lies: A Piece for Three Voices and a Bawd* (AL), London: Vintage, 1995.

——, *Art Objects* (AO), London: Vintage, 1996.

——, *Gut Symmetries* (GS), London: Granta, 1998.

——, *The PowerBook* (PB), London: Vintage, 2001.

——, *The World and Other Places* (WOP), London: Vintage, 1999.

Web Reading

Key website: http://www.jeanettewinterson.com/

'Salon Interview', http://archive.salon.com/april97/winterson970428.html
http://w1.181.telia.com/~u18114424/

http://www.themodernword.com/scriptorium/winterson.html

Conclusion: The Novel
Today and Tomorrow

The most valued novels are sometimes those produced outside of the mainstream. The vitality of the genre is not to be witnessed solely in the works routinely celebrated in the press and in the prize awards, but also in the alternative voices that often most strongly encourage the reader to see, in Paul Ricoeur's words, 'oneself as another'.

In this the novel may be seen as still a radical cultural force, in postcolonial writing, in the British novels that are written from Scotland, Wales, or that varied phenomenon inadequately described as Black Britain. Pronouncements of fiction's decline usually focus on the mainstream and not on challenging work from the margin, which is often the principal place from which socially important novels are written. Which is why Andrew Marr's comments, mentioned at the start of the Introduction, are helpful, when he says that the novel makes no claim to extend the limits of how we understand the world except when it exposes the reader to culture overseas. The novel has always aimed at opening the reader to the experiences of other people and other ways of living, but Marr is wrong to conclude that seeing oneself as another requires that other to be from a distant country. The novel enables the individual to understand freshly because it delivers the world from the perspective of another; which is to say that, if the novel is successful, then the reader, encouraged to see the world through someone else's eyes, creates an other of the self.

The novel has perhaps always flourished most at the margin. The exiles and émigrés of modernism included few writers who did not feel marginalized: Woolf by her sex, Lawrence by his class, Forster by his sexuality, many others by their nationality – these were also marginal writers in that they sold few books in comparison with the contemporary literary heavy-weights; and it took a revolution in publishing and marketing in the 1980s to make the literary novel significantly profitable once more. It has also been said that the 'great' English novel of the twentieth century was Irish, while a notable feature of the last thirty years is that a large proportion of important novelists writing in English have been postcolonial authors. 'British' writing is thus a very different concept from the one it was a hundred years ago, and includes authors who have relocated and migrated. Some were not born in England, some no longer live there (Rushdie for example was born in Bombay and now lives in New York); some set most of their work elsewhere (e.g. Ishiguro) and others follow the stylistic examples of American authors (e.g. Amis). V. S. Naipaul, the most recent winner of the Nobel Prize is a British novelist, but only because of the Empire.

Naipaul's Nobel citation referred to his invention of a new kind of writing: one that collapses boundaries between the novel and life-writing. He is one of those who does occasionally pronounce the novel dead: his tribute in the *Times*, written by the editor of the *New Statesman*, Jason Cowley, glossed this by saying that Naipaul means the novel as a familiar mould of plot, character, and event; as opposed to Naipaul's hybrid 'novels' of autobiography, social inquiry, reportage, and invention (*Times* 12 October 2001: 15). Yet, it is probably Naipaul's postcolonial perspective over 50 years that has injected something new into the novel. His books, alongside works by many other non-English writers – some of them, like W. G. Sebald, resident in England but not writing in English have introduced questions of ethnicity, nationalism, and the politics of belonging to the mainstream of fiction. These questions, alongside ones of gender and sexuality, history and apocalypse, science and the New Physics, have multiplied both the form and the content of the literary novel, transforming its production and reception since the discussion of the 'literature of exhaustion' in the 1960s and 1970s. Those pronouncements on the death of the novel proved to be revealingly premature because they marked an end, not to fiction, but to the model of the novel with which critics were working. Since the 1980s, fiction in Britain has had a remarkable resurgence, though its cultural centrality, seemingly self-evident 50 years ago, has sometimes come into question. The 'crisis' in the novel resulted not in ossification but in rejuvenation. As a consequence, critical perspectives have changed, focussing less on formal and spiritual aspects and more on issues of ethnicity and sexuality, gender and the body, history and memory.

While the novel's future position in cultural life is uncertain, the importance of narrative and the written word is less so, even though these features, far older than the novel, may appear in new forms. It is notable that the events of 11 September 2001 were, for many people, most affectingly considered by novelists, but not in novels. The broadsheets turned to writers such as Martin Amis and Salman Rushdie to best express what many others were feeling. Of these articles, some of the most praised were written by Ian McEwan for the *Guardian*, on 12 and 15 September. These were essays which in their discussions implicitly reflected upon the inadequacy of McEwan's major genre, the novel, to speak of what had happened: for reasons of immediacy as well as morality. In a printed text, commenting on events that almost everyone reading would already have witnessed McEwan noted that reality always outstrips the imagination and then observed that for most viewers the pictures obliterated the commentary.

Most importantly, what McEwan asserted is something that the novel has frequently been used to argue: that, in contemplating life, the exercise of the imagination enables, in George Eliot's words from 'The Natural History of German Life', 'the extension of our sympathies'. McEwan maintained that the nature of empathy is to see oneself as an other – and the basis for compassion and empathy is the imagination.

Also writing in the *Guardian*, Martin Amis echoed McEwan's view, by arguing that 'we' need to look beyond nationalisms, religions, and ethnicities to develop further our 'species consciousness'. Species-consciousness (*Gattungsbewußtsein*) was a concept Marx outlined in the *Economic and Philosophical Manuscripts*. Here he argued that an awareness of ourselves 'as members of a human community is not an intellectual construct ... but the natural outcome of our relationship to the natural world, not least because from the beginning, the existence of human beings as a species has demanded collaborative, socialized activity. Without it our survival as a species is simply inconceivable' (Karl Marx, *Selected Writings*, edited by D. McLellan, Oxford: Oxford UP, 1977, 91).

Species consciousness, which currently figures in a number of contemporary discourses, from those centred on eco-criticism to those attempting to project a 'new humanism', might be something that the novel, the exemplary literary product of national consciousness, will continue to be well equipped to promote in the future. However, the universal language of visual imagery, despite its association with the homogenizing forces of globalization and the vested interests of, among others, media corporations, may have more *power* in the future 'to extend our sympathies', just as it has more power to diminish them. Yet, the novel is no more likely to diminish as an art form now than it ever was. What it will do is continue to mutate and proliferate its forms, including the graphic novel and the hypertext novel, responding to new understandings of identity, in a globalized world where almost everything is 'post' something else, and continuing alongside new media to offer one of the most sophisticated, subtle, and sensitive ways of understanding human experience. Seeing oneself as another, which is at the heart of this understanding, is common to the novels discussed in this study as it is to most important and original imaginative fiction. Winterson's work, for example, is repeatedly concerned with the emotional and corporeal connections between individuals. In the 'key novels' considered in her chapter above she works at the interface between story-forms and bodies, drawing parallels between the ways we write ourselves into words and onto flesh.

Another of the chief concerns of the novelists discussed in these chapters is the questioning of boundaries or the transgression of borders. For example, in the work of these twelve writers, the nation is simultaneously treated at length and put into relief by transnational identifications, by contrasts with other nations, and by globalized cultures. Writers as seemingly diverse as Amis, Ishiguro, and McEwan have each offered a kind of 'state of the nation' narrative in *London Fields*, *The Remains of the Day* and *Amsterdam*, while Welsh's novels repeatedly pass comment on the subject of the 'condition of Scotland'. Many writers from Barnes and Rushdie to Amis and McEwan have looked at England tangentially through the history and politics of another country, while other countries, from Pakistan to Bulgaria, have been the subject of numerous 'British' novels of the period. For Kureishi and Smith, both born in England, the reconfiguring of identity takes place inside the nation, negotiating what Rushdie has called 'the new empire within Britain'. Though both writers have been compared to Rushdie, they are less directly concerned with the migrant's experience and the translation of identities across national borders. The younger generation within *The Buddha of Suburbia* and *White Teeth* see connections with other nationalities but their cultural positioning concerns finding a place, or reflection, from within rather than without.

Swift, Barker, and Ishiguro find an image of modern Britain by investigating the past, but it is perhaps Zadie Smith, the youngest writer, who presents the fullest, if flawed, overview of postwar changes, tracing genealogies into the past to get to the heart of the present. Certain writers in this study also concentrate on the preoccupations of identity since the 1970s: sexuality in Winterson and Kureishi; gender in Barker and Carter; popular culture in Welsh and Kureishi; class in Barker and Swift; the eclipse of old England in the 1950s in McEwan and Ishiguro; new ethnicities in Smith and Kureishi; consumerism in Amis and Welsh. The interaction of families, within and across generations, has been the particular preserve of Graham Swift, though the theme surfaces strongly in other writers, from Ishiguro to Smith.

The British novel from the late 1960s to the 2000s retains a clear experimental streak in writers from B. S. Johnson to Lawrence Norfolk, but the comparatively anti-intellectual dominant cultural climate has kept to a minimum self-conscious or postmodernist successes, like Barnes's *Flaubert's Parrot* and Byatt's *Possession*. The British novel also maintains an excellent tradition of social satire in the works of Martin Amis and indeed Zadie Smith, writers well received in the US, but few writers seem to have made a claim for the 'great British novel', partly because the theme lacks the romance and grandeur of 'the great American novel' and partly because Britain's imperial legacy has suggested a different project. Books like *Waterland* or *Lanark* are outstanding examples of the national or regional novel, but Britain's variety is rarely attempted, let alone successfully represented by contemporary novelists, and the 'English' novel of ideas often has too little to offer as a self-reflection beyond the whimsy of *England, England*. Instead, history and ethnicity have been the strong themes and these have been imaginatively scrutinized to great effect in the novel since the 1970s.

Though there may be almost no British writers who engage with the present as persuasively as Don DeLillo or Philip Roth, on the one hand, Milan Kundera and Michel Houellebecq on the other, history has been ranged over and interrogated in dialogue with the present since novels like John Fowles's *The French Lieutenant's Woman* (1969) offered a model for British historiographical metafiction. A. S. Byatt's 1990s work (alongside several of Peter Ackroyd's novels and more recently Sarah Waters's) is particularly associated with the reinscription of Victorian Britain in works such as

Possession (1990), *Angels and Insects* (1992) and *The Biographer's Tale* (1999). She has argued that the project of 'writing the self' in fiction has been overtaken by novelists returning to historical fiction for radical difference through the combination of the unknowable and imaginable. This applies to writers in the fabulist European tradition, such as Lawrence Norfolk, Penelope Fitzgerald, Angela Carter, and Tibor Fischer, but also those who work in a more realist form, such as Barker. There has also in this period been a reconsideration of history's relation to narrative by historians themselves, from Hayden White to Simon Schama, alongside the imaginative approach to literary biography in such works as Peter Ackroyd's *Dickens* (1990) and D. J. Taylor's *Thackeray* (1999). Even Martin Amis returned to the past in *Time's Arrow*, while Graham Swift constructed a Victorian back-history in *Ever After* (1992), building on his intertwining of personal, local, natural, and political history in *Waterland* (1983). Carter's baroque *Nights at The Circus* (1984) is an exploration of ideas about gender and sexuality set in London, St. Petersburg and Siberia at the end of the nineteenth century, while Ackroyd has mined London's history in works such as the Victorian psycho thriller *Dan Leno and the Limehouse Golem* (1994), and Beryl Bainbridge has utilized the Crimean War in *Master Georgie* (1998). Carter's final novel, *Wise Children* (1991) is a review of the twentieth century, recounting the adventures of two 'stage girls' born on New Year's Day, 1900, which is also the momentous birth date of Liza Jarrett Wright, the heroine of Pat Barker's *The Century's Daughter* (1986). The First World War and its aftermath was a major reference point in the 1990s, revisited in a range of novels from Barker's *Regeneration Trilogy* (1991–95), through Sebastian Faulks's Western Front novel *Birdsong* (1993), to Adam Thorpe's *Nineteen Twenty-One* (2001). The interwar years and the Second World War formed the backdrop to McEwan's first novel mostly set before his own birth, *Atonement* (2001), and also to Ishiguro's *When We Were Orphans* (2000), as well as Louis de Bernières' *Captain Corelli's Mandolin* (1995), Faulks's *Charlotte Gray* (1999), and Rachel Seiffert's *The Dark Room* (2001). The past has thus offered fertile territory for exploring a society little known to readers, without a need to make direct sense of the accelerated, pluralistic culture of the present. The vogue for historical novels also has not passed with the turning of the millennium, though there is perhaps a new trend emerging of novels that revisit the more recent past, exemplified in Jonathan Coe's *What a Carve Up!* (1994) and *The Rotters' Club* (2001).

A sustained concentration on the effects of history has also characterized more explicitly postcolonial fiction of the last 40 years, which has brought to the British novel, alongside the transatlantic English of Amis and the Scots English of Kelman and Welsh, new styles and Englishes that have flourished in other countries: the London Caribbean English of Sam Selvon, the pidgin, Creole, and gangster rap of Victor Headley, and the Indian English of G. V. Desani, perfected by Rushdie. Alongside the works of Rushdie, Kureishi, and Smith, there has been a more general and noticeable shift to a concern with the politics of relocation, reclaimed pasts, 'black Atlantic' culture, and ethnic difference. For example, the Guyanese poet David Dabydeen has vividly repainted the past in *A Harlot's Progress* (1999), and metaphorically re-built it in *Disappearance* (1993), which recounts the experience of a young Guyanese engineer constructing sea defences for a cliff-top village near Hastings. Powerfully imagined by other writers who have built on the legacy of Sam Selvon and George Lamming, such as Caryl Phillips, some of this historical re-envisioning has also been recognized in novels by whites, including Barry Unsworth's Booker prize-winning condemnation of the eighteenth-century slave trade, *Sacred Hunger* (1992). After the historiographical metafiction of the 1980s, the 1990s might fairly be characterized overall in terms of postcolonial issues such as decolonization, diaspora, and cultural diversity, as mentioned in the Introduction. Rushdie represents only the tip of the iceberg of authors concerned with Indian, Pakistani, and Bangladeshi postcolonial identities, which includes Amitav Ghosh (e.g. *The Shadow Lines*, 1988), Sunetra Gupta (*The Glassblower's Breath*, 1993), Vikram Seth (*A Suitable Boy*, 1993), Amit Chaudhuri (*Afternoon Raag*, 1993), and Monica Ali (*Brick Lane*, 2003). In parallel with the emergence of these authors, who either do live or have lived in England, has developed a good number of important British writers with roots in the Caribbean and/or Africa, including Caryl Phillips (e.g. *Cambridge*, 1992), Fred D'Aguiar (*Feeding the Ghosts*, 1998), Ben Okri (*The Famished Road*, 1990), Bernadine Evaristo (*The Emperor's Babe*, 2001), Joan Riley (*The Unbelonging*, 1995), Buchi Emecheta (*Joys of Motherhood*, 1979), Courttia Newland (*Society Within*, 1999) Abdulrazak Gurnah (*Paradise*, 1994), and Diran Adebayo (*My Once Upon a Time*, 2000). The late 1990s in particular has seen a noticeable shift in dominant from writing that has looked at Britain from the point of view of migrancy to fiction that has opened up new black British urban perspectives, in for example, the work of Newland and Adebayo. Alongside these are also the excellent writers whose work is informed by other national traditions, such as the Sri Lankan-born Romesh Gunesekera and the British-Chinese Timothy Mo.

Overall, the books that have been examined in this study scrutinize a range of subjects from the oldest myths of racial and gendered identity to modern addictions like television and drugs. Contemporary British fiction is now enormously varied but much of it in recent decades has shared a common concern in issues of historical and ethnic identity. These have emerged as conspicuous themes after the preoccupation with gender and form in the 1970s and alongside conjectural writing on the effects of Thatcherism and capitalism in the 1980s. Fiction in the twenty-first century is increasingly pluralistic as a new generation of novelists redraws the fictional map, fusing the styles and themes of the last thirty years with those emerging on a cultural scene in which diversity and plurality thrive, such that, in terms of the contemporary British novel, while it may be decreasingly clear what 'British' and 'the novel' mean there are growing signs of a willingness and an ability to chronicle the contemporary.

Index